I0124511

# Mobilizing
## Global
## Knowledge

**UNIVERSITY OF CALGARY**
Press

# Mobilizing Global Knowledge

**Refugee Research in an
Age of Displacement**

Edited by
**SUSAN MCGRATH
AND JULIE E. E. YOUNG**

© 2019 Susan McGrath and Julie E. E. Young

University of Calgary Press
2500 University Drive NW
Calgary, Alberta
Canada T2N 1N4
press.ucalgary.ca

This book is available as an ebook which is licensed under a Creative Commons license.
The publisher should be contacted for any commercial use which falls outside the terms
of that license.

LIBRARY AND ARCHIVES CANADA CATALOGUING IN PUBLICATION

Title: Mobilizing global knowledge : refugee research in an age of displacement / edited by
    Susan McGrath and Julie E. E. Young.
Names: McGrath, Susan, 1946- editor. | Young, Julie E. E., 1978- editor.
Description: Includes bibliographical references and index.
Identifiers: Canadiana (print) 20190103000 | Canadiana (ebook) 20190103043 | ISBN
    9781773850856 (softcover) | ISBN 9781773850863 (Open Access PDF) | ISBN 9781773850870
    (PDF) | ISBN 9781773850887 (EPUB) | ISBN 9781773850894 (Kindle)
Subjects: LCSH: Refugees—Research.
Classification: LCC HV640 .M63 2019 | DDC 305.9/06914072—dc23

The University of Calgary Press acknowledges the support of the Government of Alberta through
the Alberta Media Fund for our publications. We acknowledge the financial support of the
Government of Canada. We acknowledge the financial support of the Canada Council for the
Arts for our publishing program.

This book has been published with the help of a grant from the Canadian Federation for the
Humanities and Social Sciences, through the Awards to Scholarly Publications Program, using
funds provided by the Social Sciences and Humanities Research Council of Canada.

Susan McGrath and Julie E. E. Young thank contributor Nergis Canefe for creating and donating
the beautiful cover painting titled *Tree of life: version non-status*. The image is a response to RRN
members who had proposed that the network should have "more branches and less roots".

Copyediting by Kathryn Simpson

Cover design, page design, and typesetting by Melina Cusano

# Contents

# Introduction: Mobilizing Global Knowledge in Forced Migration Studies and Practice

*Susan McGrath and Julie E. E. Young*

> *Scholars from other societies and traditions of inquiry could bring to this debate their own ideas about what counts as new knowledge and what communities of judgement and accountability they might judge to be central in the pursuit of such knowledge.*

Arjun Appadurai

Reflecting on more than ten years of work in conceptualizing and building a network for refugee research, we pose the challenge—to ourselves and others—of "ethical networking" for research and practice. Research partnerships and collaborations have become the standard for funded research in recent years (Bradley 2007; McGrath et al. 2011; Landau 2012). A key question driving our work on the Refugee Research Network (RRN) was how to collaborate ethically—or at least how to think ethically when building a research network. Moreover, through our work together, we sought to generate and disseminate knowledge in ways that are accessible to multiple audiences and that would improve the well-being of refugees.

We recognize, and share concerns about, the politics of knowledge production in forced migration contexts. The global nature of the RRN means that partners are across the so-called north/south divide, with different resources and capacities. It is an environment where people in the more marginal regions of the world risk being "simply producers of data for the theory mills of the North," as Appadurai (2000, 5) has warned, and where donors, primarily from the north, are setting forced migration research agendas—often with the primacy of "policy relevant" research (Bradley 2007; Landau 2012). We have aspired to bring disparate cultures of knowledge production into effective relation with one another, which Jazeel and McFarlane (2007) describe as "responsible learning"—along the lines of the "strong internationalization" that Appadurai (2000) describes in the epigraph, in which scholars from a broad range of societies and traditions of inquiry determine what counts as new knowledge.

This edited volume reflects on the lessons learned through our work as the RRN, a global network of academics, practitioners, and policymakers built around relationships among refugee research centres across the global south and north in Bogotá, Cairo, Chicago, Johannesburg, Kampala, Kolkata, London, Melbourne, Oxford, Sydney, Tehran, Toronto, and Washington. The RRN emerged out of a vision to establish a collaborative network that has a wide-ranging and progressive impact on refugee research and policy in Canada and globally. This volume seeks to capture and reflect on how we tried to build networks for knowledge production and mobilization and what we were able to accomplish together, as well as the challenges of bridging silos, sectors, and regions and engaging across global north-south tensions. The RRN guided the formation of eight multidisciplinary research clusters addressing major questions in the field, three regional networks (Canada, Latin America, and Asia Pacific), and two issue-specific networks (emerging scholars and global refugee policy). These "networks within the network" have functioned relatively independently to generate new knowledge on key issues facing refugees and those who work to protect them.

The key question motivating this collection is: what are the contributions of a research network to thinking about the broader ethical, methodological, and practical questions in the field of refugee studies? Contributors reflect on the process of building networks in the context of research on refugees, displacement, and forced migration. Thus the book bridges scholarship on the practice of building networks for knowledge production and dissemination and scholarship on the process of doing research with and about refugees (including questions of ethics and methodologies). In this introduction, we identify and examine some of the ethical questions raised by networks and partnerships in the field of refugee studies, which is already fraught with (neo)colonial relationships and power dynamics.

Our RRN work has highlighted how knowledge production and dissemination are contingent on human relationships. It has shown us that building equitable and interactive learning and sharing experiences requires mutual trust, respect, and reciprocity within the community of practice. What is more, supportive relationships in turn promote healthy networks capable of adapting and responding to shifting cultural and political terrains. It reminds us that effective and useful research and advocacy must also be combined with a conscious and directed commitment to the democratization of knowledge production within and beyond the community. This is especially relevant in the context of a research community and field of research that has traditionally been dominated by scholars in the global north while the questions and issues raised in research and practice are most acutely experienced and addressed by actors in the global south.

In this book we review the vision that guided us, the practices that we believed were ethically grounded, the outcomes of the network, and the challenges and barriers to full success. These reflections incorporate two evaluations conducted with our partners. One was completed at about year three and covered in Hynie et al. (2014); another was a mapping of the knowledge activities, strategies, and needs of our regional networks and partners that was conducted in 2014 with interviews of eleven of our thirteen institutional partners (Oakes 2015).

## The Vision and Practice of Ethical Networking and Knowledge Making

Our goal was to build a "network of networks" that would promote fair and equitable connections throughout the field of refugee and forced migration studies. We envisioned a dynamic web of global connections and relationships that would stimulate the development of new research partnerships and projects and encourage the sharing of findings with policymakers, practitioners, and advocates who work as part of the international refugee regime. We adopted a dialogical and participatory approach that would: 1) expand our awareness of the global knowledge regime on refugee and forced migration issues; 2) improve communication concerning this knowledge across academic, policymaking, and practice sectors in the global south and north; and 3) build alliances and active involvement in the development of national and international policy frameworks and humanitarian practices affecting refugees and forced migrants. A belief in public entitlement to knowledge, as well as the centrality of knowledge mobilization and translation of academic scholarship in that process, inspired our partnership approach. Our guiding principles included the notion that knowledge should be accessible and available in different forms and formats with an emphasis on open source and open access, as well as the conviction that knowledge should not remain within academic institutions, behind pay walls—especially in places where universities are public institutions (as in Canada). While national and global policies are a key factor in how forced migration and refugee situations are addressed, there are also differences in the willingness of researchers to share knowledge with policymakers. Part of our aim with the RRN was to promote engagement across sectors that would also facilitate the active participation of our partners in the global south in setting the agenda for the field. This approach acknowledged the geopolitics of forced migration, in the sense that it is actors in the global north that dominate the field of study, while also confronting the perceived "myth of difference" in the nature and study of asylum between the global north and south (Chimni 1998). This volume captures and reflects on how we tried to build networks for knowledge mobilization and what we were able to accomplish together as well as the challenges of bridging silos, sectors, and regions.

We sought to practice *networking* in an ethical manner consistent with our vision. We tried to be transparent in our processes, with a clear governance model and participatory decision-making. We convened all institutional members of the network in person annually, alternating between Toronto and the sites of the biennial meeting of the International Association for the Study of Forced Migration (IASFM) that were typically organized at the site of one of the partners, e.g., in Cairo, Kampala, Kolkata, and Bogotá. During the year, between the annual in-person meetings, we held video conferences. These processes did not always run smoothly, e.g., Egyptian officials refused entry to our Iranian colleague to attend the Cairo conference, the timing of the meetings did not fit everyone's schedule, the technology was not always adequate to support everyone's participation, and time differences meant that some people were asked to stay up late and/or get up early in the morning for these virtual meetings. The in-person connections and ongoing virtual contacts, although often difficult to maintain, were important in building trusting relationships that have endured among many of the partners.

We also needed to be aware of the social and economic inequities within the hierarchies of our institutions, across our disciplines, and among academic institutions globally. We sought to engage and support students to participate in the research and attend conferences where they could begin to build their own networks. While most of the research assistants were York University students or at least Canadian, we did transfer some funds to centres in the south (Cairo, Johannesburg, Kolkata) to fund students to support local research initiatives such as literature reviews, conference organizing, and digitizing of reports. One of the most successful networks of the RRN has been that developed and led by early career scholars and practitioners, the Emerging Scholars and Practitioners on Migration Issues (ESPMI) network (see chapter 10). Despite a paucity of resources they have maintained strong leadership and have been highly productive, e.g., founding and producing the open access journal *Refugee Review*.

Sustainability over the longer term is an important aspect of an ethical practice. We hope such sustainability can be achieved through IASFM with some support from the Centre for Refugee Studies at York University. IASFM has agreed to offer seed funding for emerging research clusters and to continue to support the travel of students—particularly students from the south—to attend the biennial conferences. The conferences provide an opportunity for research centre directors to meet, share recent research projects and practices, and explore possible collaborations. CRS will continue to maintain the RRN website and social media tools, including the very active Facebook group (discussed in chapter 9).

We sought to *generate knowledge ethically* with the formation of research clusters that addressed key issues including one that studied ethical research methods in forced migration (see chapter 13). Criteria for the clusters were created in consultation with the RRN institutional members and based in discussions of emerging and pressing research issues. Modest amounts of funding (typically CAD $7,000–10,000 each) were allocated as seed money to support the development of research clusters of academics and students (see chapter 11 on the importance of this initial funding support). Applications were reviewed and approved by the executive committee. Consistent with funded research projects, priority was given to the co-applicants of the original proposal who were primarily Canadian academics. This domination of the research by scholars based in Canada was an ongoing tension, despite our efforts to involve a broader range of academics in the research clusters and networks.

The multidisciplinary research clusters have generated new knowledge on key issues facing refugees and the global refugee regime. Beyond the contributions outlined in this volume, several other clusters engaged with substantive issues of research, policy, and practice. For example, the Age & Generation in Migration Contexts cluster (led by Christina Clark-Kazak) developed the concept of social age in migration, recognizing the different impacts that migration has on different populations, while the Detention & Asylum cluster (led by Jennifer Hyndman and Stephanie Silverman) documented the increase in the detention of refugees with a view to supporting the development of policy and practice interventions that eliminate or ameliorate this practice. Partners also made contributions in three areas of refugee law research: comparative research on safe country of origin policies (led by Delphine Nakache and Idil Atak); a series of workshops on critical issues in international refugee law (organized by James Simeon); and comparative research on refugee status determination systems (led by Donald Galloway). The latter helped to launch the Canadian Association of Refugee Lawyers (CARL), and produced a report on Canada-US border policy and the politics of refugee exclusion (Arbel and Brenner 2013). Finally, the Gender & Sexuality cluster (led by Jennifer Hyndman) produced an annotated bibliography of scholarship that addresses claims for asylum based on persecution related to gender and sexuality. This cluster's collaboration has included colleagues from the Refugee Law Project (RLP) at Makerere University, Kampala (Uganda), whose research takes place in a highly discriminatory state with many sexual minority claimants. The second phase (guided by Wenona Giles) focused more broadly on advancing gender equity, including access to university programs by women.

Beyond the focus on forming research clusters that are networked locally and globally, a parallel strategy pursued by the RRN has been the *dissemination of the knowledge* in multiple forms and formats. We sought to use the best forms to reach different populations including academics, practitioners, policy actors, and refugees. Online tools were identified early on as important mechanisms, and one of our primary strategies was producing a website accessible in five languages.[1] Social media tools are also providing opportunities and potential for dialogue. Chapter 9 explores the perils and possibilities of social media as a forum for engagement within and between multiple sectors, particularly for academics who seek to make their research available to all who might benefit from it. As a vehicle for dissemination and information sharing, the primary website has been successful, with 120,699 unique users and 402,171 page views between the inception of the site in 2010 and October 2018. The website provides access to: a database of academic and grey material, a search engine, broadcasts of current events and education programs, and space for moderated group discussions—both public and private. As of October 2018, the RRN Facebook group had 38,813 participants and the RRN Twitter feed 3,312 followers. Dissemination also takes place through other electronic formats such as listservs and e-blasts. When an item is broadcast, it can reach between 50,000 and 60,000 people globally.

## Contributions to the Field of Refugee Studies

One of the most noteworthy accomplishments of the RRN was its development of a model of individual and institutional partnership that strives to bridge the social and economic inequities inherent in "south/north" relationships. The goal was to establish fair and equitable partnerships that promote engaged and participatory knowledge generation in a context rife with unequal capacities and inequitable access to resources. RRN's model of research partnership is based on respectful interpersonal relationships—with person-to-person contacts, and open and transparent communications—because we recognize the structural inequalities among researchers in low and high-income countries. This model guided the formation of the thematic clusters and regional and thematic networks that have achieved relative independence. RRN member institutions indicate that they value the way in which the project opened "spaces of encounter" and networking, and call for the RRN to become more decentralized and to work from a more regional perspective—to have fewer roots and more branches.

The RRN was supported by a short-lived, and since reframed, funding program called the Strategic Knowledge Research Cluster—now called Partnership Grants—operated by Canada's Social Sciences and Humanities Research Council (SSHRC). In a sense our project was unique, in that during its funding cycle the RRN was the only project with partners outside of Canada. In addition, the grant was explicitly to support networking as opposed to the traditional research agenda; in other words, the funding was meant to be put towards generating knowledge through the formation of research clusters with an emphasis on connectivity. Despite a funding program based on supporting networking, there was an expectation of traditional research outputs. This disconnect between how the funding stream was framed and what the funder expected from this funding raised important questions about how to evaluate networks and how to demonstrate effective networking. In their study of the transnational partnerships of African universities, Koehn and Obamba (2014) recommend that evaluations of partnerships include consideration of issues such as shared vision, relationship dynamics, mutual capacity building, and sustainability rather than merely the current quantitative and qualitative metrics.

While traditional metrics of academic impact focus on publications, we feel the building of a network is itself an impact. The challenge is to demonstrate effective networking. Our approach through the RRN was to bring people together around key research areas: across issues, research methodologies, and regions. The resultant "network of networks" coalesced around shared thematic or regional interests and continues to evolve, expand, and regroup. Key to the emergence of these networks was creating spaces—for personal contacts and relationships to be formed, for research questions to emerge, for connections to be made. Moreover there had to be different kinds of spaces—from regular face-to-face meetings, to virtual spaces, to smaller workshops, to larger conferences. One of our colleagues suggested that the RRN could be viewed as having two major roles: one concerned with knowledge dissemination and the other aiming to provide leading researchers in the field with a space to connect and collaborate. To this participant, it is the second role that makes the RRN unique and necessary. As they put it: "What RRN does for me and for the centre, which would not be as easily replicated, is having a venue and a process through which we can talk with our peers and colleagues to form the kind of relationships that allow us to move from 'it's nice seeing you' to 'let's collaborate,' 'let's actually do a full partnership.'"

Similarly, another colleague underscored that the role of the RRN should be to help sustain personal and professional relationships by also providing a space where researchers and practitioners can meet face-to-face and discuss joint work opportunities. As they explained: "So I think to me it's more about can you create the right spaces in which people can find one another rather than can you orchestrate collaborations kind of as a starting point." The project sought to work through shared knowledge areas of interest that built upon different motivations for creating knowledge as well as different uses of the knowledge produced. A key area of contribution of the RRN was its role as connector of research clusters. As one of our colleagues put it:

> It is important to show [through the RRN and IASFM] that different centres are saying that these are important topics and that they can't be researched independently . . . and a way to actually do more collaborative research is through maybe linking up multiple grants so that I have a grant and someone else has a grant, then the RRN can be the connector of these grants. And so, if you're working on, for example, refugee protection outside of the legal framework, I don't have to imagine I am doing the whole ball of wax. But if that is something we all agree is a topic of relevance, then there could be ways to show, look there is a topic and this institution is holding this grant to address it and this institution is holding this grant . . . so that at some level we can show that we are mutually reinforcing our work and not imagining that one centre is the source of that big research.

The RRN has been a place where Canadian and international researchers working on issues of forced migration could turn for current research and new ideas. It has been lauded as a learning community that provided researchers in early and middle career stages with opportunities for personal and professional growth (see chapters 10 and 11). Colleagues from less established and more geographically isolated research centres found that the RRN helped to broaden their exposure and strengthened their ties with institutions, NGOs, and peers in other disciplines and regions (see, for example, chapter 12). The RRN's ability to create networking opportunities was repeatedly cited as its greatest strength. What seemed to work best was not only the kind of peer-to-peer encounters that the RRN created but also the way that it opened these spaces of encounter: the RRN created an informal and stimulating atmosphere that allowed members to network at their own pace and through their own interests. It provided partners the space in which to feel out the research landscape and exercise agency and agility in choosing the topics and peers with whom they wished to collaborate. This informal atmosphere relied on a degree of improvisation, engendering unexpected partnerships and collaborations (see, for example, chapter 11 on how the spaces created for networking led to contributions in reconceptualizing environmental displacement).

When reflecting on the trajectory of the field of refugee studies, one of our RRN colleagues highlighted that an important part of deepening and expanding the field has been the work of scholars from the south in critiquing the dominance of scholars and researchers in the north. Not only did this critique provide room for new perspectives and the re-evaluation of key concepts, it also marked an important shift in critical forced migration discourse. As one of our RRN colleagues explained: "The post-1989 political situation also contributed to these developments. Focus on terror brought to the forefront the critique of the role of the global north in producing forced migrants in the south in the name of anti-terror operations. Pakistan and Iraq are burning instances of this."

Although our focus is on the impacts of the networks, the RRN did produce significant research products: forty-one workshops and conferences, six books, six special journal issues, forty-six separate journal articles, eleven reports, four annotated bibliographies, a new online journal, and five conference presentations on the RRN research process. Training and mentoring students has been a priority throughout the project. Since 2009, the RRN project has directly funded 132 students (117 graduate and fifteen undergraduate; eighty-eight Canadian and forty-four foreign students) from across disciplines to work under the supervision of leading scholars on emerging research issues and attend the IASFM conferences.

SUSAN MCGRATH AND JULIE E. E. YOUNG

In summary, the impacts of the RRN can be measured in five areas: 1) expansion of the field with new networks of researchers, practitioners, and policy actors created both regionally and globally; 2) generation of new knowledge on major issues in the field; 3) global mobilization of new and existing knowledge in accessible forms and formats; 4) training and mentoring of students to provide future leadership in the field; and 5) advancement of the practices of global research and knowledge generation.

## Mapping the Challenges

The RRN has experienced significant barriers and challenges, some alluded to above. The difficulties are very much linked to the achievements. The broader political, intellectual, cultural, and institutional contexts continue to shape how researchers in the north and south encounter and conduct research (see chapter 1). The relationships among the RRN and its partners are never outside the historical continuities that shape north-south relations—and the sense that for many years, knowledge has been "trafficked" out of the south to the benefit of scholars, institutions, and funders in the north. As one of our colleagues frames it: "For a long time, the research agenda of forced migration was dominated by the scholars and thinkers from the global north. Researchers of the global south were expected to work on case studies that would support the meta-narratives produced in the north. However, with the influx of a new group of scholars from the global south in the last two decades that picture changed substantially . . . They pointed out that categorization of forced migrants into rigid groups of refugees, IDPs, forced migrants, economic migrants, etc. is unhelpful to say the least. They also pointed out that forced migrants were always vulnerable people irrespective of whether the particular vulnerability came from poverty or a political situation within a society." This context pushed some of our colleagues to focus their resources on intra-regional collaboration rather than on the north-south collaborations that research funders have been pushing for the past decade. They argued not only that intra-regional collaborations tended to be more productive and more mutually respectful, but also that such collaborations ensured that northern researchers would not continue to dominate knowledge production in the field of forced migration. Two of the chapters here focus on the formation of regional networks (see chapters 3 and 12).

While there was a general sense that the RRN could do more to democratize and decentralize the production of knowledge in the field of forced migration, it was also acknowledged that the RRN's global platform did create room for southern partners to connect and collaborate with one another. As one of our colleagues based at an institution in the global south explained, the RRN has been central to their regional network's ability to strengthen dialogue with other southern partners beyond the region: "One of the good outcomes of the RRN is that it allowed us to enter in contact with other southern partners like ourselves, in fact, it's thanks to RRN that last week I was in India meeting with a partner there . . . RRN provided the possibility to develop south-south dialogues."

Structural and bureaucratic barriers have inhibited the full participation of some partners, especially those in the south whose access to funding is significantly more limited. Differential access to funding remains a major challenge in how research thinking, agendas, and collaborations are developed and taken up. What is more, it speaks to how vastly different the RRN experience has been for individual members of the network even at the institutional level (i.e., the network of research centres). Funding was flagged by most participants in our mapping of the network, particularly those in the global south and newly established centres in the north, as a major factor affecting their research agendas and collaborations. With most available funding distributed by agencies and foundations in the global north, there are limited pathways and structures for joint funding with institutions in the south. The problem of funding is tied to the fact that funding sources in the north for forced migration research are increasingly difficult to access, disproportionately focused on issues in the north, and as such largely out of reach for research institutions in the south (Chimni 1998; Landau 2012; Oakes 2015). This inaccessibility of resources places enormous pressure on institutions in the south and affects their ability to develop and influence research agendas of their own. At the same time, as one colleague noted, influencing policy requires building local legitimacy: "If they (local grassroots organizations) want to have a policy influence, they cannot let anyone know they have been funded (from institutions in the north) otherwise it will look like foreign agents are meddling in domestic affairs. It's not to say that your work (i.e., RRN) isn't important and couldn't be used here but disseminating through the RRN might be counter-productive (for local grassroots organizations). We also need to be thinking though, who is it that you want to influence and how can you get a local voice to be saying these things because that is what is going to be heard; not a voice with a Canadian accent." Southern colleagues were not only dissatisfied with the dearth of joint funding opportunities but also keen to highlight that the RRN's Canadian and international focus, and its focus to date on speaking to a global audience, did not do much for them regionally. There was a clearly articulated desire for the network to become more decentralized and to work from a more regional perspective. This raises a crucial question about how to be relevant and responsive to regional needs and contexts while at the same time functioning as a global platform for research, collaboration, and dissemination. It is a question that has broader application to research, policy, and practice in the field of refugee studies given that there are global and regional/local interests and contexts to consider.

## Overview of Sections and Contributions

This edited volume asks RRN members to think about their work in a slightly different way than they are perhaps used to: it does not merely present a summary of what they did in their clusters and networks but rather showcases the lessons they have learned about the practice of networking and the value of working across disciplines, sectors, and regions—as well as the tensions involved in such partnerships. The book is organized into three sections: 1) Power and Politics in Refugee Research; 2) Emerging and Developing Research Approaches and Tools; and 3) Knowledge Production and the Ethics of Network Formation.

### *Power and Politics in Refugee Research*

This section of the book focuses on the geopolitical contexts of refugee researchers and how those contexts influence the practice and understanding of research on forced migration. The relationships among researchers, civil society actors, and policymakers are considered, particularly the challenges that researchers face in the negotiations of these relationships across sectors. The murky process of influencing public policy through research and advocacy is addressed. Colleagues in the global south experience unique difficulties in conducting their research and navigating the power imbalances and resource questions. They are also demonstrating new approaches to generating knowledge on forced migration and the importance of drawing distinct areas of work into the conversation.

In his chapter "Capacity, Complicity, and Subversion: Revisiting Collaborative Refugee Research in an Era of Containment," Loren B. Landau documents the challenges of conducting refugee research in Africa. He argues that the cross-continental research partnerships most researchers in the south rely upon to fund their work come with substantial risks of heightening inequality and of becoming complicit in the prevailing global strategies of migrant containment. Landau warns us that international research partnerships can simultaneously expose and (re)enact the inequalities, structural constraints, and historically conditioned power relations implicit in the production of knowledge; they can risk entrenching the very north-south dichotomies they seek to overcome.

In "Rethinking Displacement: Transitional Justice and Forced Migration Studies," Nergis Canefe argues for the necessity of bringing the study of forced migration together with the study of transitional justice, especially in the global south where the majority of the world's dispossessed populations strive to survive. She insists on the need to build upon the knowledge of collaborative networks, scholarly and activist organizations, and practitioners in select locales in order to contribute to the study of human suffering induced by mass political violence in the hands of states turned against their own peoples. This includes examining the underlying social disenfranchisement, socio-economic predicaments, normative challenges, and rights of the displaced in the context of transitional justice projects enacted in postcolonial landscapes of nationhood. As such, establishing connections of documentation and research that attend to the ethics of witnessing is essential. Her chapter provides a conceptual debate and an interdisciplinary foundation for such a framework to be established within the larger context of forced migration studies.

Susan Kneebone documents the challenges and impacts of the Asia Pacific Forced Migration Connection (APFMC), which was launched with the support of the RRN in November 2013. She organized APFMC as a hub to bring together scholars of forced migration in Australia and the Asia Pacific region, which she describes as a contested and contentious space. Her chapter "The Asia Pacific Forced Migration Connection: Linking Activists, Advocates, and Academics" presents the political context of the Association of Southeast Asian Nations (ASEAN) and how the researchers of APFMC have navigated the troubled geopolitical waters of the region. The chapter demonstrates the importance of researcher independence as well as the freedom to network widely and engage political and civil society actors through invited participation in roundtables, publications, and conference papers.

The Borderless Higher Education for Refugees (BHER) project is an international partnership of Kenyan and Canadian universities and a Kenyan non-governmental organization that, with the support of the UN-HCR, provides post-secondary opportunities to students in the Dadaab refugee camp in northeastern Kenya. Dadaab is one of the largest and most insecure refugee camps in the world. Hyndman and Giles (2017) have documented refugees' educational needs in these situations, and the plan to develop a response was in the original RRN proposal. In their thoughtful chapter, "Transitions from Knowledge Networked to Knowledge Engaged: Ethical Tensions and Dilemmas from the Global to the Local," Wenona Giles and Don Dippo—the leaders of BHER—document the challenges and opportunities for educators attempting to work within and across the social, political, economic, and cultural differences of the camps and the local communities. Drawing from the work of Hannah Arendt and postcolonial theory, the chapter presents a transformative model of education guided by ongoing efforts to enter into ethical student-teacher encounters.

Finally, Paula Banerjee and Ranabir Samaddar dissect the discourse of security/insecurity in terms of migration, which they argue is the most contentious issue in the life of a nation. In their chapter "Insecure Nation, Insecure Migrant: Postcolonial Echoes from India's Northeast," they study the historical conditions that saw migration emerge as a matter of nationalized security marked by collective violence and collective politics. Their case study is the region of Assam in northeast India and the complexity of forced migration across the borders in that area, where mobile populations are perceived as dangerous. The chapter demonstrates the deep colonial roots of violence in the region and how discourses of the military, social and physical insecurity, and the contentious politics of nationhood all combined to ensure security against mobile populations with women being particularly vulnerable.

## Emerging and Developing Research Approaches and Tools

The second section focuses on the development of research approaches and tools to enhance the study of situations of forced migration. From its inception in 2008, the RRN has been committed to finding equitable and accessible means and forms of knowledge mobilization, dissemination, and translation. Members were interested not only in how to collaborate on research but also how to share and communicate knowledge. We also debated what our collective contributions to the field of refugee studies might be, including interventions on the ethics and politics of knowledge production and how to teach forced migration and refugee issues. The chapters in this section focus on ethical, methodological, and practical questions related to the production and dissemination of knowledge in this field that raises pressing global concerns for policymakers, practitioners, and educators.

Since 2013 an interdisciplinary team of social and computer scientists with NGO advisors based at Georgetown University and its Institute for the Study of International Migration (an RRN institutional partner) has been working on developing a simulation tool that could act as an early warning system to enable governments and international humanitarian organizations to formulate contingency plans, establish appropriate policies, and deliver shelter, food, medicines and other supplies to areas likely to receive large numbers of refugees and displaced persons. In their chapter "Big Data and Early Warning of Displacement," social scientist Susan F. Martin and computer scientist Lisa Singh review their research methodologies (including state-of-the-art information retrieval techniques) and identify the challenges (including the ethical issues) that need to be addressed in order to develop more timely and reliable evidence-based systems for detecting and forecasting forced migration.

One of the regional networks supported by the RRN is the Canadian Association for Refugee and Forced Migration Studies (CARFMS). Since its launch with its first conference in 2008, CARFMS has been continually growing and developing its contributions to refugee research beyond the annual meetings. In the chapter "Building and Sustaining a Web Platform for Researchers, Teachers, Students, and Practitioners in the Field of Refugee and Forced Migration Studies," former CARFMS President James C. Simeon documents the development of CARFMS' Online Research and

Teaching Tools and Practitioners Forum (ORTT&PF), a multi-functional online tool designed as a resource for the field of refugee and forced migration studies. A work in progress, it is an open access website that strives to provide information on the key terms, concepts, methods, and theories relevant to the field. A Practitioners' Forum is intended to provide a private online space where members can engage in conversations and debates.

Documents leading up to the 2018 Global Compact on Refugees called for "better data about migration" (Guterres 2017, 4), data that is "reliable, comparable, and timely" (UNHCR 2018, 5). Demographers have long advocated for a greater role in the scientific study of refugee and forced migration; two of the world's leading demographers, Ellen Percy Kraly and Mohammad Jalal Abbasi-Shavazi, make important contributions to this discussion in their chapter "The Promise and Potential of the Demography of Refugee and Forced Migration." They demonstrate how demography can contribute toward a better understanding of refugees and forced migration by focusing on levels and trends of displacement, characteristics of refugees, and pathways by which refugees and forced migrants adapt and are integrated into host societies. Demographic theory and population modelling are valuable tools to better understand the vulnerabilities and resiliencies of refugees and to inform the current debate by states about their mutual roles and responsibilities to refugees, migrants, and host communities.

In their chapter "Disseminating Knowledge in the Digital Age: The Case of the Refugee Research Network," William J. Payne and Michele Millard document the evolution of the RRN's knowledge mobilization strategies and particularly the use of social media tools in reaching out to different groups and disseminating research findings. When the RRN was formed in 2008, the website was envisioned as the main vehicle for dissemination; as new technologies emerged in the interim, the website came to exist in a dynamic relationship with the network's social media presence. The authors provide a guide to developing an engaged social media audience with commentaries on the utility of the different tools including some dos and don'ts. Drawing on the ten years of experience with the RRN, they offer insights into the opportunities and limitations of social media as a forum for engagement across multiple sectors.

## Knowledge Production and the Ethics of Network Formation

This section of the book examines the different kinds of partnerships that emerged within the broader RRN: global, cross-cultural, interdisciplinary. Contributions focus on the process of building these networks within the network and offer unique lessons learned from each case. Contributors reflect on: what networking and partnership mean; the difference that networking made to their research; how networking builds capacity; and the importance of different contexts to how partnerships and networks are built. It also examines the approach of working through clusters of researchers and assesses to what extent and in what ways this form of collaboration influenced the ability to see connections. A key organizing principle for the project was to connect seemingly disparate research interests, questions, and agendas—to draw from individual research programs and link together those scholars who were doing work that was related either quite directly or more implicitly. Contributions to this section reflect on the value of working as a research cluster and how to think about research as a network or unit.

In their chapter "New, Emerging, Emerged? Navigating Agency, Technology, and Organization in Developing the Emerging Scholars and Practitioners on Migration Issues (ESPMI) Network," Brittany Lauren Wheeler and Petra Molnar provide an overview of ESPMI's trajectory as a working group and network. They document the challenges and successes of: weaving together in-person and social media-based engagement; identifying and critiquing the network's mission; weighing the utility of institutional support and traditional funding sources; and maintaining momentum in endeavours that rely upon the contributions of a network of volunteers. ESPMI members felt a strong commitment to the field of refugee studies and sought a meaningful place to contribute. They focused primarily on initiatives that encouraged intergenerational, interdisciplinary, and other cross-boundary engagements. By identifying project-based work, establishing a network of professional connections, and developing the opportunity to publish and access research and initiatives, ESPMI has charted a largely grassroots course toward creating a space for scholarly and professional support, especially regarding knowledge production by its members.

In their chapter "What Constitutes Environmental Displacement? Challenges and Opportunities of Exploring Connections across Thematically

Diverse Areas," Pablo Bose and Elizabeth Lunstrum explore the successes and challenges of the RRN's Environmental Displacement cluster. This collaborative cluster brought together researchers from diverse locations and at different points of their academic careers to work on issues of common interest. Their reflections focus on four areas in particular: 1) the origins and structure of the networking model; 2) making the case for "environmentally induced displacement" as a substantive conceptual field, and their main organizing concept; 3) how the cluster enabled other interventions into knowledge production concerning this main organizing concept; and 4) reflections on what has worked in this model and what remain as challenges moving forward.

In her chapter "Bittersweet Symphony: Challenges and Lessons Learned from Network Building in Latin America," Beatriz Eugenia Sánchez-Mojica traces both the development and the demise of the Latin American Network for Forced Migration (LANFM)/*Red latino americana de migración forzada*, reflecting on the "lights and the shadows" of the unfinished process. In 2010, at a workshop hosted by Roberto Vidal (Javeriana University) and Sánchez-Mojica (Los Andes University) in Bogotá, thirty academic and community researchers agreed to form the first ever network focused on forced migration in Latin America. The chapter documents four highly productive workshops and the successful hosting of the 2014 conference of the International Association for the Study of Forced Migration in Bogotá. However, in the absence of crucial resources, the network could not be sustained. Sánchez-Mojica suggests that the current context in Latin America is more propitious for collaborative research than it was in 2010 and sets out guidelines for the possible resumption of LANFM.

Christina Clark-Kazak explores lessons learned in developing an international network on research methodologies and knowledge production in forced migration. Her chapter "Partnering on Research Methodologies in Forced Migration: Challenges, Opportunities and Lessons Learned" describes both the successes and challenges of this network, with a view to contributing to more sustainable partnerships in the future. It highlights the importance of developing specific, concrete initiatives around which network members can rally and the need to take advantage of opportunities that present themselves, including by adding methodology activities into existing initiatives and events. The group also learned about the challenges of funding projects *about* methodology, in contrast to more traditional, empirically driven research collaborations. Moreover, despite an explicit focus on power and attempts to decolonize forced migration, the network still reflected and reproduced knowledge asymmetries that privileged participation from those in the global north.

We are deeply grateful to our RRN colleagues for their thoughtful reflections on their work and for the guidance they provide to the field of forced migration studies as it continues to negotiate partnerships of knowledge production in a geopolitical context of immense inequality. Their contributions guide us through valuable lessons learned as they managed significant challenges in striving to achieve ethical practices in research and networking. These colleagues offer strategies and tools to those researchers and practitioners who share our commitment to the fair and equitable generation of knowledge in Appadurai's (2000) tradition of "strong internationalization."

## Notes

We are indebted to Wesley Oakes, a former doctoral student at York University, who conducted the research and wrote the *RRN Mapping Report* (2015) upon which we are drawing here.

1    www.refugeeresearch.net.

## References

Appadurai, Arjun. 2000. "Grassroots Globalization and the Research Imagination." *Public Culture* 12, no. 1: 1–19.

Arbel, Efrat, and Alletta Brenner. 2013. *Bordering on Failure: Canada-US Border Policy and the Politics of Refugee Exclusion.* Cambridge, MA: Harvard Immigration and Refugee Law Clinical Program, Harvard Law School.

Bradley, Megan. 2008. "On the Agenda: North-South Research Partnerships and Agenda Setting Processes." *Development in Practice* 18, no. 6: 673–85.

Chimni, B. S. 1998. "The Geopolitics of Refugee Studies: A View from the South." *Journal of Refugee Studies* 11, no. 4: 350–74.

Currie, Melissa, Gillian King, Peter Rosenbaum, Mary Law, Marilyn Kertoy, and Jacqueline Specht. 2005. "A Model of Impacts of Research Partnerships in Health and Social Services." *Evaluation and Program Planning* 28, no. 4: 400–412.

Hyndman, Jennifer, and Wenona Giles. 2017. *Refugees in Extended Exile: Living on the Edge*. Abingdon-on-Thames: Routledge.

Hynie, Michaela, Susan McGrath, Julie E. E. Young, and Paula Banerjee. 2014. "Negotiations of Engaged Scholarship and Equity through a Global Network of Refugee Scholars." *Scholarly and Research Communication* 5, no. 3: 1–16.

Jazeel, Tariq, and Colin McFarlane. 2007. "Responsible Learning: Cultures of Knowledge Production and the North-South Divide." *Antipode* 39, no. 5: 781–9.

Jentsch, Birgit. 2004. "Making Southern Realities Count: Research Agendas and Design in North-South Collaborations." *International Journal of Social Research Methodology* 7, no. 3: 259–69.

Koehn, Peter, and Milton Obamba. 2014. *The Transnationally Partnered University: Insight from Research and Sustainable Development Collaborations in Africa*. New York: Palgrave Macmillan.

Landau, Loren B. 2012. "Communities of Knowledge or Tyrannies of Partnership: Reflections on North-South Research Networks and the Dual Imperative." *Journal of Refugee Studies* 25, no. 4: 555–70.

Nakabugo, Mary G., Eimear Barrett, Peter McEvoy, and Ronaldo Munck. 2010. "Best Practice in North-South Research Relationships in Higher Education: The Irish African Partnership Model." *Policy & Practice: A Development Education Review* 10 (Spring): 89–98.

Oakes, Wesley J. 2015. *RRN Mapping Report*. Toronto, ON: Refugee Research Network, York University.

Shantz, Elizabeth. 2012. *Knowledge Translation Challenges and Solutions Described by Researchers*. Waterloo: Canadian Water Network.

*Power and Politics in Refugee Research*

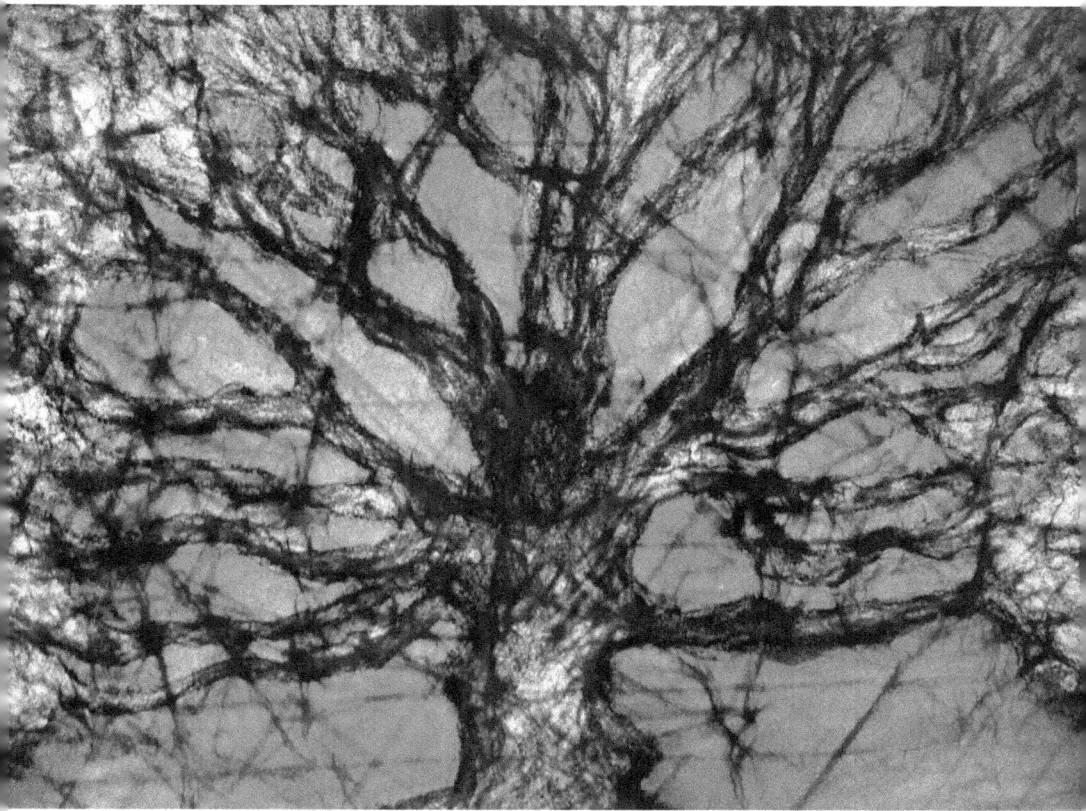

# Capacity, Complicity, and Subversion: Revisiting Collaborative Refugee Research in an Era of Containment

*Loren B. Landau*

## Introduction

Power imbalances are intrinsic to every social relation. In research or teaching collaborations spanning geographic and economic divides, these imbalances can be acute. There are often benefits of such partnerships—new data, louder voices, effective advocacy—but there may also be a high price to pay. Indeed, the most lasting consequence of such collaborations may be to legitimize the presence, perspectives, and budgets of relatively empowered scholars and institutions. Ideally partners are aware of privilege and work towards equity in ways that erode long-standing structural and institutional constraints. As the introduction makes clear, this was the primary goal of the Refugee Research Network (RRN). However, such explicit self-awareness is rare and there are times when that awareness is absent or privilege is expressly overlooked. This oversight, combined with misaligned expectations and incentives, can ultimately disempower precisely those the relationships ostensibly aim to assist (cf. Cooke and Kothari 2001). A deluge of resources flowing into refugee and migration research due to the "European migration crisis" will likely heighten these risks. This chapter explains why this may be and offers suggestions for how groups with fundamentally different and inequitable endowments can interact in ways that are just, sustainable, and mutually beneficial to themselves and the populations they serve: students and displaced people.

With increased Western and donor interest in migration within Africa and the Middle East, pressure for translocal research partnerships is growing. Motivations include, inter alia, the neo-imperialist (attempting to generate data to frame migration prevention interventions [see Curzi 2016]), the paternalistic (building capacity at poor universities), and the scholarly (how to better assess translocal processes). More politically correct engagements lean towards the paternalistic and political: aiming to level scholarly playing fields by enabling marginalized partners to shape a global research agenda and improve research quality. They also frequently seek to relay southern perspectives to northern policymakers and scholars.[1] These are important and potentially worthy objectives inasmuch as they improve the quality of scholarly teaching and research while addressing (or at least seeking to) the "dual imperative" in refugee research: making an academic contribution while meeting ethical obligations to assist the often-vulnerable populations on which we build our professional success (see Jacobsen and Landau 2003).

However well meaning, research partnerships also come with substantial risks of heightening inequality and becoming complicit in global strategies of migrant containment.[2] Insufficient funding, administrative hiccups, shifting interests, or an ill-informed choice of partners all play a part—although these are by no means unique to cross-continental collaborations. There are also factors at once distinct and more fundamental behind these shortcomings. International research partnerships enact and expose the inequalities, structural constraints, and historically conditioned power relations implicit in the production of knowledge. These include unequal resource endowments and discordant incentive structures and funding schemes. As Zingerli (2010, 222) suggests, "research partnerships are not an easy remedy for inherent asymmetries and inequalities." Indeed, partnerships risk entrenching some of the north-south dichotomies they seek to overcome (see Standing and Taylor 2009).

With increased pressure for collaboration due to northern funding regimes and African scholars' need for recognition and resources, African

LOREN B. LANDAU

scholars frequently trade their most valuable international currency—legitimacy and local insight—for financial resources, travel opportunities, and prestige.[3] But these exchanges may work against the long-term success of southern partners in satisfying the dual imperative: contributing to scholarship while addressing real world problems. Northern scholars may recognize and work against these trends and Africans may find creative subterfuges, but the general trend is nonetheless worth debating. In an era where Europe—in particular—is funding substantial research projects across Africa with the goal of preventing migrants and refugees from "escaping" the continent, the risks go beyond entrenching academic inequality. By responding to Europe's obsession with containment, cross-continental partnerships risk not only distorting local research agendas but doing so in ways that may ultimately work against the populations we study.

Many of the challenges faced in refugee or displacement research networks echo north-south academic relations generally. Nonetheless, displacement research is infused with distinguishing forms of politics and ethics. Indeed, the field's close ties to practitioner communities—direct service providers, donors, humanitarian agencies, advocacy groups—reinforces two enduring inequalities and distortions within partnerships and transnational collaborations:

- The structural position of northern and southern researchers means that northern researchers can convert information generated through policy-oriented projects into scholarly outputs while offering critical perspectives from the security of tenured offices. Yet the emphasis on promoting "local insight into local problems" often fixes scholars geographically and analytically. Moreover, for reasons described below, local scholars are often wary of overtly criticizing the officials or agencies supporting their salaries. For those working in the south—particularly in acutely under-resourced African universities—needs for funding and policy recognition reinforce a dependence on policy actors.

- An emphasis on global governance and international best practices inadvertently positions people at the centre of international cooperation as the collective voice. In most cases this means northern partners become the voice for southern actors whose language is too fragmented and particularistic to be globally legible. In an era in which global governance concerns are dominated by a containment compulsion, this may mean southern scholars are increasingly caught between the Scylla of irrelevance and inaction and the Charybdis of complicity.

## Perspectives on African Displacement Research

Before continuing, a few qualifications are in order. First, I am concerned here almost exclusively with work based in the social sciences rather than the natural sciences or more applied fields (e.g., social work, law, and engineering). Second, for my purposes, northern universities are schools in Europe, Australia, or North America. Southern ones are those elsewhere in countries characterized as middle or low income. There is enormous diversity within both north and south (see Mouton 2010), but it is the research collaborations spanning this divide that concern me here. My perspective is informed largely by my experience with sub-Saharan African universities and work at a South African institution. My colleagues and I are often nominated as "southern" partners despite South Africa's relative wealth, which privileges us vis-à-vis the rest of the continent. Nonetheless, I hope others from the continent will consider this something of a southern perspective on partnerships, perspectives that remain "few and far between" (Bradley 2006, 4).

My comments here are intentionally general and imprecise. Other chapters in this collection offer more concrete examples and insights (see chapters 3, 4, and 12). This chapter refines comments I made in a similar forum half a dozen years ago in a paper initially commissioned by the Refugee Research Network (RRN).[4] The discussion has continued since then, and I have noted a growing awareness among some "northern" partners regarding the nature of partnership. In many instances, these simply translate into higher levels of frustration given the structural obstacles we all face. Moreover, while many universities have become more aware of the hazards of partnership, the political economy of knowledge production has shifted in dangerous ways given the large-scale commitment from the United States and Europe—two of the largest donors to humanitarian

LOREN B. LANDAU

action and research—to create a global technology of containment (see Landau 2019).

## Revisiting the Dual Imperative in Refugee Research and the Political Economy of Knowledge Production

In 2003, Karen Jacobsen and I argued that most displacement related research seeks to influence agencies and governments to develop more effective responses. This orientation stems in part from our research subjects, whose experience of violent conflict, displacement, and human rights violations compels us to work—whether from compassion, charity, or self-interest—to reduce their burdens and vulnerability. Many of us remain swayed by David Turton's (1996, 96) admonition that research into suffering can only be justified if alleviating that suffering is an explicit objective.

While concerned with refugees' rights and welfare, university-based scholars typically premise research on a belief that sound inquiry can and should serve multiple masters. Indeed, for those facing disciplinary tenure committees, scholarly audits, or publication demands, policy recommendations are never enough. Moreover, for universities to offer critical thought and reflection on the local and global societies of which they are part, they must also reserve distinct space for non-policy oriented research, theorization, and provocation (see Rodgers 2004; Bakewell 2008). It is encouraging to see questions of displacement gaining increased prominence in expressly scholarly fields like economics, political science, and anthropology within Europe and North America. This has not been the case across much of Africa. If anything, African-based migration research has become increasingly policy or activist oriented.

The relative absence of African (and other) voices from scholarly debates diminishes our understanding of the world while allowing a relatively privileged, geographically concentrated group of scholars to set global academic agendas. Even if the majority of the world's refugees and migrants and the bulk of the humanitarian interventions are located in the south, southern-based scholars are hard to find in the leading (i.e., most broadly cited) scholarly journals on the topic. Even more infrequently does their work on displacement appear in disciplinary journals or interdisciplinary outlets oriented towards the academy. Where they appear, it is usually through country case studies or as secondary authors. Rarely do they proffer multi-sited comparative studies; even more infrequently do they include multiple countries. One must dig deep to find a theoretically informed critique of aid modalities, concepts, or academic theory and methods written by an African scholar working at a southern institution. While northern scholars may struggle to justify more practical work, African-based researchers often remain excluded—or exclude themselves—from anything but case studies and policy driven reports.

The highly localized orientation and limited conceptual vocabulary of African-based refugee research can be explained by a set of interrelated circumstances: 1) extended isolation from global scholarly publications and dialogues; 2) the limited amount of course work required to complete advanced degrees, particularly those who have conducted work within the British system; and 3) the practical orientation of many African universities and state-funded research organizations. Due to these and additional factors described below, scholars trained and working at African universities often express a limited impulse to produce for anyone other than a local audience or audience concerned with the particularities of specific cases. When provided chances to define questions that are more conceptual or theoretically promising, few of the African-based scholars with whom I have collaborated take the opportunity to do so. Instead, their inquiries are typically framed by policy issues or immediate normative concerns. The idea of conducting "demand-led research" in which southerners are asked only to drive research that can solve pressing social problems or otherwise "unleash southern potential" risks reinforcing this tendency (see Nair and Menon 2002).

The strict local and policy focus also compromises one of African scholars' most significant comparative advantages: the ability to identify what might be invisible or inexplicable to outsiders, where local empirics challenge global presuppositions either practical or scholarly. Consequently, collaborations often see southern scholars generating data on narrowly defined topics while northern scholars synthesize, analyze, and theorize (see Zeleza 1996; Chimni 2009). Schweigman and van der Werf (1994) call this the Ganuza dilemma. The absence of a strong or unified southern intellectual agenda creates the space/necessity for northern partners to dominate decision-making and research directions. Encouraging southern partners to collect and relay "local knowledge" further incentivizes deep, sometimes myopic, local engagement. At an immediate level this

LOREN B. LANDAU

may satisfy all involved, but it does little to overturn northern dominance of global academic discourse. As discussed below, a range of institutional factors further reinforces this status quo.

Conceptual and theoretical narrowness are by no means unique to forced migration research, but the topic itself further limits the scope of our inquiry. A field founded to satisfy a humanitarian and academic impulse and supported by policy or rights-oriented funding, refugee research has conceptually encircled itself. Rather than drawing extensively on the insights of other fields—and thereby contributing to them—self-identified refugee researchers focus almost exclusively on displaced peoples, their activities, and interventions oriented exclusively towards them. In many cases, researchers draw on (and speak to) literature that is similarly blinkered in ways that work against contributions to established disciplines. Instead, we see the repeated focus on refugee vulnerability, exploitation, and bureaucratic ineptitude. Our tendency to see refugee rights and welfare as the sole, important outcome also leads us to ignore interests and actions that may indirectly prejudice (or promote) the displaced. This is especially true in the global south where refugees may have distinct, but by no means uniquely acute, vulnerabilities (see Kihato and Landau 2016).

## Thinking Locally, Acting Globally?

Beyond generating scholarly work, many north-south partnerships aim to channel information from where refugees are (i.e., the south) to the northern policymakers and organizations behind the global humanitarian enterprise. This is an important function and one potentially well served by collaborations with representatives strategically placed around the world. Nonetheless, such relationships are not without their shortcomings and risks, four of which I raise here. First, they presume research is a powerful tool for achieving policy change. Second, they typically suppose substantial and unproblematic gains of channelling southern voices to policymakers in the north. Third, inasmuch as the previous two points are true, such collaborations effectively generate institutional configurations where northern scholars choose and shape the southern voices that get heard. Lastly—and building on points made above—the framing of much new migration research may well make Africans complicit in an emerging containment regime.

First, does research influence policy change? Sound research design, representative sampling, and objectivity may be the hallmarks of good academic and policy-oriented research, but there are often only weak correlations between research quality and practical influence. Even when research is commissioned or funded by governments and aid agencies, it is often ignored if the recommendations are politically or financially inconvenient. This is clearly not limited to displacement research; all research is more likely be used if it confirms existing principles or furthers policymakers and advocates' interests (Argyris 1982; Feldman and March 1981). Moreover, given the pace at which humanitarian interventions are planned, by the time good research is ready to share, we are often left fighting yesterday's policy battles. Researchers able to offer shiny, cleverly packaged solutions score newspaper and television coverage in ways that help their careers far more than those they claim to aid. African scholars are rarely able to package their work in these ways—nor should they—and their recommendations and critiques often get overshadowed by global perspectives that may have little local relevance.

Faced with researchers' frustrations at their work being ignored and funders' anxiety that their investments are coming to naught, the typical response has been to spend more money on dissemination and develop ever more elaborate strategies for getting policymakers and researchers in the same room. This has produced some successes—but precious few given the time, energy, and money put into it. Indeed, there are reasons to doubt whether such research initiatives can produce substantial policy change in their lifespan. Where it does produce change, it likely will come only by capitalizing on opportunity windows opened by circumstances well beyond our control. That African policymaking processes are often so obtuse and arbitrary—or shaped by donors and international organizations—means that the kind of forums and initiatives used in Europe or North America are unlikely to drive policy exchange. Instead, they may be formed to legitimize government decisions or as a tool for northern policy influence (via their southern partners) as has been the case regarding the dissemination of particular norms around trafficking and border management (Segatti 2011a). The use of the media to mobilize public opinion may be equally unsuccessful where the press is controlled or largely irrelevant (as is public opinion in policymaking).

Rather than throw more money at dissemination, we should shift thinking about research use in important ways: instead of simply producing more sophisticated work on policy outcomes, we need to better understand policymaking processes. There has already been some work on policymaking around refugee concerns (see, for example, Schmidt 2008; Handmaker 2001; Segatti 2011b). This is important, but we must go further. As with many other aspects of refugee related research, we are overly bound by our focus on displacement and the humanitarian space. In many instances, the policies that matter will not be about migration, per se, and may only tangentially mention refugees and migrants (see Landau and Amit 2014). As such, we must complement our work on humanitarian issues with analyses of housing, agriculture, security, and a range of other issues and an effort to understand (a) how these policies intersect with our concerns and (b) how those policies are made and how they might be proactively reformed. This means not only nesting forced migration research within broader migration studies, but actively identifying and exploring intersections between forced migration and other fields of inquiry. This does not mean losing our focus but may instead mean forging collaborations with the substantial number of scholars working in these areas. While more careful analysis of policymaking processes may disabuse us of our often-naive notions of how policy is made (and our ability to influence it), those continuing this campaign will have better strategies for doing so.

## Channelling African Voices

Speaking of policy influence, forced migration studies places a disproportionate emphasis on global governance, donor policies, and international organizations. There is value in working at this level, but the most immediate and important changes will be achieved through local and regional (or even sub-regional) initiatives. Even where there are sensible modifications to existing regional or international instruments, such global frameworks provide protection only when supported by highly specific national and sub-regional dynamics: the local politics, not the principles, of protection are what typically matters most (see Kihato and Landau 2016). However, Scholey (2006) argues (in her work on peace building and human security) that where research is framed in policy terms, it is typically informed by global or northern policy concerns, rather than the immediate, concrete problems facing communities grappling with armed conflict. This has been the case for our field, where discussions of UN reform, resettlement, international legal frameworks, and the global aid regime have shaped research agendas in ways that exclude local meanings of those terms or other issues of relatively greater importance. Obsessions with the global migration and refugee compacts or the "European refugee crisis" are yet further examples.

Rather than supporting our research interests, our relationships have generated a kind of coercive isomorphism: we either fall in line with others' agendas or we risk losing much needed financial support. Where so many new research projects across Africa are expressly oriented towards generating data for European policymakers, there are particular dangers of complicity. Undoubtedly, improving our understanding of African migration and displacement can be valuable. I, for one, have long advocated the need to promote African-based interventions that can aid and absorb those who move by choice or compulsion. However, when the data is intended to feed European efforts to discourage movements within or out of Africa, Africa-based scholars may quickly become complicit in an enormous and highly funded containment apparatus.[5] A call for increased attention to local political processes and other local dynamics (social, economic, etc.) gives cause to question just how useful networks and efforts are to influence global policymaking. While many value participating in high level dialogues, we must recognize that international laws and policies (and often even domestic ones) may make little difference to most migrants. More than a decade ago, Chimni (1998, 352–6) persuasively argued that the field had been wilfully apolitical and asocial in its approach to improving refugees' lives and refugee-related scholarship. While there have been some improvements, we could and should go further. This means looking closer by complementing global generalizations with local or regional perspectives.

Returning again to the symbolic value attached to information reveals an additional dimension of collaboratively generated knowledge. In some instances, northern institutions' imprimatur enhances a finding's credibility and the likelihood that it will be considered. For many years, the City of Johannesburg hired British and American consultants to provide models from London, New York, or other first world cities. More recently, the UNHCR in Pretoria has begun building intervention programs on a two-week research project by the Women's Refugee Committee while largely ignoring years of locally generated research. If policy influence is the goal, there may be instances where southern researchers must reinforce the northern experts' power in global debate, swallow their pride, and hand over results to those who will get heard.

While we can accept partnership and invisibility as the price we pay for influence, the issue here is a simple one: as long as these partnerships continue to depend on northern partners to set the research agenda, manage funding, and provide legitimacy, southern-based scholars will rarely have the opportunity to participate in global dialogues on their own terms. That information is so frequently relayed via northern partners (or synthesized and then presented by them) only furthers the imbalance. Most obviously, northern scholars are in a position to act as gatekeepers, filtering out "noise" by silencing those who work against their agendas and presenting only that information which they find convincing, relevant, or otherwise suitable. (As a scholar working in South Africa, I confess to excluding local and regional voices from joint projects where I felt they were misguided or counterproductive. This is a similarly damaging form of paternalism that can only be countered through dialogue and radical generosity.) While refugees and others may benefit in some way from engagements done under these auspices—notwithstanding the points raised above—the work of southern scholars inadvertently confirms northern scholars' position as experts, theorists, and the most powerful critics. It is, after all, northern scholars who choose and shape the southern voices that are being heard. Given the increasingly powerful position that experts play in international humanitarianism (see Barnett 2011), these further academic and global political hierarchies.

Some will undoubtedly respond that as unfortunate as northern involvement may be, this is the price scholars pay. However, trading visibility and autonomy for policy influence is no guarantee of success. Across much of the south, political authorities view northern involvement in research projects as nefarious neo-imperialism. In some instances, the presence of northern partners (even if they are living and working in the south) can cause work to be summarily dismissed as a product of meddling outsiders. In the worst circumstances, a reasonable policy option may be partially or completely stigmatized if it becomes conceptually linked to political outsiders or foreigners. The consequences are likely to depend heavily on local political systems, the timbre of civil society-state relations, and the qualitative content and strategies surrounding other advocacy issues. That said, where authorities are looking for reasons to ignore unflattering analyses, donors' insistence on branding can work against their stated objective of policy change. If we accept that local or national policies are equally (or more) important than global frameworks, we must take these politics seriously.

I am increasingly convinced that effective policy influence demands a twofold adjustment. On the one hand, we need to understand and work to influence policy at the intersections of the "humanitarian space" with other policy fields whether those of urban management, environmental science, or health and nutrition. On the other, we need to "go local." International law, global policy, and multilateral donors are important, but substantive policy change in that realm is hard to achieve and its effects are dilatory and diffuse. We need to seek solidarities on multiple scales, largely with those empowered to make structural or political changes. In most cases, these are people and interests outside of the humanitarian community. The "low-hanging fruit" are often at the national or even sub-national level, where change is both easier to achieve and more likely to produce immediate effects. This demands a level of critical local literacy, not local knowledge mobilized for global interests. As such, we must be acutely aware of how partnerships towards these ends can both endanger our efforts to influence policy and marginalize the voices and autonomy of southern partners.

## Reshaping Partnerships

Responding to the dual-imperative for refugee research in the south—or at least in Africa—means confronting the political economy of knowledge production and recognizing the limits of scholarship in achieving changes in policy and practice. As scholars, there are limits to what we can do about general funding patterns and the fragility of scholarship across sub-Saharan Africa. Yet if we are serious about building African capacity and influence, we ought to carefully consider the nature of interaction and the intended and unintentional outcomes of our north-south partnerships.

The following are a series of practical steps that can help improve research generated in the south and the success of future collaborations.

*Take Small Steps Wisely*: Research consortia partners are often selected more for their geography and ability to legitimize collaboration than their intellectual interests or endowments. The results include motley crews that lack focus, have little personal rapport, and struggle internally for resources. While not always avoidable, more energy spent in selecting partners and greater upfront openness about objectives, resources, and expected outcomes can help ensure more fruitful collaboration. Even in existing networks, there are benefits of starting small with concrete projects involving relatively few partners. This may help avoid a "lowest common denominator" approach to research and the kind of pressure where southern partners are overwhelmed by a dominant "northern" or comparative agenda that marginalizes the value of small-scale research (this is the kind of tyranny of consensus that Cooke and Kothari outline). As "The Nairobi Report" suggests, successful small-scale collaborations can be the base for broader projects managed by people who have established a functional and productive working relationship (British Academy 2006). Whenever possible, these partnerships should be forged as early possible. Once a project has been conceptualized (or a funding proposal submitted), the die is cast: no matter how much an ancillary partner may "push back," the parameters are already established.

*Open the Gates*: Partnerships should be at once more specific and more broadly conceived. Collaborations between a refugee studies person in the north and a refugee studies person in the south will tend to reproduce or strengthen existing knowledge and presuppositions with additional case study materials. Given the close connection of policy and the field, this limits the work's audience and its potential scholarly impact. It may also reinforce a global hierarchy of knowledge production. Both enhancing our research agenda and broadening our policy impact demands building links with people outside of the humanitarian field. These people can provide both technical expertise and insights and, equally importantly, connections to policymakers outside our comfortable stovepipes and silos. In the long term, this can open new funding sources and break the close and potentially damaging dyads of refugee researchers and practitioners.

*Fences Make Good Neighbours*: Alternatively, call a spade a spade. Too many north-south collaborations are shrouded in the politically correct language of partnership, a fiction that disguises inherent inequalities with the relationships and differences in objectives and endowments. To address these, there should be a full assessment of the participants' resources and objectives from the get-go. In instances where objectives differ substantially, project leaders should walk away or consider devolving financial resources to allow individuals or small groups to continue work. Where this is not possible, partners should define their roles from the beginning. If this means southern partners are to act as research assistants and data generators, so be it. At least they will know where they stand and the risks and benefits associated with their position. Full accountability and transparency in budgeting and planning will also help southern partners to assess the degree to which they are partners or participants.

*Live within Our Means*: To secure funding, applicants often make elaborate claims about their scholarly and practical impact. This may win grants, but it often levies too many demands on overcommitted partners who will not be fully compensated for their time. A series of smaller projects that require less ongoing participation may ultimately be more likely to be completed and cost effective. The heavy demand for policy influence at all stages of research also draws scholars uncomfortably close to the policy community, sacrificing autonomy and reinforcing a consultancy culture.

*Pay the Bills; Pay in Advance*: Partnerships must recognize that southern partners' participation in research collaborations is often as much (or more) about securing financial resources as intellectual inquiry or policy impact. To encourage substantive collaboration and scholarship, budgets must consider the full cost of involvement. Where long-term partnership is desired, support must cover scholars' university salaries and other opportunity costs associated with such participation. It must also provide the research infrastructure required to conduct the work (e.g., travel, logistics, printers) and the somewhat extortionate overheads African universities typically charge on funds they manage (in exchange for managing them poorly) (see British Academy 2006, 10). If such payments are prohibitive, alternative arrangements may be considered such as short-term and highly focused writing retreats or other fora in which partners are able to dedicate—albeit for a short period—their full attention to a given project or collaborative initiative.

*Buy Local*: Inasmuch as policy influence remains an objective, greater emphasis should be placed on building relationships with local advocacy organizations and with partners outside of the refugee field. Although there are reasons why southern scholars may not wish to be publicly associated with policy critics, where the options for such associations exist they are likely to produce more immediate change and at least partially avoid channelling information to northern institutions in ways that enhance their expertise and voice.

*Replant and Replenish*: Senior scholars across Africa have strong incentives for monopolizing fields in their respective countries. It is typically these people who attract international attention and get drawn into global or multi-region partnerships. This both fortifies their dominance of local scholarship and lessens the likelihood of full participation in collaborative initiatives. Insisting on the independent participation of doctoral students and early career scholars can help to multiply the voices being heard both in and out of their respective countries. This will especially be the case if such participation enables scholars to gain experience in proposal and grant writing and research management, skills that will ultimately provide them with a level of autonomy (see chapter 10). As with other aspects of collaborations, selection for participation should be done carefully and transparently to avoid providing senior scholars with further patronage opportunities. Care must also be taken as such arrangements are potentially paternalistic and risk creating imbalances where senior scholars in the north are working with less established scholars elsewhere.

*You Get What You Negotiate*: African and other southern scholars often underestimate their importance to northern researchers' legitimacy, research funding, and ability to do research. While there are some risks to doing so, African scholars are often able to play on northerners' liberal sensitivities and genuine desire for collaboration to assert their interests and demands. If such negotiations fail, southern scholars should walk away or be clever enough to realize what they are getting into. While we must honour our commitments, we must also ensure that even the most unequal relationships become mutually beneficial. If this requires slyness or subterfuge, so be it. Some of the most effective and radical forms of social change have started with little more.

## Notes

1 See Bradley 2006; Katz and Martin (1997); Baud 2002; Zingerli 2010. For more general critiques, Zeleza 1996.

2 For a broader discussion of this theme, see Haraway 1991.

3 See Freschi 2011.

4 An earlier version of this chapter was published as Landau 2012.

5 For more on Europe's efforts to develop containment technologies, see Knoll and de Weiker 2016; Brachet 2016; and Perrin 2012.

# References

Argyris, C. 1982. "How Learning and Reasoning Processes Affect Organizational Change." In *Change in Organizations: New Perspectives on Theory, Research, and Practices*, edited by P. S. Goodman, 47–86. San Francisco: Jossey-Bass.

Bakewell, Oliver. 2008. "Research beyond the Categories: The Importance of Policy Irrelevant Research into Forced Migration." *Journal of Refugee Studies* 21, no. 4: 432–53.

Barnett, Michael. 2011. *Empire of Humanity: A History of Humanitarianism*. Ithaca: Cornell University Press.

Baud, Isa S. A. 2002. "North-South Research Partnerships: An Institutions Approach." In *North-South Research Co-operation: Comprehensives Approaches to Development and Innovation*, edited by J. Bouma and Opschoor, 51–90. Amsterdam: KNAW.

Brachet, Julien. 2016. "Policing the Desert: The IOM in Libya beyond War and Peace." *Antipode* 48, no. 2: 272–92.

Bradley, Megan. 2006. *North-South Research Partnerships: Literature Review and Annotated Bibliography*. Ottawa: International Development Research Centre.

The British Academy and The Association of Commonwealth Universities. 2006. *The Nairobi Report: Frameworks for Africa-UK Research Collaboration in the Social Sciences and Humanities*. London: The British Academy.

Chimni, B. S. 2009. "The Birth of a 'Discipline': From Refugee to Forced Migration Studies." *Journal of Refugee Studies* 22, no. 1: 11–29.

———. 1998. "The Geopolitics of Refugee Studies: A View from the South." *Journal of Refugee Studies* 11, no. 4: 350–74.

Curzi, Corallina L. 2016. "The Externalisation of European Borders: Steps and Consequences of a Dangerous Process." *Open Migration*, 12 July 2016.

Cooke, Bill, and Uma Kothari. 2001. "The Case for Participation as Tyranny." In *Participation: The New Tyranny*, edited by Bill Cooke and Uma Kothari, 1–14. London: Zed Books.

Feldman, Martha S., and James G. March. 1981. "Information in Organizations as Signal and Symbol." *Administrative Science Quarterly* 26, no. 2: 171–86.

Freschi, Laura. 2011. "African Universities: Creating True Researchers or 'Native Informers' to NGOs?" *Aidwatch Archive*, 4 May 2011. Accessed 8 Dec 2018. http://www.nyudri.org/aidwatcharchive/2011/05/african-universities-creating-true-researchers-or-%E2%80%9Cnative-informers%E2%80%9D-to-ngos.

Gaillard, Jacques F. 1994. "North-South Research Partnership: Is Collaboration Possible between Unequal Partners?" *Knowledge and Policy* 7, no. 2: 31–63.

Handmaker, Jeff. 2001. "No Easy Walk: Advancing Refugee Protection in South Africa." *Africa Today* 48, no. 3: 91–113.

Haraway, Donna. 1991. *Simians, Cyborgs and Women: The Reinvention of Nature*. New York: Routledge.

Hathaway, James. 2007. "Forced Migration Studies: Could We Agree Just to 'Date'?" *Journal of Refugee Studies* 20: 349–69.

Jacobsen, Karen, and Loren B. Landau. 2003. "The Dual Imperative in Refugee Research: Some Methodological and Ethical Considerations in Social Science Research on Forced Migration." *Disasters* 27, no. 3: 95–116.

Katz, J. Sylvan, and Ben R. Martin. 1997. "What is Research Collaboration?" *Research Policy* 26, no. 1: 1–18.

Kihato, Caroline W., and Loren B. Landau. 2016. "Stealth Humanitarianism: Negotiating Politics, Precarity, and Performance Management in Protecting the Urban Displaced." *Journal of Refugee Studies* 30, no. 3: 407–25.

Knoll, Anna, and Frauke de Weijer. 2016. "Understanding African and European Perspectives on Migration: Toward a Better Partnership for Regional Migration Governance?" Discussion Paper No. 203, November 2016. Maastricht: European Centre for Development Policy Management.

Landau, Loren B. 2019. "A Chronotope of Containment Development: Europe's Migrant Crisis and Africa's Reterritorialization." *Antipode* 51, no. 1: 169–86.

———. 2007. "Cognitive and Institutional Limits on Collecting and Processing Data on Populations at Risk: Preliminary Reflections on Southern African Responses to Displacement." In *Tools and Methods for Estimating Populations at Risk from Natural Disasters and Humanitarian Crises*, edited by National Research Council, 217–35. Washington, DC: The National Academies Press.

———. 2012. "Communities of Knowledge or Tyrannies of Partnership: Reflections on North-South Research Networks and the Dual Imperative." *Journal of Refugee Studies* 25, no. 4: 555–70.

Landau, Loren B., and Roni Amit. 2014. "Wither Policy? Southern African Perspectives on Understanding Law, 'Refugee' Policy and Protection." *Journal of Refugee Studies* 27, no. 4: 534–52.

Lubkemann, Stephen C. 2010. "Past Directions and Future Possibilities in the Study of African Displacement." Unpublished scoping study. Uppsala: Nordic Afrika Institute.

Mauss, Marcel. 1990 [1922]. *The Gift: Forms and Functions of Exchange in Archaic Societies.* London: Routledge.

Mouton, Johann. 2010. "The State of Social Science in Sub-Saharan Africa." In *World Social Science Report*, edited by International Social Science Council, 63–7. Paris: UNESCO.

Nair, K. N., and Vineetha Menon. 2002. "Capacity Building for Demand-Led Research: Issues and Priorities." Policy Management Brief 14. Maastricht: European Centre for Development Policy Management.

Perrin, Delphine. 2012. "The Impact of European Migration Policies on Migration-Related Legislative Activity in Maghreb Countries: An Overview of Recent Reforms." In *European Migration and Asylum Policies: Coherence or Contradiction?*, edited by Cristina Gortázar, María-Carolina Parra, Barbara Segaert, and Christiane Timmerman, 251–60. Brussels: Bruylant.

Rodgers, Graeme. 2004. "'Hanging Out' with Forced Migrants: Methodological and Ethical Challenges." *Forced Migration Review* 21: 28–9.

Segatti, Aurelia. 2011a. "Reforming South African Immigration Policy in the Postapartheid Period (1990–2010)" In *Migration to South Africa: A Regional Development Issue*, edited by Aurelia Segatti and Loren B. Landau, 31–66. Washington: The World Bank; Paris: The French Development Agency.

———. 2011b. "The Southern African Development Community: A Walk Away from the Free Movement of Persons?" In *A Regional Approach to Free Movement*, edited by Antoine Pécoud. Paris: UNESCO and New York: Berghahn Books.

Standing, Hilary, and Peter Taylor. 2009. "Whose Knowledge Counts? Development Studies Institutions and Power Relations in a Globalised World." *IDS Bulletin* 28, no. 2: 79–85.

Schmidt, Anna. 2008. "Negotiating Policy: Refugees and Security in Tanzania and Uganda." Paper presented at the ISA's 49th Annual Convention, "Bridging Multiple Divides," San Francisco, CA, 26 Mar 2008.

Scholey, Pam. 2006. "Peacebuilding Research and North-South Research Partnerships: Perspectives, Opportunities and Challenges." In *A Decade of Human Security: Global Governance and New Multilateralisms*, edited by Sandra J. McLean, David R. Black, and Timothy M. Shaw, 285–99. London: Ashgate.

Schweigman, C., and Ineke van der Werf. 1994. *Development-Related Research Collaboration: A Second Look at the Role of the Netherlands.* Amsterdam: Royal Tropical Institute.

Turton, David. 1996. "Migrants and Refugees." In *In Search of Cool Ground: War, Flight, and Homecoming in Northeast Africa*, edited by Tim Allen, 96–110. Trenton: Africa World Press.

Zeleza, Paul T. 1996. "Manufacturing and Consuming Knowledge." *Development in Practice* 6, no. 4: 293–303.

Zingerli, Claudia. 2010. "A Sociology of International Research Partnerships for Sustainable Development." *European Journal of Development Research* 22, no. 2: 217–33.

# Rethinking Displacement: Transitional Justice and Forced Migration Studies

*Nergis Canefe*

## Introduction

This article investigates a critical set of intersections between mass political violence, dispossession/displacement, transitional justice, politics of regime transformation, and human rights law. In the field of forced migration studies, displacement and dispossession-related restorative justice projects—and more specifically, issues such as right of return, compensation, and amelioration of state-induced ills for displaced peoples—are emerging as new areas of examination. Traditionally speaking, however, forced migration and transitional justice are two areas of scholarship attended by different academic communities. Similarly, often separate groups of activists and victims' advocates, scholars, jurists, policymakers, agencies, and donors address causes of concern and strategies pertaining to each area disparately. In the following pages, I assert that it is both possible and necessary to bring together the work done by these various actors and groups. In this vein, I highlight the benefits of conjoining these two approaches to dispossession, dismemberment from the national polity, and resultant experiences pertaining to displacement-induced human suffering. In order to point out future possibilities of this envisaged synergy, I offer a critical discussion of select works on transitional justice as they relate to forced migration and vice versa. Here, it is essential to note that the suggestions and findings articulated in this chapter are in tandem with the insights offered by Loren B. Landau on the issue of collaborative research (see chapter 1), as well as the urgent call for paying closer attention to the links between chronic state criminality and forced migration that Paula Banerjee and Ranabir Samaddar make in this volume (see chapter 5). It would also be pertinent to suggest that the conversation led by Christina Clark-Kazak (see chapter 13) on cross-disciplinary dialogue and ethical commitments to working with human suffering fits well with the spirit of this particular quest for establishing synergies of knowledge production and knowledge dissemination.

The nexus of transitional justice and forced migration studies could be approached from multiple angles and perspectives: empirical and theoretical, analytical and normative, historical and contemporary, local, regional, and global. Here I urge that regardless of the angle taken, we must pay close attention to the historical fault lines pertaining to structural inequalities, imposed divisions, and violently secured borders, which reveal dynamics of power struggles between states and their own people. This point is particularly important regarding the neocolonialist and late-Orientalist tendencies that exist in the depiction of global refugee crises. The politics of studying historical and social transformations in the global south are such that forced migration movements create an aura of perpetual or at least chronic crises in the postcolonial and postimperial geographies of modern statehood. In this context, analyzing mass dispossession of political subjects in post-conflict settings runs the risk of becoming an end in and of itself. Indeed, forced migration studies have long suffered from an oversight caused by a determined concentration of scholarship on numbers and short-term survival strategies. As a result important aspects of dispossession—such as duties and responsibilities of states and non-state actors, politico-legal aspects of forced migration movements, interventions of civic bodies, international organizations, and normative changes in the wider field of human rights law as they relate to displacement, societal peace-making, and political justice—are often overlooked.

# Methodological Interventions

The study of mass political violence created by states turning against their own peoples requires an interdisciplinary effort. Analyses of underlying causes of social disfranchisement, socioeconomic predicaments leading to marginalization and targeting of select groups, challenges pertaining to remembrance of violence, and restoration of the rights of the displaced all fall under the purview of this effort. These events and processes almost always take place in the context of transitional justice projects enacted in postcolonial/neocolonial landscapes. Essential to these kinds of endeavours is the establishment of connections between documentation of violence, deliberation on its causes, and research keen to understand patterns, as well as an overall awareness of the ethics of witnessing when academics engage with human suffering. To this end, we must first determine the reasons for the largely single-focus study of forced migration despite the fact that it could not be isolated from sociopolitical and economic factors and processes. This act of contextualization is essential to develop a counter-discourse on forced migration.

To this end, this chapter is divided into three sections. The first section canvasses theoretical exercises that identify patterns and unique approaches to forced migration that differ from dominant practices and debates on the subject. This is done in the specific context of linking transitional justice projects with forced migration in the global south. The second section engages with lessons learned from post-conflict restorative justice projects and their specificities in select regions as these relate to forced migration. It is often the powerful rather than weak postcolonial states that experience mass political violence related displacements. Of these, here I reflect on the post-conflict experiences of the displaced populations in select cases to underline the innate relationship between societal and political justice and to reiterate the detrimental effects of dispossession and forced movement for society at large. The last section presents a critical debate on the concept of mobility in its application to the forced migration and transitional justice studies nexus as a burgeoning field. In particular, I examine non-conventional approaches to forced migration, conundrums pertaining to statelessness, ethics of witnessing, and profitable intersections between qualitative and quantitative research. My observations support the need for developing in-depth knowledge of the disparity, disjuncture, and at times abyss that exists between the instrumentalized and orderly realm of transitional justice studies as they are often practiced in the global north and the complicated and layered realities of post-conflict histories pertaining to forced migration in the global south (see chapter 5 for an examination of struggles over security and nationhood in India's Northeast).

## Of the People, By the People, For the People? Sixty Shades of Dispossession

The "unwanted peoples," refugees, exiled and displaced populations, stateless peoples, and other subjects of forced migration have always played a significant role in the economic, political, and social life of sovereign states (see chapter 5). Since 1945, millions of people have been subjected to partitions, forced population exchanges, purges, and cleansings as part of the nation-building processes in the postcolonial and later neocolonial world orders (Hansen 2003; Castles et al. 2013). However, the majority of the people who suffered and continue to suffer such fates are rarely captured by the legal definition of refuge/refugee/asylum (Goodwin-Gill 2014). Forced migration studies must broaden its scope and incorporate some of the foundational debates pertaining to postcolonial and neocolonial statecraft as well as practices denoted under the umbrella term transitional justice in order to make full sense of these trends of systematic dispossession.

In international law, a refugee—as enshrined in the 1951 Refugee Convention and subsequent protocols—is someone who "is unable or unwilling to return to their country of origin owing to a well-founded fear of being persecuted for reasons of race, religion, nationality, membership of a particular social group, or political opinion." What emerged at the global scale in terms of state-induced displacements is a much more complicated picture than what is captured by this codification. Statelessness, permanent limbo of internal displacement, dispossession via partition, unrecognized minority status, forcibly resettled returnees are also a regular part of this equation of building states via displacing peoples (Canefe 2017). This multi-faceted nature of displacement is revealed best from the vantage point of transitional justice studies. Meanwhile, developing an understanding of the causes and consequences of displacement, forced migration, and statelessness—not to mention actually dealing with the challenges posed by these recurrent and cyclical phenomena—is often left on the margins of transitional justice scholarship as well. In other words, both fields suffer from dangerous short-sightedness concerning the structural causes of long-term human suffering related to internal, state-induced, or state-condoned conflict and related mass violence and forced movement of peoples. This lacuna is most curious when one considers the fact that according to UNHCR estimates, by 2016 there were a total of 65.6 million forcibly displaced people worldwide, of whom only 22.5 million were refugees and asylum seekers, including 5.3 million Palestinian refugees under UNWRA's mandate.[1] Figuratively speaking, the displaced make a permanent country in no man's land.

Here, I attempt to establish tangible links between lack of societal peace, structural causes of human suffering, recurrent patterns of political violence—all of which constitute the traditional subject matter of transitional justice—and forced migration in the global south. However, this issue does not concern only the postcolonial states being caught up in such a web of violent entanglements. It is also a matter directly involving international agencies, NGOs, and scholars of transitional justice and forced migration studies located in the global north where the big donors are based. This is key since the aforementioned actors fund and frame much of the resettlement or reconciliation efforts and thus give a particular direction to forced migration studies. Notably, in these joint endeavours international actors and organizations' emphasis is first and foremost placed on the maintenance of state boundaries and sovereign sanctity. Specifically, since the 1970s transitional justice policies have largely been associated with victims' advocacy movements and they rely on the use of legal mechanisms aimed at moving forward in the aftermath of mass societal and political violence (McEvoy and McConnachie 2013; Sharp 2014). This is commonly encouraged and funded by think tanks, institutions, and research hubs, and endorsed by independently funded civil society/ sponsor organizations and research institutes, many of which are funded by the global north.

In a somewhat contrarian vein, in the following pages I question this confined definition pertaining to transitional justice and its often heavily prescriptive presumptions about sociopolitical and historical change from the point of view of the debates taking place in the global south through the lens of forced migration, displacement, and related forms of human suffering. In order to evaluate the long-term political significance and deep-seated socio-ethical dimensions of forced migration movements, one has to look beyond the traditional transitional justice arsenal of policy measures and legal arrangements. In this regard, I posit that denial of the right of return; selective uses of amnesties; governmental and social orchestrations of political amnesia to ensure the forgetting of the experiences of traumatized and displaced groups; failures of legal and pseudo-legal accountability measures; and limitations of restorative justice schemes including compensation and redistribution programs all become strongly evident when examined from the vantage point of forced migration and displacement. Those who were forced to leave are often not wanted back, today or tomorrow. In this regard, conceptually guided comparative work allows for global pattern recognition in statecraft and maintenance of legitimacy in postcolonial and postimperial settings through displacement and dispossession. Lack of it, on the other hand, often locks us into regional troubleshooting exercises with short-term gains (Fletcher and Weinstein 2015).

While law is a tool for responding to violence and exposing abuses of power, law is also utilized to obfuscate and legitimate abuses of political authority. As such, it is puzzling that for many decades, scholarship concentrated mainly on the "corrective" aspects of legal and semi-legal practices associated with transitional justice measures and movements in the global south. This preference led to a widespread instrumentalization of our understanding of sociopolitical change in the aftermath of mass conflict and displacement (Vinjamuri and Snyder 2015; MacDonald 2017). In mainstream literature on forced migration, which is often event specific, rarely has enough attention been paid to the issue of creating new forms of justice capable of questioning the legitimacy of prior political or legal practices that led to both institutional and societal involvement in and subsequent denial of mass violence leading to the very events of displacement. There is also a major concern about the cooption of transitional justice projects by governments for political gain. Concerning reinterpretations of a traumatic past by a "new regime," there are real politico-ethical confrontations that take place since what is at stake is imagining the future of the society as a whole while coming to terms with its past. Until recently, these concerns have largely been amiss in the scholarship that habitually emanates from important research centres and international think tanks. Such institutions include the International Center for Transitional Justice (New York, USA), Peace Research Institute (Oslo, Norway), and special programs organized by MacArthur, Carnegie Endowment, and Ford Foundations, Hans Böckler Foundation in Germany, or Open Society Institute and Helsinki Citizens' Assembly chapters across Europe. Projects funded by these circles regularly concentrated on "solid criteria" such as legislative efforts and litigation processes to prove that a "transition to democracy" is underway in a given constituency.

In this chapter, my take on the issue of transition in post-conflict societies underlines the importance of relying on the expertise and work of scholars, activists, and legal practitioners located in the global south. These actors have decades-long experience in regional hubs of forced migrations, which in turn allows us to unpack problematic assumptions associated with standard approaches to transitional justice projects, institutions, and practices. It is of paramount importance that we focus on non-conventional measures and policies that will advance not just institutional but genuine political reconciliation, as well as a social acknowledgement of responsibility for mass atrocities and displacements. Such a hybrid approach could establish a much-needed platform of comparative work and exchange among the scholars situated in the global south and institutions and research centres in North America and Europe. Based on the experiences emanating from cases in the Middle East, Southeast Asia, Latin America, and Africa, it is time to pay closer attention to the implications of historical trends in the study, funding, and institutionalization of transitional justice projects and programs particularly as they relate to human displacement (Drumbl 2016; Rowen 2016). Only then could we start asking new questions and put the older, repetitive ones to rest.

## The Transitional Justice Canon: Contextual Challenges

Societies in the global south that confronted the challenges of transitional justice schemes often have a postcolonial/postimperial background and have long been grappling with traditions and legacies of "deep states." Whether in Asia, Africa, the Middle East, or Latin America, many states owe their existence to repeated waves of forced migrations, displacements, and population exchanges in the form of partitions following declarations of independence or ethnic cleansing and civil wars related to regional warfare (Chatty 2014; Samaddar 2016). Many also have a multiplicity of victims' groups whose traumas and losses are yet to be acknowledged through restorative justice measures. These cases provide the foundation for comparative work on global trends in post-conflict social transformations and the politics of justice in the aftermath of mass political violence. Thus they aid us in developing a new understanding of the connection between modern statehood and forced migration (see also chapter 5 on the linkages between state formation and the securitization of migration).

A transitional justice industry emerged in the 1990s, keen to embrace a "checklist" approach to acute crises in the global south. This trend in scholarship and policymaking, however, rarely resulted in increased attention to historical socioeconomic inequalities and root causes of mass political violence, displacement, and systemic abuses of power. As transitional justice projects struggle to deliver un-tempered truth, all-encompassing societal justice and reconciliation continues to prove elusive. Disproportionately hefty demands are placed upon transitional justice schemes to provide guarantees for long-term political peace. As a response, we witness the burgeoning of an alternative discourse from the global south where there is a marked shift in the definition of the very term justice (Uhlin et al. 2017; Waldorf 2018). In keeping with this call for rethinking justice in postcolonial and neocolonial contexts, critical practices and discourses in the field strive to pay respect to the social history of societies affected by mass political violence, internal warfare, crimes against humanity, and overall legacies concerning imbalanced state-society relations (Samaddar 2017). This kind of scholarship also aims to redefine the territory covered by the canonized legal-political language of economic and social rights. The relevance of such interventions is twofold: to gather historically specific information, genealogies, strategies, and interventions that characterize a region, and to reach overall conclusions based on long-term trajectories of how post-conflict societies deal with mass human suffering and political violence in a comparative and globally relevant politico-legal framework.

Many of the key features of this new politics of transitional justice become evident within the context of forced migration. Almost every case of "transitional justice" emanating from the global south includes a history of partitions, forced population exchanges, and civil strife leading to mass displacements (Mitra et al. 2017). Hence scholars, policymakers, and citizens' groups engaged in transitional justice on the ground had to build up extensive knowledge and capacity to work with victims of forced migration through grassroots mobilization, ad hoc human rights advocacy programs, channelling of humanitarian assistance, and critical scholarly research, knowledge dissemination, political network building, and involvement in policy deliberations aiming for a dialogue for reparations. Transitional justice related work reflecting on the experiences of academics/activists in Latin America and India readily attests to the large arsenal of experience that challenges the boundaries of established canon on the subject (Shaw and Swatuk 1994; see also chapter 12 for discussion of networking around transitional justice in the Latin American context). Critical knowledge of these cases provides overall conclusions concerning how to address forced migration and mass displacement as a key component of socio-economic and political change. Such a juxtaposition of transitional justice and forced migration studies allows us to redraw boundaries of scholarly knowledge pertaining to human suffering induced by historical inequalities in postcolonial and neocolonial contexts.

While creating strict categories of when, to whom, and for what transitional justice projects are expected to apply, global institutions and funders construct and dictate models that focus on specific sets of actors for predetermined targeting of societal conflicts and political crimes. This often results in dangerously narrow interpretations of societal, political, and structural violence and somewhat artificial timeframes for change and restitution. It also excludes key actors, social groups, and classes in subsequent sociopolitical negotiations and selectively emphasizes criminal proceedings. The concomitant narrowing and depoliticization of transitional justice projects constitutes a prime reason for the habitual separation of transitional justice and forced migration studies. As such, there is a need to reformulate justice from the grassroots level rather than employing traditional, top-down institutional models in regions of the world heavily affected by long-term political violence. At times, seemingly unstructured movements lacking official recognition could be much more effective in developing ways of coping with past political and societal violence as well as addressing present-day inequalities. They present an immense potential that could be translated into programs of action with a clear vision and a new form of post-conflict politics. Scholars, communities, and activist networks from the global south contend that such diverse inputs into transitional justice projects, especially with reference to displaced populations, are vital for achieving long-term sociopolitical change and peace. This approach would also deepen our understanding of mass political violence at a global scale to initiate genuine responses to human suffering.

Another key and often overlooked area of study is the relationship between transitional justice projects and socio-economic restructuring programs that aim to reverse systemic underdevelopment (Sharp 2016). While this subject occupies a central place in debates on the political economy of the global south, it is largely absent from the arsenal of topics covered by Western academia, barring a few notable exceptions (Duthie 2014). Development is formulated in a very particular way in the context of problems, concerns, and future trajectories pertaining to societies "in transition." Often, NGO and INGO funded work emanating from the global north focuses mainly on the potential impact that transitional justice projects and policies may have on a state's ability to compete for international assistance or to embark on economic reconstruction programs in the aftermath of a crisis. The particular language used in this setting suggests a link between development, finance market stability, and societal justice (Franzki and Olarte 2013). Despite recurrent calls for a more locally rooted and politically engaged approach to rebuilding "capacities," internationally funded transitional justice projects and operations remain heavily influenced by this neoliberal mindset spiced with a tinge of neo-colonialism and a dash of old-fashioned Orientalism. By and large, their aim is to transform "war-torn societies" of the global south into derivative liberal democracies.

Last but not least, here I will advance the proposition that social movements and politics of everyday life should not be secondary in our understanding of what transitional justice stands for. They should be accorded a primary status. The instrumental approach to transitional justice focuses too much on purportedly objective sources of legitimacy, such as courts or state departments at the expense of events, movements, confrontations, and changes materializing at the local level and manifesting themselves in everyday life (Teitel 2015). As transitional justice became part of the new global liberal ethos of peace building in the late 1980s, it became linked with a broad, positivist, and largely elusive definition of peace itself. Such an application-oriented definition of peace does not resonate with the needs of the populations directly affected by drawn out conflicts. The peace-building model of transitional justice aims primarily at rebuilding state institutions and only as an afterthought attends to the reconstruction of social relations (Jeffrey and Jakala 2015). The very state that became a battleground is made the anchor upon which the future of a whole social and political system is predicated, a weakness that we must fully address. We must redefine what transitional justice is for the communities that are meant to be transitioning from perpetual suffering and structurally sustained rights violations to a future where human dignity is paramount. If the past is the memory of our present, the future is its hope. In this regard, exclusive focus on the state, which failed to protect the vulnerable or perpetrated mass crimes against the very groups and classes later declared as victims, is a trap we must learn to avoid. This would be a breath of fresh air in both conceptual and political terms.

To summarize, it is true that there is a growing number of studies and research institutions devoted to transitional justice. However, it is rare to find strong and dedicated voices talking about issues and content that are not limited to politically sterilized conversations on the subject matter. Even less frequent are enterprises that directly address the issue of forced migration in the context of post-conflict peace building and sociopolitical change (Mihail 2010). And yet, any endeavour that wishes to effect change and transformation in the global south must address forced migration as part of the canopy of solutions envisaged. Addressing the links between transitional justice as a sociopolitical project, forced migration as a means of state building and maintenance, and conditions of postcoloniality is similarly paramount for forced migration studies (Turton 2003; Canefe 2017). We must push for a greater appreciation of the unevenness of mobility, drawing attention to the rigidity that many forced migrants experience in their daily lives and the premature closure of the option of return by the limited focus of transitional justice projects on those who remained inside the nation-state borders. Displacement could also allow for dissent and resistance to grow by mobilizing collective identities and supporting alternative discourses of political agency. By excluding these vital voices from transitional justice schemes, societies engage in a dangerous pretense that such communities never existed or left of their own accord.

Law, justice, and hope are genuinely intertwined. Critical debates redefining the scope and contents of transitional justice must therefore weave together questions about the legitimacy of law, including refugee law and restorative change, hence speak of hope while engaging in assessments of the status quo. Similarly, debates on the past must assume the regenerative format of remembering and reintroducing memories of traumatic events as a bridge to our understanding of the present. Examples for this kind of endeavour could easily be drawn from Rwanda, Sri Lanka, and India (Kaushikee 2017; Longman 2017; Seoighe 2016). Without gazing into the future, and daring to imagine how things could be different, one cannot move beyond the weight of present circumstances of displacement and dispossession. Conflicts end, but dispossession does not until and unless it is acknowledged and remedied. Looking into the future requires political will and social engagement beyond any project that relies solely upon legalistic and institutional solutions. The Colombian peace process and the developments in the Great Lakes region and in South Africa constitute key examples revealing the making and remaking of states, nations, and even regions by means of forced migration. Forced migration creates unfinished business in terms of acknowledgment of the pain, suffering, and strife of displaced populations and the way they are forced to keep silent—sometimes for decades. Existing debates on both transitional justice and forced migration must be reframed around the inherent connection between these two fields of analysis, especially within the critical context of the global south.

## In Lieu of a Conclusion: Mobility, Statehood, and Violence

Mobility is inherent to our understanding of both forced and voluntary migration. "Displacement"—whether it leads to movement of people across borders and their permanent resettlement or to internal, repetitive, temporary movements within a state's borders—always involves the corporeal movement of people and the undoing of habitats, life worlds, and identities. In this regard, human mobility could both induce and take away aspirations, longings, and memories, and has a powerful impact on the future of affected communities, both those remaining behind and those that have left. Furthermore, displacement involves not only the mobility of people; it also brings domestic crises to regional and global audiences.

The presence of the dispossessed is a regular feature of the contemporary system of states. In the case of forced migration, effects of displacement are amplified by the collapse of livelihoods of people on the move, whose immediate rehabilitation becomes the priority for aid and development agencies. As such, mobility is defined as integral to the right to life by some, and yet as a burden for others.

Displacement is a process that could last many months or even years. During this process, different types of mobility emerge depending upon whether the displaced are located in urban areas or camps, whether they have easy access to the basic resources they need for survival, whether they are fearful of renewed violence, levels of environmental stress, and whether or not they expect or aspire to return home. Overall, human displacement cannot be fully understood in its political, cultural, economic, and technological complexities without looking at the dynamic and systemic nature of interlocking forms of mobility. The endeavour of addressing it also requires a solid ethical commitment in terms of not overriding its root causes, and not treating it as a cause itself rather than the symptom that it is. Despite the clear overlap between mobility and forced migration, however, relatively little work has combined these two bodies of research and thinking. While both forced migration and mobilities literatures are well established in their own right, there is a range of areas in which the two approaches would substantially benefit from cross-fertilization and a more fluid interchange in both theoretical and empirical terms (Urry 2000, 2003; Sheller and Urry 2006). Attending as much to moorings as to mobility and as much to fixity as to flow could be an apt beginning point in this regard (Hannam et al. 2006). Forced migration is a particular kind of mobility that involves total undoing of the possibility of remaining in one's habitus and thus fixity. A genuine engagement between theories of mobility and forced migration promises to provide a new window onto this complex relationship with space/place and security/freedom. Through studying situations in which mass movements start due to diminished chance of livelihood and survival, both fixity and flow assume novel meanings (Canzler et al. 2008).

In its traditional format, mobility studies tended to be consumed by the temptation to treat the forced migrant as a figure outside the global north. This Orientalist vision of the world divided the globe into advanced capitalist regions with predictable, peaceful mobilities and the postcolonial and postimperial global south with unpredictable, chaotic mobilities triggered by violence, governance deficits, and abuse of state power. As an alternative, a critical, historically informed focus on forced migration could fruitfully connect mobilities research with debates on entangled and contested modernities. This would then allow us to embed theories of statehood, global political economy, regimes of accumulation, and restructuring of labour markets within the context of various forms of both imposed and forced mobility (Eisenstadt 2000; Preyer and Sussman 2015; see chapter 5 for an example of such an analysis). Such a critical gaze is particularly pertinent at a moment when the global balance of power is shifting with new political and environmental consequences, and when the vision of global flows and borderless horizons of supposedly endless opportunities is now taking hold in emerging regional economies such as those in India, China, Turkey, and Brazil. In many parts of the world, increased circulation of labour is uncritically seen as a promising sign of a global move forward to better lives, further development, and interconnectedness. The resultant romanticization of mobility through its association with freedom, liberation, and self-fulfillment is particularly detrimental to developing a global analysis of imposed and forced migration flows and population exchanges. Even critical thinkers such as Gilles Deleuze and Félix Guattari and Michel de Certeau equate mobility with power. This viewpoint is blind to the sociopolitical reality that mobilities are socially, economically, and legally differentiated and not all lead to better lives (Elliot and Urry 2010). In keeping with these reservations about decontextualized understandings of mobility, many of the ways in which movement is imposed upon populations indicate the use of mobility as a tool in subjugating and disciplining populations rather than delivering paradise. Mobility thus becomes a last resort and is to be associated with deep-seated insecurities rather than freedom. The lack of an endpoint or destination, the constant movement from one location to another, and the persistent uncertainty about the future that many forced migrants, environmentally displaced people, political refugees, and the *sans papiers* have to live through is indeed no cause for celebration.

In hindsight, during the post-Second World War era the refugee has not featured as prominently as the foreigner, the flâneur, or the stranger—other than in a few select bodies of work, such as Hannah Arendt's oeuvre (Diken 1998; Isin and Nyers 2014). It was never made into a pivotal figure in understanding modernity, change, or even oppression. More recent accounts on refugees, exile, and dispossession still fail to take proper note of the reluctance of the refugee regarding their condition (Agamben 2000; Derrida 2001). This relative neglect of the refugee and the forced migrant is indicative of the inclination of writers, scholars, and intellectuals to favour the more singular and elite term "exile." Given the widespread and systemic nature of forced migration, the preference of common metaphors and symbols used to represent displacement indicating individualized, and often elite, circumstances is indeed worrisome vis-à-vis the history of social sciences itself. As long as dislocation is expressed in singular rather than collective terms, and as an individual choice rather than as a result of sociopolitical circumstances and due to structural inequalities, we are bound to associate mobility with better lives, more choice, and a presumed use of agency (Kaplan 1996; Doughty and Murray 2016).

Forced migration is often regarded as puzzling since there is no migration without, at some point, a conscious and volitional choice to move, however constrained and imposed this choice might be (Turton 2003; Steinberg 2016). Under-theorization of communities and individuals whose numbers reach millions and for whom movement is an undesirable necessity as a result of factors outside their control, is a serious deficit affecting multiple fields of study. Processes of purification that have shaped modern Western imaginaries dictate that colonial and imperial logics of population control and demographic engineering through displacement of the subaltern subjects are normalized through the construction of a hiatus between now and then: the time of such chaos is supposedly over for the societies of the global north. In this sense, forced migration studies invites us to rethink the history of modernity in a way that recognizes the legacy of these double gestures of colonization and expulsion, incorporation and erasure, crises and status quo, et cetera. Without these entangled and yet silenced histories of colonialism, partition, and exploitation, state borders are perpetually reinforced as inalienable despite their innate porousness and indeterminacy (Appadurai 2006; Elden 2009). And yet, the systemic and dynamic character of global capitalism reveals itself as disorganized movements in the global south (Gregory and Pred 2007; Springer and Le Billion 2016). Systemic violence, the threat of persecution, and the fear of impending disasters routinely producing movements and moorings cannot be simplified as an internal problem of the societies in the global south. The common understanding of war as a cataclysmic, one-off conflict between two parties in one place over a relatively short period of time is dangerously outdated in the face of longer periods of conflict engulfing diverse groups in multiple places and including multiple actors in addition to states (Kaldor 2001; Van Creveld 2009).

In this regard, conceiving the state as a fluid and highly adaptable entity (perhaps almost a shape-shifter) is a crucial step towards understanding contemporary global and regional regimes of regulation pertaining to migrants, refugees, asylum seekers, and *sans papiers*. Responses of the state to populations on the move involve quantification techniques that allow for their counting, codification, classification, and categorization. This is raw governmental power—producing and reproducing subjects as calculable units (Painter 2006). It is also an intensely political process since judgments are made about who can move, who gets counted, and who becomes part of the "unknown masses" on the move. The security sought by states through these techniques of containment and selection creates further insecurities. For the forced migrant, spatial and temporal mobility thus become co-constitutive of new forms of dispossession. Displaced persons are kept repetitively, gradually, seasonally, and/or locally mobile as a result of the dire necessities of survival. Mobility thus becomes a way of life rather than an exceptional event (Malkki 1996; Bauman 2001; Nyers 2003).

The historical and geographical variability of regimes of citizenship offers yet another potentially fruitful field to explore the synergy between forced migration studies and mobility. The fluid notion of membership rights varies according to the cultural context and sociopolitical climate in which it circulates, with profound consequences for migrants in terms of the rights and responsibilities they are entitled to (Dikeç et al. 2009). Furthermore, commonplace innovations in border controls such as points-based systems of immigration management, privatization of detention facilities, and the use of quasi-legal mechanisms such as safe third country rules and remote-control strategies of policing global mobilities raise the broader question of global policy transfers (Anderson 2010). Key to this issue is the degree to which policies replicate subversive techniques and disciplining measures as they travel, or become "self-fertilizing" based on the combination of policy perspectives adopted from different places (Prince 2010). In this context, as well, forced migration scholarship throws into relief a vast array of challenging situations in which mobility, uncertainty, risk, and fear interact. Geographies created through these routes, encounters, retentions, and escapes are becoming increasingly volatile. Textures of ordinary lives in countries and regions where forced migration has become a central and persistent practice of social and political control shape identities in ways that cannot be confined to migration studies alone (Mountz 2015). This emergent ontology of exclusion surrounding the regulation of mobility by states and other institutional actors is highly relevant to discussions on the relationship between forced migration and transitional justice. It also calls into question the impact of asylum-sector research that effectively rewrites and reinterprets the narratives of displaced peoples because they often act, however unwittingly, as part of the broader governmental apparatus through which populations are subjected to control. We could go as far as arguing that helping to alleviate the worst humanitarian consequences of dispossession inadvertently leads to the marginalization of immigrant communities (Tickell and Peck 2003; May et al. 2007). This is a methodological as well as a political problem. In conclusion, there is great potential for the transitional justice and forced migration nexus to provide a platform for the production and dissemination of cross-cutting research and activism on topics such as: gaps in human rights law, norms, and standards pertaining to dispelled and disposed populations; post-conflict processes as they relate to displaced peoples; global justice and peace movements including refugees and exiles who wish to return home; and our understanding of human mobility at the age of global capitalism in general. Bringing these two lenses together allows us to see forced migration like a sentence stopped in the middle, and encourages us to think of various endings to it rather than seeing refuge and resettlement as the ultimate destination.

## Note

1    See UNHCR figures for 2017 at http://www.unhcr.org/figures-at-a-glance.html [accessed 9 Dec 2018].

# References

Agamben, Giorgio. 2000. *Means without End: Notes on Politics*. Minneapolis, MN: University of Minnesota Press.

Anderson, Bridget. 2010. "Migration, Immigration Controls and the Fashioning of Precarious Workers." *Work, Employment and Society* 24, no. 2: 1–18.

Appadurai, Arjun. 2006. *Fear of Small Numbers: An Essay on the Geography of Anger*. Durham: Duke University Press.

Bauman, Zygmunt. 2001. *Community: Seeking Safety in an Insecure World*. Cambridge: Polity Press.

Canefe, Nergis. 2017. "Migration as a Necessity: Contextualising the European Response to the Syrian Exodus." *Refugee Watch* 48.

Canzler, Weert, Vincent Kaufmann, and Sven Kesselring. 2008. *Tracing Mobilities: Towards a Cosmopolitan Perspective*. London: Ashgate.

Castles, Stephen, Hein De Haas, and Mark J. Miller. 2013. *The Age of Migration: International Population Movements in the Modern World*. Houndmills, Basingstoke, Hampshire: Palgrave Macmillan.

Chatty, Dawn. 2014. "Anthropology and Forced Migration." In *The Oxford Handbook of Refugee and Forced Migration Studies*, edited by Elena Fiddian-Qasmiyeh, Gil Loescher, Katy Long, and Nando Sigona, 74–85. Oxford: Oxford University Press.

Derrida, Jacques. 2001. *Cosmopolitanism and Forgiveness*. London: Routledge.

Dikeç, Mustafa, Nigel Clark, and Clive Barnett. 2009. *Extending Hospitality: Giving Space, Taking Time*. Edinburgh: Edinburgh University Press.

Diken, Bulent. 1998. *Strangers, Ambivalence and Social Theory*. Aldershot: Ashgate.

Doughty, Karolina, and Lesley Murray. 2016. "Discourses of Mobility: Institutions, Everyday Lives and Embodiment." *Mobilities* 11, no. 2: 303–22.

Drumbl, Mark A. 2016. "Transitional Justice Moments." *International Journal of Transitional Justice* 10, no. 2: 203–10.

Duthie, Roger. 2014. "Transitional Justice, Development, and Economic Violence." In *Justice and Economic Violence in Transition*, edited by Dustin N. Sharp, 165–201. New York: Springer.

Eisenstadt, Samuel N. 2000. "Multiple Modernities." *Daedalus* 129, no. 1: 1–29.

Elden, Stuart. 2009. *Terror and Territory: The Spatial Extent of Sovereignty*. London: University of Minnesota Press.

Elliott, Anthony, and John Urry. 2010. *Mobile Lives*. London: Routledge.

Fletcher, Laurel E., and Harvey M. Weinstein. 2015. "Writing Transitional Justice: An Empirical

Evaluation of Transitional Justice Scholarship in Academic Journals." *Journal of Human Rights Practice* 7, no. 2: 177–98.

Franzki, Hannah, and Maria Carolina Olarte. 2013. "Understanding the Political Economy of Transitional Justice." In *Transitional Justice Theories*, edited by Susanne Buckley-Zistel, Teresa K. Beck, Christian Braun, and Friederike Mieth, 201–21. New York: Routledge.

Goodwin-Gill, Guy S. 2014. "The International Law of Refugee Protection." In *The Oxford Handbook of Refugee and Forced Migration Studies*, edited by Elena Fiddian-Qasmiyeh, Gil Loescher, Katy Long, and Nando Sigona, 36–47. Oxford: Oxford University Press.

Gregory, Derek, and Allan Pred. 2007. *Violent Geographies: Fear, Terror, and Political Violence*. London: Routledge.

Hannam, Kevin, Mimi Sheller, and John Urry. 2006. "Editorial: Mobilities, Immobilities and Moorings." *Mobilities* 1, no. 1: 1–22.

Hansen, Randall. 2003. "Migration to Europe since 1945: Its History and Its Lessons." *Political Quarterly* 74, no. 1: 25–38.

Isin, Engin F., and Peter Nyers. 2014. *Routledge Handbook of Global Citizenship Studies*. New York: Routledge.

Jeffrey, Alexander S., and Michaelina Jakala. 2015. "Using Courts to Build States: The Competing Spaces of Citizenship in Transitional Justice Programmes." *Political Geography* 47: 43–52.

Kaldor, Mary. 2001. *New and Old Wars: Organised Violence in a Global Era*. London: Polity Press.

Kaplan, Caren. 1996. *Questions of Travel: Postmodern Discourses of Displacement*. Durham, NC: Duke University Press.

Kaushikee. 2017. "Justice and Reconciliation in the Aftermath of Mass Atrocities and Collective Violence: The Restorative Justice Lens." In *Restorative Justice in India: Traditional Practice and Contemporary Applications*, edited by R. Thilagaraj and Jianhong Liu, 151–66. San Francisco: Springer.

Longman, Timothy. 2017. *Memory and Justice in Post-Genocide Rwanda*. Cambridge: Cambridge University Press.

MacDonald, Anna. 2017. "Transitional Justice and Political Economies of Survival in Post-conflict Northern Uganda." *Development and Change* 48, no. 2: 286–311.

Malkki, Liisa. 1996. "Speechless Emissaries: Refugees, Humanitarianism, and Dehistoricization." *Cultural Anthropology* 11, no. 3: 377–404.

May, Jon, Jane Wills, Kavita Datta, Yara Evans, Joanna Herbert, and Cathy McIlwaine. 2007. "Keeping London Working: Global Cities, the British State, and London's New Migrant Division of Labour." *Transactions of the Institute of British Geographers* 32, no. 2: 151–67.

McEvoy, Kieran, and Kirsten McConnachie. 2013. "Victims and Transitional Justice: Voice, Agency and Blame." *Social & Legal Studies* 22, no. 4: 489–513.

Mihai, Mihaela. 2010. "Transitional Justice and the Quest for Democracy: A Contribution to a Political Theory of Democratic Transformations." *Ratio Juris* 23, no. 2: 83–204.

Mitra, Iman K., Ranabir Samaddar, and Samita Sen. 2017. *Accumulation in Post-Colonial Capitalism*. Singapore: Springer.

Mountz, Alison. 2015. "Political Geography II: Islands and Archipelagos." *Progress in Human Geography* 39, no. 5: 636–46.

Nyers, Peter. 2013. *Rethinking Refugees: Beyond State of Emergency*. New York: Routledge.

———. 2003. "Abject Cosmopolitanism: The Politics of Protection in the Anti-Deportation Movement." *Third World Quarterly* 24, no. 6: 1069–93.

Painter, Joe. 2006. "Prosaic Geographies of Stateness." *Political Geography* 25, no. 7: 752–74.

Preyer, Gerhard, and Michael Sussmann. 2015. *Varieties of Multiple Modernities: New Research Design*. Leiden: Brill.

Prince, Russell. 2010. "Policy Transfer as Policy Assemblage: Making Policy for the Creative Industries in New Zealand." *Environment and Planning A* 42, no. 1: 169–86.

Rowen, Jamie R. 2016. "'We Don't Believe in Transitional Justice:' Peace and the Politics of Legal Ideas in Colombia." *Law & Social Inquiry* 42, no. 3: 622–47.

Samaddar, Ranabir. 2017. *The Politics of Dialogue: Living under the Geopolitical Histories of War and Peace*. New York: Routledge.

———. 2016. "Forced Migration Situations as Exceptions in History?" *International Journal of Migration and Border Studies* 2, no. 2: 99–118.

Seoighe, Rachel. 2016. "Discourses of Victimization in Sri Lanka's Civil War: Collective Memory, Legitimacy and Agency." *Social & Legal Studies* 25, no. 3: 355–80.

Sharp, Dustin N. 2014. "Emancipating Transitional Justice from the Bonds of the Paradigmatic Transition." *International Journal of Transitional Justice* 9, no. 1: 150–69.

———. 2016. "Transitional Justice and Liberal Post-Conflict Governance: Synergies and Symmetries, Frictions and Contradictions." PhD diss., Leiden University.

Shaw, Timothy M., and Larry A. Swatuk. 1994. *The South at the End of the Twentieth Century: Rethinking the Political Economy of Foreign Policy in Africa, Asia, the Caribbean and Latin America*. Houndmills, Basingstoke, Hampshire: Palgrave Macmillan.

Sheller, Mimi, and John Urry. 2006. "The New Mobilities Paradigm." *Environment and Planning A* 38, no. 2: 207–26.

Springer, Simon, and Philippe Le Billon. 2016. "Violence and Space: An Introduction to the Geographies of Violence." *Political Geography* 52: 1–3.

Steinberg, Jonny. 2016. "The Vertiginous Power of Decisions: Working through a Paradox about Forced Migration." *Public Culture* 28, no. 1: 139–60.

Teitel, Ruti G. 2015. *Globalizing Transitional Justice: Contemporary Essays*. Oxford: Oxford University Press.

Tickell, Adam, and Jamie Peck. 2003. "Making Global Rules: Globalization or Neoliberalization?" In *Remaking the Global Economy: Economic-Geographic Perspectives*, edited by Jamie Peck and Henry Wai-chung Yeung, 163–81. London: Sage.

Turton, David. 2003. *Conceptualising Forced Migration*. Refugee Studies Centre Working Paper No. 12. Oxford: University of Oxford.

Uhlin, Anders, Jewellord Nem Singh, Jean Grugel, and Lorenza B. Fontana. 2017. "Claiming Justice in the Global South." In *Demanding Justice in the Global South*, edited by Jean Grugel, Jewellord Nem Singh, Lorenza B. Fontana, and Anders Uhlin, 177–94. Houndmills, Basingstoke, Hampshire: Palgrave Macmillan.

Urry, John. 2000. *Sociology beyond Societies*. London: Routledge.

———. 2003. *Global Complexities*. Oxford: Polity

Van Creveld, Martin. 2009. *Transformation of War*. New York: Simon and Schuster.

Vinjamuri, Leslie, and Jack Snyder. 2015. "Law and Politics in Transitional Justice." *Annual Review of Political Science* 18: 303–27.

Waldorf, Lars. 2018. "Legal Empowerment and Horizontal Inequalities after Conflict." *Journal of Development Studies*. https://doi.org/10.1080/00220388.2018.1451635.

# The Asia Pacific Forced Migration Connection: Linking Activists, Advocates, and Academics

*Susan Kneebone*

The Asia Pacific Forced Migration Connection (APFMC) was launched in November 2013 to create a hub to bring together research scholars of forced migration in Australia and the Asia Pacific region, and to connect with relevant civil society organizations, especially the Asia Pacific Refugee Rights Network (APRRN). As I will explain in this chapter, APFMC has had considerable success in raising awareness of normative frameworks in the face of challenges that arise from the context of forced migration in Asia Pacific generally, and more specifically the Southeast Asian (SEA) context. APFMC has responded to the regional institutional and normative context of forced migration and thereby provided a link between global "north" and "south" discourses on these issues (Chimni 2009). It has worked directly with scholars and organizations within the region and has challenged the perception that human rights responses to forced migration are Eurocentric (Davies 2008). Overall, the regional institutional framework, which provides challenges for the participation of civil society organizations (CSOs) vis-à-vis states in the region, has provided opportunities to APFMC to contribute to the debate on these issues. Some of these opportunities crystallized during the 2015 Andaman Sea crisis when it is estimated that as many as 6,500 persons, many of whom were stateless Rohingya, departed from Myanmar and Bangladesh mainly by boat, only to be turned away by Thailand, Malaysia, and Indonesia.

First, I explain the regional Southeast Asian institutional context, including the lack of focus on forced migration, before elaborating on the challenges and opportunities this environment provides for developing a network. I will differentiate the work of APFMC from organizations such as APRRN that sometimes compete with "top-down" actors such as UNHCR and IOM for "protection space." In this chapter, I highlight the participation of two academics in the APFMC and the Asia Dialogue on Forced Migration (ADFM), which is described as a "Track II" regional institutional dialogue: Sriprapha Petcharamesree and Alice Nah. The latter was also one of the founding members of APRRN demonstrating the interrelationship between APFMC and other actors in the region.

## The Region and Its Institutions

The Asia-Pacific region essentially contains two subregions within Asia: South Asia (Afghanistan, Sri Lanka, India, and Bangladesh) and Southeast Asia. The latter comprises countries in the Mekong River Delta (Myanmar, Thailand, Lao PDR, Cambodia, and Vietnam) that are linked from Thailand through the Malaysian Peninsula to Malaysia and Singapore. Indonesia and the Philippines are also part of this SEA region. An important unifying factor is that these countries are all members of the ASEAN Community.[1] The unique nature of that community and the exclusion of CSOs from direct participation within ASEAN was a key driver for the establishment of the APFMC.

In SEA, there are three main causes of forced migration. The first is displacement arising from conflict and hostilities, leading to both internal and external displacement. This creates internally displaced persons (IDPs) and asylum seekers/refugees, many of whom are stateless persons who lack a formal nationality. The region is both a source of refugees and a region of transit. Whilst the majority of refugees originate from Myanmar, many refugees are from Afghanistan and countries in Africa and the Middle East. Malaysia and Thailand are the two major destination and transit countries, whereas Indonesia is largely a country of transit for refugees intending to travel to Australia. A second cause of forced migration is displacement resulting from development or uneven development

**FIGURE 3.1**
Map of ASEAN Countries. Source: Colourbox 10558323.

within countries and within the region (Kneebone and Debeljak 2012). Such displacement may lead to smuggling and exploitative labour migration, amounting to human trafficking. Aside from this specific example of displacement, much labour migration within the region involves persons who migrate to work in semi and low-skilled occupations because of lack of opportunities in their home state. Singapore, Malaysia, and Thailand are the main receiving countries, and the sending countries are the Philippines, Indonesia, Vietnam, Cambodia, and Lao PDR. A substantial proportion of such migration is "irregular" or "informal"—that is, it begins as or subsequently becomes migration outside of legal channels. Natural disasters are a third cause of forced migration in the region; the region has achieved a substantial degree of cooperation on disaster management (following events such as the 2004 Boxing Day tsunami in the Indian Ocean and Cyclone Nargis in Myanmar in 2011).

The largest groups of forced migrants in SEA are asylum seekers/refugees and semi/low-skilled migrant workers. It is estimated that 5 million of 13.5 million workers from ASEAN states are working in other ASEAN countries (International Labour Organization 2005). The UNHCR, which has a mandate over both statelessness and refugees, projected in 2017 (UNHCR 2017a), that in the ASEAN countries that comprise Southeast Asia, there were 1.5 million stateless persons (comprising 40 per cent of the world's stateless population) and that 519,816 were refugees and 79,580 were asylum seekers. This population also included over 502,000 IDPs, mainly in Myanmar, Indonesia, and the Philippines where there are ongoing internal conflicts. The main country of origin of asylum seekers/refugees within SEA is Myanmar. UNHCR has estimated that 500,000 refugees from different ethnic groups have fled Myanmar over several decades in search of protection from ethnic conflict and violence prior to 2017 (UNHCR 2017a). The Rohingya refugees are the largest group from Myanmar; UNHCR has estimated that 168,500 fled Myanmar from 2012 to 2016 (UNHCR 2017b). The world and the region were alerted to the plight of the (mostly stateless) Rohingya fleeing persecution in Myanmar by the discovery of twenty-six bodies in a mass grave of smuggled Rohingya in a trafficking camp in southern Thailand in early May 2015 (di Gaetano 2015). As the Rohingya crisis that escalated in 2015 illustrated, asylum seekers may be both stateless persons and refugees whilst at the same time also undocumented migrant workers and smuggled and trafficked persons. From August to December 2017, over 600,000 Rohingya fled from Myanmar to Bangladesh (UNHCR 2017a). The number of refugees and asylum seekers in Malaysia is currently approximately 154,000 of whom 91 per cent are from Myanmar. In Thailand there are about 106,000 refugees (mostly in nine camps on the Thai-Myanmar border), and about 9,500 asylum seekers in urban areas (UNHCR 2017c).

As Petcharamesree (2016) has explained, the term "forced migrant" is not well known or accepted in the ASEAN/SEA context. Under the two regional processes that operate in SEA—namely ASEAN and the Bali Process (Conference on People Smuggling, Trafficking in Persons and Related Transnational Crime)—the focus is on "securitizing" migration by eliminating human smuggling and trafficking (Kneebone 2014a). The issues of human smuggling and trafficking are well covered by normative and institutional frameworks in SEA and ASEAN, which include inter-state cooperation and arrangements with CSOs at the national level as well as with international non-government organizations (INGOs) (Kneebone and Debeljak 2012). On the issue of labour migration, there is a well-mobilized civil society approach, which has a semi-formal relationship with ASEAN (Kneebone 2014a). Although this group was frustrated in its efforts (at the recent 30th ASEAN Summit held in Manila the draft declaration on promoting the rights of migrant workers was again shelved) it does have a voice (Regional Civil Society Statement, 18 July 2017). For this reason, a large focus of APFMC is on asylum seekers/refugee issues, which are dealt with at the state level under ASEAN and the Bali Process, and where it is difficult for individual CSOs to be heard.

## Challenges and Opportunities for APFMC: Filling the Gaps

In its efforts to contribute to "norm enhancement" the APFMC has an opportunity to fill the normative gap on refugee protection, as the institutional norm entrepreneurs, states, and the regional processes appear to have rejected the international refugee protection and human rights normative frameworks. Although the UNHCR, and more recently the International Organization for Migration (IOM), play a large role in advocating for and protecting asylum seekers/refugees, this role is often contested by CSOs as privileging the international perspective at the expense of the local. As an "outside-insider" APFMC has the advantage of being a non-state actor that can engage both in the region and outside on issues of refugee protection through scholarly outputs including media.[2]

## The Institutional and Normative Gap: The Rejection Theory

Whilst countries within the Southeast Asian region have considerable experience with providing shelter to refugees, and indeed have signed up to the complementary instruments that guarantee non-refoulement (such as the International Convention on Civil and Political Rights and the Convention against Torture), there is a persistent reluctance to recognize their international status in refugee law and to accord them protection in domestic law (Alexander 2008). As the 2015 UNHCR Overview of South East Asia pointed out (and the situation is unchanged): "Only three States are parties to the 1951 Refugee Convention and only one State has signed the 1954 Statelessness Convention" (UNHCR 2015). The UNHCR Overview laments the "lack of asylum laws and diversity of national legal frameworks, as well as government practices and protection environments in the region's countries." As UNHCR explained, states in SEA "generally consider refugees and asylum-seekers to be illegal migrants, who as such are susceptible to detention, expulsion, refoulement and other serious protection risks" (UNHCR 2015).

Despite the experience of states in sheltering and processing refugees fleeing from Indochina in the 1970s and 1980s, and their participation in the Comprehensive Plan of Action (CPA) for Indo-Chinese Refugees brokered by ASEAN, which operated from 1989–96 (Kneebone and Rawlings-Sanaei 2007, 11–18), this experience failed to imbue norms of refugee protection in the region (Davies 2008). Further, this context encouraged states in the region to consider that the refugees were the responsibility of the "developed" world. In the SEA region, as Petcharamesree (2016) explains, there is a lack of "norm entrepreneurs" advocating for refugee rights at the state level, as they are largely characterized as irregular migrants in national laws. She points out that despite the creation of the ASEAN Community, with its plethora of institutions, in reality the interests of "national governments predominate." These interests centre on issues of national security (Petcharamesree 2016). Although ASEAN has produced a "soft-law" instrument that promotes the right to seek asylum as well as human rights (Kneebone 2014), during the 2015 Andaman Sea crisis it was individual states rather than ASEAN that took the initiative to convene a meeting (despite calls for ASEAN to intervene) (Petcharamesree et al. 2016). This is in contrast to the CPA situation, which was an ASEAN-led initiative supported by UNHCR.

## The Normative Gap: Human Rights, Democracy, and the Security Discourse

The lack of academic engagement with these issues is a manifestation and consequence of the institutional and conceptual gap in refugee protection in SEA, which the APFMC can harness. For example, at the 14th Asian

**TABLE 3.1**: Search of SCOPUS Journals 2007–17, Based on the Country of the Organization to Which the Author Is Affiliated

| | Asylum Seeker | Refugee | Migrant Worker | Migrant | Migration | Forced Migration |
|---|---|---|---|---|---|---|
| Singapore | 23 | 145 | 179 | 518 | 738 | 20 |
| Philippines | 5 | 31 | 52 | 127 | 222 | 8 |
| Indonesia | 10 | 39 | 26 | 77 | 129 | 14 |
| Thailand | 12 | 92 | 79 | 163 | 230 | 27 |
| Vietnam | 0 | 0 | 0 | 0 | 0 | 0 |
| Malaysia | 18 | 85 | 64 | 198 | 309 | 20 |
| Australia | 816 | 2395 | 440 | 3179 | 5224 | 382 |
| UK | 1484 | 5302 | 1211 | 7992 | 14308 | 949 |
| Global | 5499 | 30853 | 6721 | 49497 | 94713 | 4202 |

Note: SCOPUS was chosen as the search as it includes both legal and social science journals.

Law Institute (ASLI) conference held in Manila in May 2017, despite the fact that migration was a denoted theme of the conference, only one panel on Institutional and Normative Responses to Migration, comprising three papers (organized by me) out of thirty-six panels (and 131 papers) dealt with the issue. One other paper by a scholar from Indonesia dealt with the issue of asylum seekers in another panel on International Law and Human Rights (ASLI 2017). The lack of regional academic engagement with issues of forced migration is demonstrated by a SCOPUS search of journals based on key words (Table 3.1 above). As can be seen, a search over the past decade demonstrates that scholars from the region engage far less with issues of asylum-seekers and refugees than others outside the region (in contrast to what Sánchez-Mojica's chapter reveals about Latin America).

Moreover, a survey of individual Asia-focused law and migration policy journals using the same keywords delivers similar findings (Table 3.2 below).

There are several explanations for this lack of engagement. As previously explained, the term "forced migrant" is not well known in the

**TABLE 3.2**: Comparison of Asian and Pacific Migration Journal (APMJ); Asian Journal of Comparative Law (AsJCL); Asian Journal of International Law (AJIL); Asian Journal of Law and Society (AJLS)

| | Asylum Seeker | Refugee | Migrant Worker | Migrant | Migration | Forced Migration |
|---|---|---|---|---|---|---|
| APMJ 2007–17 | 6 | 88 | 51 | 277 | 281 | 18 |
| AsJCL 2007–17 | 1 | 0 | 2 | 2 | 0 | 0 |
| AJIL 2011–17 | 0 | 1 | 3 | 3 | 2 | 11 |
| AJLS 2014–17 | 0 | 0 | 4 | 3 | 3 | 4 |

Notes: The APMJ is an interdisciplinary journal on human migration in the Asia-Pacific region. It has been published by Sage since 1992. The APMJ is based in the Scalabrini Migration Center, Philippines. The AsJCL has been published by Cambridge University Press since 2006. It is an initiative of the Asian Law Institute (ASLI) of the National University of Singapore. The Asian regional international law focus of the journal is widely conceived, and includes research applying an "Asian" approach to global issues. The AJLS is the most recent of the four journals, published by Cambridge University Press since 2014 on behalf of KoGuan Law School of Shanghai Jiao Tong University. The journal publishes socio-legal articles relevant to Asia generally.

region; rather the focus of states is on the irregular status of the migrant, who is seen as threat to the state. As one commentator on the region has said, there is a fear of the "outsider" and the desire to control borders in the region: "There is the perpetual fear of the outsider and the fear that foreigners will create trouble within the borders of the state and, if present in sufficient numbers, lead to changing identities of the nation itself" (Skeldon 2000). As Caballero-Anthony has explained, within the region migration is "elevated by the state above the course of normal politics" and is viewed through a "security lens" (Caballero-Anthony 2008, 165).

Within the SEA region, refugees are perceived as a political problem and a threat to border security (Goodwin-Gill 2008, 8). As Vitit Muntarbhorn has explained in relation to Thailand, refugees are seen as a political embarrassment, and as a threat to state sovereignty and national security (Muntarbhorn 2004; Nah 2007, 37). In Malaysia, refugees recognized by the UNHCR are at risk of being sanctioned as "illegal migrants." Refugees are seen in traditional security terms as a potential threat to social cohesion and as posing "transboundary challenges." This has a deep resonance with the ASEAN process, which emphasizes state sovereignty, non-conflict, and consensual decision-making.

A distrust of human rights mirrors the characterization of forced migrants as illegal migrants. The region has long been characterized as being distrustful of human rights or seeing them as another postcolonial example of Eurocentric measures being imposed by a foreign state. It reflects the democratic deficit that exists in SEA states and the tentative, indeed precarious, role of CSOs in some states such as Cambodia and Thailand. Thus the APFMC is provided with an opportunity, as unlike CSOs it does not claim a democratic gap-filling or public accountability role (Petcharamesree 2013). Unlike local actors, it does not put itself in direct conflict with the state.

The development of the notion of human rights in modern law is linked to the principle of popular sovereignty, as human rights focus on the responsibility of the democratic state (Habermas 1996). In this region, the concept of human security (Edwards and Ferstman 2010, 3) is promoted as an alternative to human rights and ASEAN is promoted as the body that protects human security rather than human rights. This idea is indeed strongly advanced by a number of Singaporean scholars (Caballero-Anthony and Cook 2013, 1–13). For example, Caballero-Anthony argues that the human security concept has developed under ASEAN into a people-centred discourse that reflects the concept of human rights. She suggests that there is "tentative consensus on locating human rights at the core of a human security community" in Southeast Asia (Caballero-Anthony 2012, 127).

Song has explained the Asian preference for a human security paradigm through focusing on the role of states (Song 2015). He argues that the concept of individual human rights is a Western construct whereby the state is seen as responsible for human rights protection, and indeed as a potential perpetrator of human rights breaches. That is, he suggests that the Western concept of human rights pits society against the state and challenges state authority. In Asia, human security is preferred by states to this confrontational concept; it recognizes the moral authority of the state as the primary guarantor of international human rights and the need for supra-national measures to solve issues of irregular migration (which he uses as a specific example). Human security is promoted as a collective concept; it acknowledges that the issues cannot be solved by one state alone.

The concept of human security fits serendipitously with ASEAN and its mode of operating. ASEAN is known to prefer decision-making through consultation and consensus-formation, and also to respect the individual sovereignty of states, which translates into the principle of non-interference. Its methods of governance and its approach to irregular migration mean that it is unlikely to insist that individual states conform to the paradigm of universal human rights that underlies the international conventions. Indeed, the issue of human trafficking is the one area of irregular migration that ASEAN has tackled very conscientiously.[3] In this context, the lack of academic engagement on contentious issues of refugees and asylum-seekers is unsurprising. For example Jonathan Rigg, the director of the Asia Research Institute's (ARI) migration group at the National University of Singapore, has said: "It is important to emphasise that ARI is a research and not a policy institute" (ARI 2017).

## APFMC, APRRN, and Top-Down Approaches: Creating a Space for Debate

ASEAN's relationship with CSOs can be characterized as one of exclusion.[4] This exclusion of CSOs within ASEAN and the Bali Process dialogue was a key driver for the establishment of the APFMC. An external actor with an independent voice, APFMC is immune from tensions between CSOs and international non-governmental organizations such as IOM and UN-HCR; it does not compete for protection space—that is not the objective. It is also sheltered from confrontation with states since it is not dependent on them for legitimacy. As an invited outsider and commentator, the legitimacy of APFMC is assumed—evidenced in particular by my role during the 2015 Rohingya crisis for example.

By contrast, APRRN is self-perceived as an advocate for refugee issues, competing with UNHCR for available protection space (UNHCR 2017a). UNHCR plays a large role in the SEA region due to the lack of national protection mechanisms. It claims to fill the vacuum of protection space created by the fact that few states in the region are parties to the Refugee Convention. In particular, it is primarily responsible for refugee status determination (RSD) in Malaysia and Indonesia. It also leads policy formulation in the region. In recent years, the UNHCR has promoted protection norms via the Asian African Legal Consultative Organization (AALCO) and other regional processes (Kneebone, 2014a). UNHCR has focussed on promoting adherence to basic principles of protection such as rescue at sea, non-refoulement, and addressing statelessness. The UNHCR attempts to fill the gap within the two regional processes, the Bali Process and ASEAN.

Nah observes that there is a negative side to this: "government officials in Asia tend to see refugees as an 'international' or 'UNHCR' problem, rather than a domestic problem" (Nah 2016). She explains that within the SEA region there is rivalry between the UNHCR and civil society for entrepreneurship of the issue. Nah (and Martin Jones) critique UNHCR's protection space approach. Jones (2014, 257) argues that it "privileges international interests, fora, and UNHCR as the negotiator; devalues the normative strength of obligations towards refugees; and, allows the underlying responsibility for the provision of refugee protection to drift from the state to UNHCR." Nah explains that local civil society actors often work under the protection of UNHCR—but also under their shadow. The APRRN 2016 Annual Report shows that it engages with UNHCR processes on a global level and works with it on a number of projects regionally (such as refugee status determination). APRRN is also dependent on UNHCR for a large proportion of its funding (APRRN Report 2016, 15–16, 28).[5]

Nah suggests that the advantage of APRRN is that it enables local civil society actors to pressure states from below; that it has a unique location vis-à-vis states. APRRN focuses on advocacy at the national level (APRRN Report 2016, 8–10); as an umbrella organization it shelters individual CSOs from national states (Kneebone 2014b, 610–13). Nah argues that working through a formalized network (in this case, APRRN) has changed the way in which local civil society actors engage in norm entrepreneurship in several important ways. She argues that it has changed the attributes of actors, helping them develop visibility, capacity, and connectedness through the formation of a "community of practice"; it has changed power-relations between them and other actors—in particular, the UNHCR; and it has facilitated the development of "regional imagination" and the practice of "scale shifting," helping local actors move beyond domestic contexts to engage with state and non-state actors through regional and international fora. It practices participatory regionalism that is intended to influence states in the region, and to shift their views that refugees are an international and UNHCR problem (Nah 2015).

APRRN also engages regionally with other umbrella CSO organizations that work differently to APRRN as they run parallel to ASEAN—in contrast to APRRN's bottom-up approach. These are SAPA (Solidarity for Asian People's Advocacy) (Kneebone 2014b, 612) and ASEAN Civil Society Conference/ASEAN Peoples' Forum (ACSC/APF). Recently 1,000 persons marched with ACSC/APF in Manila to complain of fifty years of exclusion of CSOs from ASEAN processes (InterAksyon 2017). By contrast, APRRN has had considerable success in advocating for the rights of individual refugees (Kneebone 2014b, 611–12).

More recently APRRN has developed regional engagement with an ASEAN side institution, namely the ASEAN Intergovernmental Commission on Human Rights (AICHR) (APRRN Report 2016, 11), which was established on 23 October 2009 pursuant to Article 14 of the ASEAN Charter. AICHR's task is to engage with ASEAN sectoral bodies and relevant CSOs to mainstream human rights across the three pillars of the ASEAN Community (AICHR 2017). In 2015–16 APRRN engaged with AICHR in relation to the Rohingya issue, and on Alternatives for Detention for children and other issues affecting asylum seekers and refugees. However, AICHR can be described as a "toothless tiger"; despite its mandate there has been little progress on human rights protection in the region. Recently for example, the ASEAN Parliamentarians for Human Rights (APHR) released a statement to coincide with ASEAN's fiftieth birthday urging ASEAN to do more to "operationalize" human rights protection (ASEAN 2017). Despite the "bottom-up" efforts of APRRN and its regional engagement it seems that refugee protection still suffers from a normative deficit in Southeast Asia.

## The Andaman Sea (Rohingya) Crisis, State (In)Action, and IOM

The response to the 2015 Rohingya crisis confirms the prevalence of both the UNHCR protection-space approach and the influential role of IOM, as states in the region continue to regard refugee protection as a humanitarian problem requiring an international response. The crisis, which came to a head in May 2015, initially produced a blame game amongst the three most affected states: Indonesia, Malaysia, and Thailand. However, when it became clear that continued pushbacks of boatloads of migrants would not solve the problem, these three states began to work cooperatively to broker a solution to the crisis. The Ministers of Foreign Affairs of Malaysia, Indonesia, and Thailand met on 20 May 2015 ahead of an international meeting on 29 May, to discuss the issue of "irregular movement of people" into their countries. The purpose of the meeting of 20 May was for: "finding a solution to the crisis of influx of irregular migrants and its serious impact on the national security of the affected countries." The joint statement issued following the meeting asserted the need to address the "root causes"; the ministers pledged to uphold their "responsibilities and obligations under international law and in accordance with their respective domestic laws, including the provision of *humanitarian* assistance to . . . those 7,000 irregular migrants still at sea" (Ministry of Foreign Affairs of Malaysia, Indonesia and Thailand 2015, emphasis added). However, they agreed only to offer them temporary shelter "provided that the resettlement and repatriation process will be done in one year by the international community."

The seventeen recommendations in the 29 May 2015 statement by states following the Special Meeting on Irregular Migration largely endorse those of 20 May, with some additional focus (Ministry of Foreign Affairs of the Kingdom of Thailand 2015). "The IOM underlined the importance of comprehensive migration management while the UNHCR called for innovative solutions to the complex problem and to ensure assistance for those in need of protection" (para 5). The recommendations focus upon preventing and responding to the issue of human trafficking and "people smuggling" rather than upon lasting solutions for refugees. Only the final recommendation [q], which referred to root causes and improving livelihoods in "at-risk communities," alluded to the protection needs of the Rohingya. This 29 May statement was followed in March 2016 by a new Bali Declaration on People Smuggling, Trafficking in Persons and Related Transnational Crime. In this instrument, the focus is again on "irregular migrants" and "mixed migratory movements" (Bali Process 2016, 5). Concrete measures suggested are to "enhance safe and orderly migration pathways, including for migrant workers," but for refugees the states are merely encouraged to "explore potential temporary protection and local stay arrangements for asylum seekers and refugees, subject to domestic laws and policies of member states" (Bali Process 2016, 6). In this respect the declaration acknowledges "the need for adequate access to irregular migrants wherever they are, by humanitarian providers especially the UNHCR and the IOM, as appropriate" (Bali Process 2016, 6). IOM plays a large role in refugee protection in the region; for example, under the Regional Cooperation Arrangement (RCA), which is a bilateral agreement between Australia and Indonesia dating from the late 1990s, IOM and UNHCR are responsible for the care and protection of asylum seekers in Indonesia. Of these two, IOM is better funded and has the largest role. During the Andaman Sea crisis, IOM statements were very influential to the final outcome of the 29 May statement and also to the March 2016 Bali Declaration. IOM stresses the "mixed flows" from Myanmar and promotes the need for regular work rights rather than durable solutions for refugees. In Malaysia currently, there is a pilot project for 300 Rohingya refugees, but the overall refugee crisis is largely unresolved. It is estimated that there are 56,000 registered Rohingya refugees in Malaysia in need of a permanent solution.

## The Asian Dialogue on Forced Migration

A new actor has entered this space in the form of the Asian Dialogue on Forced Migration (ADFM), which developed out of the Centre for Policy Development (CPD)—an Australian-based lobby group. The ADFM was conceived as a "Track II" dialogue, comprised of individuals with "very significant expertise in the field of forced migration." These are academics, ex-government experts, ex-international organization experts, think tank staff, and international organization members (CPD 2015). Because of the close links of some of its members with governments, it is now closely aligned with the Bali Process. This alignment flags the advisory role that ADFM sees itself playing in the international environment. The Fourth Meeting of the ADFM, held in Jakarta in March 2017, "deepened its policy contributions" to both the Bali Process and ASEAN. The Bali Process has in turn requested that the ADFM continue to provide policy advice to its member countries. At this meeting, the ADFM agreed to work toward contributing to the Global Compacts on Migration and Refugees (ADFM 2017). Importantly, two of its members are Sriprapha Petcharamesree and Alice Nah, each of whom had previously participated in APFMC workshops, and whom I recommended to the CPD when it was establishing the ADFM in 2015. The ADFM has been quite vocal in its critique of regional inaction in the Andaman Sea crisis (Petcharamesree et al. 2016).

## Conclusions

The context for refugee protection in Southeast Asia is a contested and contentious space, created by the lack of state take-up on responsibility and burden-sharing for lasting solutions. This response reflects a perception that refugee protection is an issue for northern states to tackle (in contrast to Landau's chapter on Africa and Sánchez-Mojica's chapter on Latin America). This lack of solidarity amongst this group of southern states is manifested by the focus on the national migration status of refugees and the preference for a "human security" approach to resolution of the issues, in place of human rights. These framings, which show the deficit of normative standards, are reflected at the regional level processes, such as ASEAN and the Bali Process. In this context it is difficult for CSOs to find a strong voice, but at the same time their exclusion creates opportunities at the intraregional level to build "local legitimacy" (see chapter 1).

In contrast to CSOs working in this area, the APFMC does not compete for protection space with international organizations or come into direct conflict with states; unlike the ADFM, the APFMC operates independently of any connection with states or state-led processes. It has the freedom to network widely through invited participation in roundtables and through publications and conference papers that emanate from APFMC, activities are disseminated globally, thereby informing the work of others.[6]

Through workshops and direct engagement with refugee advocacy groups (e.g., Justice Hong Kong, Human Rights Watch Australia, Refugee Council of Australia, Refugee Legal) APFMC forms a bridge between academia and advocacy. It works with other refugee networks and their leaders, such as professor Susan McGrath from the Refugee Research Network (RRN) and professor David Cantor, director Refugee Law Initiative (RLI) and the Kaldor Centre (University of New South Wales). Through its work with engaged academics such as Sriprapha Petcharamesree and Alice Nah, the APFMC creates links across other networks and is linked to other networks. It is indeed a model networking network.

## Notes

Thanks to Thomas Harré and Reyvi Mariñas for research and editorial assistance.

1 ASEAN (Association of South East Asia Nations), founded in 1967, originally involved five states—Singapore, Malaysia, Thailand, Philippines, and Indonesia—to promote "common political interests as well as a forum for private business and community-level interactions." Brunei was added in 1984, Vietnam in 1995, Lao PDR and Myanmar in 1997, and Cambodia in 1999.

2 For example, in May–June 2015 at the height of the Andaman Sea crisis I was interviewed by media (television and radio) based in Singapore on at least six occasions.

3 A prominent recent example is the ASEAN Convention on Trafficking in Persons (2015).

4 Although note that in the Chairman's Statement of the recent 30th ASEAN Summit, the importance of dialogue between ASEAN and CSOs was held up as being of importance in terms of successfully attaining the ASEAN Vision 2025.

5 According to the financial statement it received $1.7 million from the UNHCR in the 2016 income period out of a total of approximately $9.3 million.

6 Recent citations include: Tan 2016; Curley and Vandyk 2016; Moretti 2016.

# References

ACSC/APF. 2017. "ASEAN Civil Society Conference (ACSC)/ASEAN People's Forum (APF)." Accessed 8 Nov 2018. https://www.forum-asia.org/?p=25084.

Alexander, Amy. 2008. "Without Refuge: Chin Refugees in India and Malaysia." *Forced Migration Review* 30: 36.

Association of Southeast Asian Nations (ASEAN) Convention on Trafficking in Persons. 2015.

ASEAN Human Rights Declaration. 2012.

ASEAN Intergovernmental Commission on Human Rights (AICHR). 2017. "Press Release: Special Meeting of AICHR, 4–6 Aug 2017, Manila, the Philippines." http://aichr.org/press-release/press-release-special-meeting-of-the-aichr-4-6-august-2017-manila-the-philippines/.

ASEAN Parliamentarians for Human Rights (APHR). 2017. "On 50th Anniversary of ASEAN's Founding, MPs Urge Regional Grouping to Evolve, Improve Rights Mechanisms." http://mailchi.mp/aseanmp/50th-anniversary-mps-urge-asean-to-evolve.

ASEAN Summit. 2017. "Chairman's Statement, 29 April 2017." http://asean.org/chairmans-statement-30th-asean-summit/.

Asia Pacific Refugee Rights Network (APRRN). 2016. *Annual Report.*Asia Research Institute (ARI). 2017. "Message from the Director." http://www.ari.nus.edu.sg/ about%20us/message-from-the-director.html.

Asian Law Institute (ASLI). 2017. "14th ASLI Conference: A Uniting Force? 'Asian Values' and the Law." http://law.nus.edu.sg/asli/14th_asli_conf/.

Bali Process. 2016. "The Bali Process on People Smuggling, Trafficking in Persons, and Related Transnational Crime." http://www.baliprocess.net/.

Caballero-Anthony, Mely. 2008. "Reflections on Managing Migration in South East Asia: Mitigating the Unintended Consequences of Securitisation." In *Security and Migration in Asia: The Dynamics of Securitisation*, edited by Melissa G. Curley and Wong Siu-lun, 165–76. New York: Routledge.

———. 2012. "The Responsibility to Protect in Southeast Asia: Opening up Spaces for Advancing Human Security." *Pacific Review* 25, no. 1: 113.

Caballero-Anthony, Mely, and Alistair D. B. Cook. 2013. "NTS Framework." In *Non-Traditional Security in Asia: Issues, Challenges and Framework for Action*, edited by Mely Caballero-Anthony and Alistair D. B. Cook, 1–14. Singapore: ISEAS-Yusof Ishak Institute.

Chimni, B. S. 2009. "The Birth of a Discipline: From Refugee to Forced Migration Studies." *Journal of Refugee Studies* 22, no. 1: 11–29.

Centre for Policy Development. 2015. "Project Briefing: Track II Dialogue on Forced Migration in the Asia Pacific." (On file with the author).

Curley, Melissa, and Kahlia Vandyk. 2016. "The Securitisation of Migrant Smuggling in Australia and Its Consequences for the Bali Process." *Australian Journal of International Affairs* 71, no. 1: 42–62.

Davies, Sara. 2008. *Legitimising Rejection: International Refugee Law in South East Asia*. Leiden, Boston: Martinis Nijhoff Publishers.

Edwards, Alice, and Carla Ferstman. 2010. "Humanising Non-Citizens: The Convergence of Human Rights and Human Security." In *Human Security and Non-Citizens: Law Policy and International Affairs*, edited by Alice Edwards and Carla Ferstman, 3–46. Cambridge: Cambridge University Press.

di Gaetano, Silvia. 2015. "How to Solve Asia's Refugee Crisis: Steps Can and Should be Taken to Alleviate the Plight of Rohingya." *Diplomat*, 28 Sept 2015.

Goodwin-Gill, Guy. 2008. "The Politics of Refugee Protection." *Refugee Survey Quarterly* 27, no. 1: 8–23.

Habermas, Jürgen. 1996. *Between Facts and Norms: Contributions to a Discourse Theory of Law and Democracy*. Cambridge and Malden: Polity Press.

InterAksyon. 2017. "Southeast Asian civil society to ASEAN, 50 years of exclusion is enough." http://www.interaksyon.com/southeast-asian-civil-society-to-asean-50-years-of-exclusion-is-enough/.

Jones, Martin. 2014. "Moving beyond Protection Space: Developing a Law of Asylum in South East Asia." In *Refugee Protection and the Role of Law: Conflicting Identities*, edited by Susan Kneebone, Dallal Stevens, and Loretta Baldassar, 251–70. London: Routledge.

International Labour Organization. 2005. *Labor and Social Trends in ASEAN 2005: Integration, Challenges and Opportunities*. Bangkok: International Labour Organization.

Kneebone, Susan. 2014a. "ASEAN and the Conceptualisation of Refugee Protection." In *Regional Approaches to the Protection of Asylum Seekers: An International Legal Perspective*, edited by Ademola Abass and Francesca Ippolito, 295–324. Burlington, VT: Ashgate.

———. 2014b. "The Bali Process and Global Refugee Policy in the Asia-Pacific Region." *Journal of Refugee Studies* 27, no. 4: 596–618.

———. 2011. "ASEAN Norms and Setting the Agenda for the Rights of Migrant Workers." In *Human Rights in the Asia Pacific Region*, edited by Hitoshi Nasu and Ben Saul, 301–38. New York: Routledge.

———. 2015. "The Labeling Problem in Southeast Asia's Refugee Crisis." *Diplomat*, 12 Aug 2015. http://thediplomat.com/2015/08/the-labeling-problem-in-southeast-asias-refugee-crisis/.

Kneebone, Susan, and Julie Debeljak. 2012. *Transnational Crime and Human Rights: Responses to Human Trafficking in the Greater Mekong Subregion*. New York: Routledge.

Kneebone, Susan, and Felicity Rawlings-Sanaei. 2007. *New Regionalism and Asylum Seekers: Challenges Ahead*. New York/Oxford: Berghahn Books.

Ministry of Foreign Affairs of Malaysia, Indonesia and Thailand. 2015. "Joint Statement: Ministerial Meeting on Irregular Movement of People in Southeast Asia." Accessed 8 Nov 2018. https://reliefweb.int/report/myanmar/joint-statement-ministerial-meeting-irregular-movement-people-southeast-asia.

Ministry of Foreign Affairs of the Kingdom of Thailand. 2015. "Summary Statement: Special Meeting on Irregular Migration in the Indian Ocean, 29 May 2015, Bangkok, Thailand." Accessed 8 Nov 2018. http://www.mfa.go.th/main/en/media-center/14/56880-Summary-Special-Meeting-on-Irregular-Migration-in.html.

Moretti, Sebastien. 2016. *UNHCR and the Migration Regime Complex in Asia-Pacific: Between Responsibility Shifting and Responsibility Sharing*. New Issues in Refugee Research Paper No 283. Geneva: Global Migration Centre.

Muntarbhorn, Vitit. 2004. "Refugee Law and Practice in the Asia and Pacific Region: Thailand as a Case Study." Thailand: UNCHR. http://www.refugeelawreader.org/en/en/english/section-v-asian-framework-for-refugee-protection/v1-protection-challenges-in-asia/core-readings-140/9456-muntarbhorn-refugee-law-and-practice-in-the-asia-and-pacific-region-thailand-as-a-case-study-1/file.html.

Nah, Alice. 2016. "Networks and Norm Entrepreneurship amongst Local Civil Society Actors: Advancing Refugee Protection in the Asia Pacific Region." *International Journal of Human Rights* 20, no. 2: 223–40.

———. 2007. "Struggling with (Il)legality: The Indeterminate Functioning of Malaysia's Borders for Asylum Seekers, Refugees, and Stateless Persons." In *Borderscapes: Hidden Geographies and Politics at Territory's Edge*, edited by Prem Kumar Rajaram and Carl Grundy-Warr, 35–64. Minneapolis: University of Minnesota Press.

Petcharamesree, Sriprapha. 2016. "ASEAN and its Approach to Forced Migration Issues." *International Journal of Human Rights* 20, no. 2: 173–90.

———. 2013. "International Protection and Public Accountability: The Roles of Civil Society." In *The UNHCR and the Supervision of International Refugee Law*, edited by James C. Simeon, 275–85. Cambridge: Cambridge University Press.

Petcharamesree, Sriprapha, Peter Hughes, Steven Wong, Travers McLeod, and Tri Nuke Pudjiastuti. 2016. "The Andaman Sea Crisis a Year On: Is the Region Better Prepared?" *Conversation*, 27 May 2016. https://theconversation. com/the-andaman-sea-refugee-crisis-a-year-on-is-the-region-now-better-prepared-59687.

Skeldon, Ronald. 2000. "Trafficking: A Perspective from Asia." *International Migration* 38, no. 3: 7–30.

Song, Jiyoung. 2015. "Redefining Human Security for Vulnerable Migrants in East Asia." *Journal of Human Security* 11, no. 1: 45–56.

Tan, Nikolas F. 2016. "The Status of Asylum Seekers and Refugees in Indonesia." *International Journal of Refugee Law* 28, no. 3: 365–83.

UNHCR. 2014. "Regional Office for South East Asia: Factsheet." Accessed 8 Nov 2018. http://www.unhcr.org/519f67fc9.html.

———. 2015. "Global Appeal 2015 Update: South-East Asia Subregional Overview." http://reliefweb.int/report/myanmar/unhcr-global-appeal-2015-update-south-east-asia-subregional-overview.

———. 2017a. "Global Focus: South East Asia 2017." http://reporting.unhcr.org/sites/default/files/pdfsummaries/GR2017-SouthEastAsia-eng.pdf.

UNHCR Regional Office for South East Asia. 2017b. "Mixed Movements in South-East Asia 2016." http://www.refworld.org/pdfid/590b18a14.pdf.

UNHCR. 2017c. "Global Focus: Malaysia." http://reporting.unhcr.org/sites/default/files/pdfsummaries/GR2017-Malaysia-eng.pdf.

# Transitions from Knowledge Networked to Knowledge Engaged: Ethical Tensions and Dilemmas from the Global to the Local

*Wenona Giles and Don Dippo*

## Introduction: From Knowledge Networked to Knowledge Engaged

In this chapter, we are interested in the impacts of a global north-south education partnership on faculty in Canada and Kenya who currently engage in the delivery of university programs to students living in and around the Dadaab refugee camps in northeastern Kenya. The Borderless Higher Education for Refugees (BHER) Partnership emerged out of the Refugee Research Network (RRN) as a project of engaged scholarship (Boyer 1990, 1996) with the goal of applying knowledge gained about displacement into knowledge transformation of both students and teachers (Hynie et al. 2014, 2). Research that led to, fostered, and accompanied the emergence of the BHER Partnership and project originated from academic relationships within the international Refugee Research Network (RRN). Its "philosophy of open source and open access . . . designed to encourage online collaboration, networking, and information sharing among researchers, policymakers, and practitioners" (Hynie et al. 2014, 4) inspired the creation of BHER in significant ways.

The partnerships involved in the development of the BHER project range from traditional macro transnational institutional and organizational relationships, such as the RRN and the BHER Canadian-Kenyan universities and NGO partnerships, to partnerships at the most interpersonal level between teachers and students. Much of what we experienced and learned about the ethics of partnerships through our involvement in the RRN runs like threads into our virtual and on-site classrooms; and much is also challenged and contested. This chapter is about our efforts to build ethical student-professor relationships with people living in Dadaab, in northeastern Kenya, in one of the largest and most insecure refugee camps in the world, while also continuously experiencing what we define with Mezirow (1995, 50) as ongoing "disorienting dilemmas."

There is a sizeable and significant literature on partnerships (e.g., Baud 2002; Chernikova 2011; Hynie et al. 2014; Jazeel and McFarlane 2007; Ogden and Porter 2000). Clark-Kazak and Landau in this volume both refer to the challenges of developing ethical partnerships or networks between global north and south participants. An important strand that links the RRN to the BHER Dadaab classroom is a claim made by members of the RRN, building on Chernikova's analysis, that "a successful partnership can support and meet different goals for the partners but that success is contingent on the partnership valuing this diversity of goals" (Hynie et al. 2014, 6; Chernikova 2011). Along these lines, respect by both teachers and students in the BHER project for each other's socio-cultural and educative experiences has been paramount to the success of BHER. As Hynie et al. also point out, respect for diversity "is challenged by the context in which community-university partnerships occur" (2014, 6; Baud 2002; Chernikova 2011).

The BHER professor-student relations are impacted by a number of contexts, all of which combine at any moment to create unexpected, puzzling, and confounding dilemmas. We explore life in the Dadaab camps and town in some detail below, and we briefly define the Kenyan-Canadian BHER partnership. However, while we recognize the centrality of obligations to funders in global north-south relations (Baud 2002, 157; Sork 2016; Jentsch 2004) and the importance of the complex uses of technologies in the transference of knowledge to marginalized populations

(Dahya and Dryden-Peterson 2016; Etim 2006), these two latter contexts are beyond the scope of the current chapter.

We begin by defining the BHER project partnership and the spaces of that project, which for the purposes of this chapter include the on-site and online classrooms and courses offered at the BHER Learning Centre in Dadaab, Kenyatta University in Nairobi, Moi University in Eldoret, York University in Toronto, and the University of British Columbia in Vancouver, where courses offered through BHER originate. We then turn to several interrelated approaches that frame our analysis. Arendt's ideas of "worldliness," its interrelationship with "political action" and the role of the university in the world provide a foundation for our thinking (Kateb 1977, 142; Arendt 2006 [1954]; Bender 1998). Conversely, postcolonial critiques have provided compelling arguments as to why some definitions of worldliness have historically been perilous paths to follow (Dirlik 1994; Hall 1996; Said 1978; Spivak 1988). Thus, we also look to ideas about the gulf between "us" and "them" and the resulting disorienting dilemmas, exploring whether worldliness and postcolonial critiques may be less contradictory when defined or guided by an ethical encounter (Butler 2004)— and if so, how. Two case studies ground this chapter: the first addresses the use of English as a language of instruction; the second concerns the presence of patriarchy in the Dadaab refugee camp classrooms.

## The Borderless Higher Education for Refugees (BHER) Project Partnerships

BHER is an international partnership of Kenyan and Canadian universities and a Kenyan non-governmental organization that, with the support of the UNHCR, work together to provide post-secondary opportunities to mainly uncertified teachers, as well as some other students living in long-term conditions of forced displacement. Most importantly for this chapter, BHER also includes professor-student relationships that can be thought of as a kind of partnership that is both local and interpersonal. On-site/online university credit courses are offered through the BHER project, enabling uncertified teachers and other refugee and Kenyan students in Dadaab to earn certificates, diplomas, and degrees in a variety of fields including health promotion, science and arts education, and geography. Refugee and local students in Dadaab and students located at partner universities benefit directly through online exchange opportunities and by being able to participate in blended courses that often include students on the home campuses with students in Dadaab. University professors routinely express that their taken-for-granted and settled ways of knowing and doing have become both unsettled and refreshed by their BHER teaching experiences. These are among the experiences we explore in the two case studies.

BHER is built upon research that began in 2005 on long-term displacement for refugees (Hyndman and Giles 2017) that revealed a dearth of attention to higher education in extended exile. Other explorations of this issue reveal the possibilities as well as challenges related to the development and implementation of the BHER project (Dippo, Orgocka, and Giles 2013; Murphy 2012, 2016). The Canadian Government funded what became known as the Borderless Higher Education for Refugees project that developed and then began to deliver university programs in Dadaab, beginning in 2013.

## Place

Access to schools and resources therein (e.g., teachers, learning materials, libraries, labs, classrooms) determine not only how youth are prepared, but also the aspirations they can build for the future. Appadurai refers to "the capacity to aspire" (2004, 59), among impoverished students, which he describes as "the social and cultural capacity to plan, hope, desire, and achieve socially valuable goals" (2006, 176). This is similar to the ontological security that Giddens describes as being predicated on a people's ability to give meaning to their lives and avoid chaos or anxiety, and that Edkins defines as essential to personal survival and based on a continuing social order that gives our lives meaning and includes "family, friends, political community, beliefs" (Hyndman and Giles 2017, 16). For Appadurai, the possibility of aspiring is linked to having access to "systematic tools for gaining relevant new knowledge" (2006, 176) that comes from education and various forms of training (2006, 167–8). Giddens and others' work on ontological security assumes a stable subject in a liberal democratic state (Hyndman and Giles 2017, 16). Edkins' and Appadurai's research, on the other hand, pertains to marginalized, poor, and militarized contexts and is thus more relevant to our understanding of educational spaces in Dadaab.

WENONA GILES AND DON DIPPO

Described as one of the largest sites of extended asylum[1] in the world, Dadaab at present is home to some 245,126 people who have fled civil war, famine, and other disasters (UNHCR 2017a, 2017b). As of March 2017, thirty-two primary schools in the camps serve 50,509 displaced children ages six to seventeen (Giles and Orgocka 2018). Only 62 per cent of school-aged boys and 52 per cent of school-aged girls were enrolled in these schools. Seven secondary schools in the camps enrolled approximately 4,838 (1,269 girls and 3,569 boys) students or 10 per cent of the secondary school age students.[2] Class sizes are immense and learning materials are scarce. Most teachers are recent secondary school graduates themselves with no particular preparation to teach. Assessment of the quality of education delivered in these schools points to several challenges, the most significant being that they are poorly resourced and the curriculum does not address adequately the psychological needs and practical knowledge and skills that these youth need. Teachers are unprepared to take on the challenge of nurturing a new generation.[3]

The BHER project provides both challenges and opportunities for educators attempting to work within and across social, political, economic, and cultural differences. The camps and local communities are complex settings where histories and politics are a defining feature of everyday life. Within camps, there are politics of inclusion/exclusion among national, ethnic, tribal, language, religious, and other groups. Between camps and local communities, there are politics of resentment and condescension. Among local communities, there are politics of distribution and competition for the economic benefits of a so-called "refugee industry" (Enghoff et al. 2010; Rawlence 2016). In such a politicized context, the idea of a professor-student partnership among those engaged in teaching and learning in the BHER project may seem presumptuous.

All professors from Kenyan and Canadian universities who have offered courses through BHER have had to deal with the complexities of offering higher education in a context of prolonged encampment. In attempting to initiate what is likely an unfamiliar professor-student relationship, they have all had to ask themselves about curriculum content. Is this course material interesting, relevant, appropriate, culturally responsive, challenging, and critical? They have all had to consider approaches to pedagogy. Are these inclusive, participatory, inquiry-driven? Will students understand, participate, and extend their knowledge and pedagogical skills? Or will they be confounded, compliant, and suspicious of new and unfamiliar approaches to teaching and learning? Will assignments be meaningful? Will technology frustrate or facilitate learning? The disorienting dilemmas associated with these and other questions are connected to the theoretical underpinnings of this chapter. In the next section, we define and question the politico-historical understandings that anchor this chapter.

## Where We Stand: "If I Am Not What I've Been Told I Am, Then It Means *You're* Not What You Thought You Were *Either*"[4]

Our approach juxtaposes Hannah Arendt's idea of worldliness, which she regarded as a mode of active engagement in the world (Arendt 2006 [1954]), with a postcolonial critique of the imposition of Western forms of education in marginalized settings throughout the world. Recognizing that "the idea of the postcolonial is located within a highly contested political and theoretical terrain" (Rizvi et al. 2006, 249), we argue that the contradictions between these two approaches are potentially diminished when brought into dialogue with ideas about the ethical encounter as defined by Butler (2004, 2009), Scarry (2011), Fassin (2011), and others.

Instead of the common and frequent aspiration for a "world class university," we follow Arendt in arguing for a worldly university and imagine what such an institution could look like. We see such a place as being engaged with the world and linked to new ways of defining prosperity, as connected to well-being and knowledge for all. A worldly university offers students, both young and older, the tools to be able to think and to judge and to be political in the world. Arendt describes freedom as having the possibility of being politically active, and worldliness as recognition of our dependency on one another. These are concepts that she prized most highly. To be political, she says, is to be alive and engaged in the world—to be human. Arendt called for educators to assume joint responsibility for the world (Arendt 2006 [1954])—promoting a worldliness by promoting the development of individuals so that they too can join in the making of that world. How then, to do so, in full recognition of the warnings from postcolonial scholars about the tragic history of powerful education "actors" enacting irreparable harm on marginalized populations (Dirlik 1994; Fanon 1984; Said 1978)?

Cultural legacies and tragic human consequences of colonialism and imperialism are well documented (e.g., Gregory 2004; Hall 1996; Jayawardena 1986; Rizvi et al. 2006; Said 1993; Spivak 1988; see also chapter 5 in this book for a discussion of colonialism and identity politics in India's northeast). And postcolonial critiques have challenged colonial and imperialist narratives that misrepresent the world (Narayan 1997) as composed of separate unequal cultures, instead arguing for and about hybridity as a philosophic value that challenges the ideological validity of colonialism as expounded during the colonial era (Bhabha 1994). The impacts of the politics of knowledge creation, control, and distribution, and its relationship to the exploitation of many in the global south continuing in the form of neocolonialism (Gregory 2004), has been disastrous in the area of education. We are reminded by Farhia Abdi (2016, 21) of the struggles by African countries to Africanize education in the postcolonial era and the tremendous struggles and indeed crises to which this has led. But as Rizvi et al. (2006, 257) succinctly point out, there is ambivalence in the relationship of education to postcolonialism: "On the one hand, it is an object of postcolonial critique regarding its complicity with Eurocentric discourses and practices. On the other hand, it is only through education that it is possible to reveal and resist colonialism's continuing hold on our imagination."

As an education project originating in the global north, BHER necessarily struggles to understand itself in relation to the historical legacy of colonialism. Local opposition to the project in Dadaab is a constant reminder that we are working among some encamped traditionalists for whom Western-style education is irrelevant, as well as militants for whom education is a threat. In academic circles in Canada and Kenya, we regularly respond to political accusations of neocolonialism by pointing out that our approach to education emphasizes a learner-centred, curiosity-driven curriculum that includes local, traditional, and scientific/academic knowledge, a participatory, inquiry-based engaged pedagogy, and an approach to course design and assignments that emphasizes "purposeful activity." This kind of teaching is more in keeping with a post-independence, nation-building project focused on cooperation and the common good (Nyerere 1968) than it is with a neocolonial educational agenda. With

Jennifer Lavia, who writes about educational practice in the Caribbean, we endorse a "pedagogy of hope . . . within the context of postcoloniality as an aspiration" and an educational practice that is "inextricably linked" with the history, politics, and culture of the region (Lavia 2006 in Rizvi et al. 2006, 258). In the BHER project, we see ideas about educational practice as intricately linked to the nature of the encounter between teachers and students.

Ideas about recognition of the other provide a place for us to comprehend the concept of the educational encounter and it is Judith Butler's ideas about recognition and the "ethical encounter" that we turn to here. She contends that "vulnerability must be perceived and recognized in order to come into play in an ethical encounter, and there is no guarantee that this will happen" (Butler 2004, 42–3). Recognizing the vulnerability of oneself and the other is a two-way experience, a reciprocal encounter (Hyndman and Giles 2017, 13). In other words, we expect in the BHER project that both professors and students will be transformed by the educative encounter, generating new subject positions for each. However, these encounters are not always easy or straightforward. Indeed, the context of our work in Dadaab is saturated with the kind of "disorienting dilemmas" (Mezirow 1995, 50), reconcilable and irreconcilable, that may always be unsettling. Writing about educative experience, Dewey says: "The belief that all genuine education comes about through experience does not mean that all experiences are genuinely or equally educative. Experience and education cannot be directly equated to each other. For some, experiences are mis-educative. Any experience is mis-educative that has the effect of arresting or distorting the growth of further experience" (Dewey 1997 [1938], 25). To engage with the students in Dadaab is to open the possibility for a truly educative experience. If that engagement enables us to imagine meaningfulness beyond the horizons of our own understanding and enlarge our capacity to recognize the personhood of someone living the tragedy of forced migration, the experience will have been educative. If, on the other hand, we are incapable of transcending the limitations of our own understandings and come away from that encounter disturbed but reassured with a singular, one-dimensional understanding of a pathetic figure of a refugee, the experience will have been mis-educative.

The BHER project promises to be rich in implications for the theory and practice of transformative learning for students, but also for teachers.

The transformation of the progressive/critical educator (Dewey 1997 [1938]) is what we focus on in this chapter. Drawing on two case studies from the BHER experience, we explore some of the emergent and ongoing tensions and dilemmas in curriculum design and program development and ask about the mis-educative potential of transformative learning. Put another way, this chapter probes whether openness to transformation (and a willingness to revisit, reconsider, and revise principles) can be mis-educative? Moreover, can a principled stance in relation to conflicting political commitments be seen as a refusal to learn?

## Case Study One: The Problem with English

"We appreciate your efforts to be respectful and not to perpetuate the colonial legacy, but get over it. You want to offer us tradition. What we want is a future." (Paraphrased comment originally made by a refugee researcher for the BHER project at a meeting in Nairobi, 2011. The subject of the discussion was whether BHER classes should be taught in Somali or English.) There are passionate academic debates about the relationship between colonial languages and Indigenous languages; between national languages and local languages (e.g., Dryden-Peterson 2006, 2011; Gichiru and Larkin 2009; Hardman et al. 2009; International Network for Education in Emergencies (INEE) 2010; Kirk 2009). One consistent theme that runs through that literature has to do with the language of instruction in schools. English is usually characterized as somewhat of an "invasive species" that inevitably extinguishes local languages. Houwer's research for the BHER project and Dryden-Peterson's conclusions in a UNHCR report both directly relate to this question of the problem with English: "In contexts of forced migration where the language of home and the host community is different, the language of curriculum, instruction, and examination is often politically and culturally contentious and a challenge to achieving positive learning outcomes" (Houwer 2011, 25, based on Dryden-Peterson 2011, 61). Dryden-Peterson (2011, 91) has argued that education is a "fourth durable solution" for refugees displaced from their home countries, indicating that the language of the host community points to local integration while the language of home points to repatriation.

Up to the present time, universities involved in the BHER project are English language institutions. Building on the aforementioned scholarship, BHER researchers advised that our teacher education program should provide instruction and training to student teachers about differences in teaching and learning in a mother tongue, or second-language, and how to address code-switching[5] among their students. It was proposed that this would not only improve learning outcomes for BHER student teachers but would respect their cultural backgrounds. Houwer quotes Hardman et al., who argue that language adaptation is "central to making the curriculum more relevant by connecting the learning to the pupil's experience, environment and culture" (Hardman 2009, 26–7; see also Abdi 2016, 26).

For the BHER project, this and other thoughtful analyses and sets of recommendations led us a) to explore the possibility of a bilingual Somali-English curriculum; and b) to develop a strategy and action plan to deal with university policies pertaining to the language(s) of instruction in our courses. At the time, we felt confident that we were indeed responding well to the challenge of being of the global north without being implicated in its globalizing, neocolonial agendas. Then we embarked on a year-long feasibility study in Dadaab and as described in the above quote, were told by refugees that they wanted English and only English in their university courses and in their schools. We were told that when schooling started in the camps some twenty years ago, they used the Somalian curriculum and Somali was the language of instruction. Then along the way, parents themselves, seeing little hope for repatriation, eventually insisted on adopting the Kenyan curriculum with English and KiSwahili, the two official Kenyan working languages, as the languages of instruction. In their view, this would better their children's chances for integration (into Kenyan society) or out migration (to the global north).

Localizing the language of the curriculum presents particular challenges in Dadaab. Somali is the mother tongue of ethnic Somalis on both sides of the Kenya-Somali border, but not of the Kenyan central state. Thus, the Kenyan curriculum was adopted in the camps out of concern for accreditation. As a result, the language of instruction in the schools is English, pointing to local integration as a durable solution. But because of Kenya's official policy of encampment, legal local integration is presently not an option. The INEE Minimum Standards advise that "learning content, materials, and instruction are (to be) provided in the language(s) of the learners" (INEE 2010, 77). This standard privileges the durable solution of repatriation, but it is also founded on extensive research that demonstrates that language comprehension is the single most important factor in the learning process. In cases where the language of instruction is not the mother tongue, it is advised that the teacher should be fluently bilingual.

We understand this divergence between international policy and scholarship on the one hand, and the desires of Dadaab students on the other, to be a disorienting dilemma and a moment rich in transformative potential. But for the progressive/critical educator, is this experience educative or mis-educative? On the one hand, it would be a mistake to dismiss the analysis and understanding put forward by the refugees as being selective or ahistorical or undertheorized; but neither do we think that the analyses and understandings offered in scholarly literature are ungrounded or overdetermined. Wholly endorsing either approach is too simplistic and closes down possibilities for coming to a more sensitive, nuanced understanding, converting the disorienting dilemma into a mis-educative experience. The educative response, the one that would be enabling, is one that would open the way for further learning that would lead to a more complex and ultimately more useful understanding.

To begin to formulate an educative response, to begin to tap into the transformative learning potential of such a disorienting dilemma, requires both acknowledging the real hopes and aspirations of refugee learners and recognizing one's own undeniable implication in English language hegemony. It requires enlarging the analysis of language use and abuse to include the histories, the politics, and the complexities of the local context. It requires seeing the global in relation to the local; the abstract in relation to the concrete; the self in relation to the Other. Openness to transformative learning requires humility, vulnerability, and a willingness to change one's mind. It is in such moments that the possibility for Butler's (2004) "ethical encounter" between a professor and student (in the case of BHER) presents itself. However, what can just as easily happen is a "specific exploitation of targeted populations, of lives that are not quite lives" (Butler 2009, 31)—a valid concern echoed in neocolonial critiques. Following the lead of Butler and others, we look for ways to traverse the discursive gulf between "us" and "them," between teachers and refugee students. Elaine Scarry's consensus-building mode of deliberation "in which a community of people gathers together to collectively present and debate information and to make a decision" (Scarry in Beckett 2013, 96) can be applied to the educative space of the BHER professor and student. She foregrounds "mutual protection" (2013, 97) and "equality of survival" (Scarry 2011, 52), which make an ethical encounter more likely.

## Case Study Two: Persistent Patriarchy

Protracted displacement in a refugee camp in Kenya, as opposed to attendance at university in the home country, turns gender relations on its head for university level students. Not only are young Somalian women's possibilities of attending high school and succeeding well enough to attend university undermined by the profound gender inequality in the Dadaab refugee camps, but most of these young women are more poorly prepared than men overall for university. It is perhaps unsurprising, then, that these women are more likely to drop out of the BHER university courses than men (Giles and Orgocka 2018).

Parents, as well as young women students in Dadaab, have expressed concerns about the safety and security of women and girls travelling to and from schools, inadequate girls-only sanitation facilities, and the inability of young women to fulfil gendered domestic responsibilities if they are in school. These anxieties have led to a high incidence of early marriages and female genital mutilation that are regarded by some parents as protective and caring responses in a context where sexual and gender-based violence is rampant. However, the point in this chapter is not to review the parents' position, but to recognize these narratives of gender inequalities. The goal is not to reiterate the counter-arguments about the history of pernicious patriarchy and neocolonialism that have contributed to the creation of long-term displacement in camps, but instead, to raise the question as to how teachers and students in Dadaab might nonetheless participate in ethical teaching encounters. Is it even possible to imagine, in such a context, the "two-way experience," the "reciprocal encounter," whereby both persons are transformed? Is a stance of vulnerability (by both teacher and student) even possible to conceive of in such an encounter? Does this disorienting dilemma have transformative potential? And can we even begin to recognize such encounters as disorienting (and will they even be dilemmas?) if we are unwilling and/or unable to doubt or reconsider our taken-for-granted political commitments?

All of BHER's policies and programs are based on a firm commitment to gender equity. BHER Kenyan and Canadian university instructors are expected to come to their virtual and on-site classrooms with a commitment to challenge patriarchy, to defy the odds and to achieve something close to gender parity in the certificate, diploma, and degree programs we offer. Is it possible to be vulnerable and open to learning in a context where patriarchy persists, without abandoning a fundamental commitment to gender equity principles and practices? We are constantly considering ways to locate more women students, include them in our programs in Dadaab, and then likewise to ensure their retention. In order to achieve a goal of 30 per cent representation of women in BHER programs, we lower entrance requirements for them, count non-academic experience, provide spaces near the classrooms for them to nurse and care for their children, allow them to repeat courses when they absent themselves from too many classes in order to deliver their babies, and provide extensive mentoring. In the autumn of 2016, we conducted workshops in the Dadaab camps to address reported gender harassment against women by some male students, with the aim of improving the safety of the learning space for women. The workshops were well attended and received.[6]

The danger for BHER instructors has been that the disorienting dilemmas that routinely present themselves as we seek to engage with people and communities in Dadaab, whose gendered customs and traditions, beliefs and values are at odds with our own, become disabling dilemmas wherein we are unable to hold onto both a strong commitment to a principle (in this case gender equity), as well as a strong commitment to openness and vulnerability. Confronted with a situation that is clearly patriarchal, our inclination is to respond (i.e., we feel "called upon" to intervene, to interfere, to disrupt the social, political, economic relations that so disadvantage, disparage, and oppress girls and women). And yet, the unfortunate history of well-meaning and well-intentioned humanitarian interventions, often perpetrated by people more like than unlike us, gives us pause (or ought to), and reminds us of the paternalism and neocolonialism that can easily be perpetuated in international development projects like BHER.

Can we begin to imagine the dilemma that would enable us to revisit our understanding and revise our "stance" vis-à-vis gender equity? Indeed, if we could imagine it, the dilemma would not be disorienting.

There are those who would argue that a human rights perspective justifies intervention; others would argue that history cautions against such interference. Which is the defensive stance and which is the principled position? Both may be a refusal to learn. If we are committed to openness and vulnerability, we must be prepared to reconsider our commitments to principles of gender equity as we understand them. If we are committed to principles of gender equity, we must admit our inability to be "open" and "vulnerable" and therefore unable to participate in the "ethical encounter." We can't have it both ways. Or can we? This is the predicament we find ourselves in. We can become paralyzed, or we can move forward with caution, humility, openness, generosity, inside the tension (of the dilemma), in conditions of uncertainty.

The work of some anti-nationalist feminists offers a possible way to live with, and possibly learn from this disorientation around gender inequity. They have long adopted a "rooting and shifting" approach in which people recognize rootedness in their own identity and culture, but at the same time try to shift so as to put themselves in a situation of exchange with others who claim other identities (see Giles and Hyndman 2004, 8). Defined as a "transversal politics of coalition building" by Italian feminists in the early 1990s, shifting does not involve self-decentring, and rooting does not make us incapable of movement. Rather, this approach calls on us to look "for connection with those among 'the others' with whom we might find compatible values and goals" (Cockburn 1998, 9, in Giles and Hyndman 2004, 8). Unlike these feminists, most BHER professors know and accept that they will engage in a teaching relationship with some students with whom they will have incompatible goals. But a transformative method espoused by BHER professors resonates with this feminist approach that has been tested by academics and activists working across ethnic nationalist boundaries in times of militarized violence and that focuses on empathy and openness rather than differences. It coincides well with Butler and Scarry, as we discuss in the first case study above, and their interest in traversing the gulf between "us" and "them," using a "reciprocal recognition" approach (an "ethical encounter," in Butler's words) and consensus-building modes of deliberation.

# Conclusion

Our argument in this chapter is that despite the challenges posed to world-liness by postcolonial critiques, these approaches are less contradictory and incongruous when defined through/guided by an ethical encounter. The transformative method that we refer to is thus embedded in a historical materialist methodology and involves at least three aspirational steps: the imperative to act as a result of an engagement in worldliness; a prohibition against doing harm in the name of good as a consequence of a critical engagement with postcoloniality; and an ongoing effort to enter into ethical student-teacher encounters. Despite ongoing disorienting dilemmas, as described through the two case studies, BHER educators have persisted in the continuing creation and recreation, the stop and restart of ethical relationships with Dadaab refugee students. This chapter is an attempt to answer why they have done so when the contestations from postcolonial critics and refugee students are so pronounced. There are the challenges of coming to terms with the politics of knowledge and the creation of a curriculum that incorporates both local and traditional knowledge and the knowledge required to meet international accreditation standards. There is the matter of knowledge critique and the obligation to call into question knowledge claims that underpin practices of inequity and exclusion. There is the challenge of understanding the relations among cultures of scholarship and cultures of violence. And still, Hannah Arendt asks whether we love the world enough to take responsibility for it. Many faculty members who have been involved with BHER strive to convey that passion, that sense of "caring for the world," to their students so as to likewise inspire them to take on the responsibility of loving and caring for the world.

## Notes

We wish to thank SSHRC for their support of the 2008 Workshop and for the 2010–13 Partnership Development Grant; the MasterCard Foundation, for generously supporting a feasibility study, a workshop in East Africa and video about the BHER project in 2011–12; and Peter Murphy, who imparted his (pro bono) expertise in the production, filming, and editing of two videos. Global Affairs Canada [formerly CIDA] very generously took an international lead in supporting the implementation of the BHER project in 2013–19.

1   Otherwise known as "protracted refugee situations" in policy discourse, UNHCR defines these as situations in which 25,000 or more refugees originating from the same country have sought asylum in another country (or countries) for at least five consecutive years.

2   EMIS 2015. The age group served by secondary schools is fourteen to twenty-one years of age. Education Management Information System (EMIS) data is used by UNICEF to maintain school data. The BHER Project Liaison in Dadaab, Philemon Misoy, gathered this data in Apr–May 2017 through communication with humanitarian agency workers in Dadaab. The EMIS derived data is thus tentative and is rapidly changing as the camps close and children and youth move out.

3   In Dadaab, where there is a dire shortage of qualified teachers, a "trained" teacher refers to a teacher who does not necessarily have any qualifications beyond completing high school but has attended any kind of training to improve their teaching skills; this may be as minimal as a three-day workshop. A "qualified" teacher has full qualifications to work as a teacher under the Kenyan education system, i.e., has earned a "P1" certificate, diploma, or degree in education.

4   In her writing on the oppression of Hawaiian women through the colonized classroom, Julie Kaomea comments on Baldwin's quote, which she says points to the importance of the inclusion of the historical perspectives of the colonized—knowledge that is not only significant and liberating to the colonized, but also to "white people who know nothing about their own history" (Baldwin 1988 [1963] in Kaomea 2006, 345).

5   According to Heller, "code-switching (is) the use of more than one language in the course of a single communicative episode" (1988, 1).

6   By 2018, and as a result of the aforementioned supports, our data demonstrate that the BHER women students, although fewer than men students, were much less likely than male students to drop out.

# References

Abdi, Farhia. 2016. "Behind Barbed Wire Fences: Higher Education and Twenty-First Century Teaching in Dadaab, Kenya." *Bildhaan: An International Journal of Somali Studies* 16: 21–35.

Appadurai, Arjun. 2004. "The Capacity to Aspire: Culture and the Terms of Recognition." In *Culture and Public Action*, edited by Vijayendra Rao and Michael Walton, 59–84. Stanford: Stanford University Press.

———. 2006. "The Right to Research." *Globalisation, Societies and Education* 4, no. 2: 167–77.

Arendt, Hannah. 2006 [1954]. "The Crisis in Education." In *Between Past and Future: Eight Exercises in Political Thought*, by Hannah Arendt, 170–93. London: Penguin Books.

Baldwin, James. 1988 [1963]. "A Talk to Teachers." In *The Graywolf Annual Five: Multi-Cultural Literacy*, edited by Rick Simonson and Scott Walker, 3–12. Saint Paul, MN: Graywolf Press.

Baud, Isa S. A. 2002. "North-South Partnerships in Development Research: An Institutional Approach." *International Journal of Technology Management & Sustainable Development* 1, no. 3: 153–70.

Beckett, Greg. 2013. "The Politics of Emergency." *Reviews in Anthropology* 42, no. 2: 85–101.

Bender, Thomas. 1998. "Scholarship, Local Life, and the Necessity of Worldliness." In *The Urban University and Its Identity*, edited by Herman van der Wusten, 17–28. Netherlands: Kluwer Academic Publishers.

Bhabha, Homi. 1994. *The Location of Culture*. London and New York: Routledge.

Borderless Higher Education for Refugees (BHER). 2016. "Building Primary/ Secondary Teaching Capabilities in the Dadaab Refugee Camps and Locally in Dadaab, Kenya by Increasing Access to Higher Education: Midyear Report— April 1–September 30, 2016." Unpublished report to Global Affairs Canada, Toronto: Centre for Refugee Studies, York University.

Boyer, Ernest L. 1990. *Scholarship Reconsidered: Priorities of the Professoriate*. Stanford, CA: The Carnegie Foundation for the Advancement of Teaching.

———. 1996. "The Scholarship of Engagement." *Bulletin of the American Academy of Arts and Sciences* 49, no. 7: 18–33.

Butler, Judith. 2009. *Frames of War: When is Life Grievable?* London and New York: Verso.

———. 2004. *Precarious Lives: The Power of Mourning and Violence*. London and New York: Verso.

Chernikova, Elena. 2011. *Shoulder to Shoulder or Face to Face? Canada's University— Civil Society Collaborations on Research and Knowledge for International Development*. Ottawa: International Development Research Centre.

Cockburn, Cynthia. 1998. *The Space Between Us: Negotiating Gender and National Identities*. New York: Zed Books.

Dahya, Negin, and Sarah Dryden-Peterson. 2016. "Tracing Pathways to Higher Education for Refugees: The Role of Virtual Support Networks and Mobile Phones for Women in Refugee Camps." *Comparative Education* 53, no. 2: 284–301.

Dewey, John. 1997 [1938]. *Experience and Education*. New York: Touchstone.

Dippo, Don, Aida Orgocka, and Wenona Giles. 2013. "Feasibility Study Report: Reaching Higher: The Provision of Higher Education for Long Term Refugees in the Dadaab Camps, Kenya." http://refugeeresearch.net/ms/bher/workshops/ feasibility-study-report/.

Dirlik, Arif. 1994. "The Postcolonial Aura: Third World Criticism in the Age of Global Capitalism." *Critical Inquiry* 20, no. 2: 328–56.

Dryden-Peterson, Sarah. 2011. *The Key to the Future: Providing a Quality Education for All Refugees*. Geneva: UNHCR.

———. 2006. "The Present is Local, The Future is Global: Reconciling Current and Future Livelihood Strategies in the Education of Congolese Refugees in Uganda." *Refugee Survey Quarterly* 25, no. 2: 81–92.

Enghoff, Martin, Bente Hansen, Abdi Umar, Matthew Owen Gildestad, and Alex Obara. 2010. *In Search of Protection and Livelihoods: The Socio-Economic and Environmental Impacts of Dadaab Refugee Camps on Host Communities*. https://reliefweb.int/sites/reliefweb.int/files/resources/C477129C7D41DCFB852577B3006B2818-Full_Report.pdf.

Etim, Felicia E. 2006. "Resource Sharing in the Digital Age: Prospects and Problems in African Universities." *Library Philosophy and Practice* 9, no. 1: 1–7.

Fanon, Frantz. 1984. *Black Skin, White Mask*. London: Pluto.

Fassin, D. 2011. *Humanitarian Reason: A Moral History of the Present*. Berkeley and Los Angeles: University of California Press.

Gichiru, Wangari P., and Douglas B. Larkin. 2009. "Reframing Refugee Education in Kenya as an Inclusionary Practice of Pedagogy." In *Beyond Pedagogies of Exclusion in Diverse Childhood Contexts: Transnational Challenges*, edited by Soula Mitakidou, Evangelia Tressou, Beth B. Swadener, and Carl A. Grant, 225–40. New York: Palgrave Macmillan.

Giles, Wenona, and Aida Orgocka. 2018. "Protracted Refugee Situations: Adolescents in Dadaab, Kenya." In *Research Handbook on Child Migration*, edited by Jacqueline Bhabha, Jyothi Kanics, and Daniel Senovilla Hernández, 416–26. Northampton, MA: Edward Elgar Publishing.

Giles, Wenona, and Jennifer Hyndman. 2004. "Gender and Conflict in a Global Context." In *Sites of Violence: Gender and Conflict Zones*, edited by Wenona Giles and Jennifer Hyndman, 3–23. Berkeley and Los Angeles: University of California Press.

Gregory, Derek. 2004. *The Colonial Present*. Oxford: Blackwell Publishing.

Hall, Stuart. 1996. "When Was 'the Post-Colonial'? Thinking at the Limit." In *The Post-Colonial Question: Common Skies, Divided Horizons*, edited by Iain Chambers and Lidia Curti, 242–59. London: Routledge.

Hardman, Frank C., Jan Abd-Kadir, Catherine Agg, James Migwi, Jacinta Ndambuki, and Fay Smith. 2009. "Changing Pedagogical Practice in Kenyan Primary Schools: The Impact of School-Based Training." *Comparative Education* 45, no. 1: 65–86.

Heller, Monica. 1988. "Introduction." In *Codeswitching: Anthropological and Sociolinguistic Perspectives*, edited by Monica Heller, 1–24. Amsterdam: Mouton de Gruyter.

Houwer, Rebecca. 2011. "Borderless Higher Education for Refugees: Pedagogical Research Area Literature Review." Unpublished BHER project report, Toronto: York University.

Hyndman, Jennifer, and Wenona Giles. 2017. *Refugees in Extended Exile: Living on the Edge*. Abingdon-on-Thames: Routledge.

Hynie, Michaela, Susan McGrath, Julie E. E. Young, and Paula Banerjee. 2014. "Negotiations of Engaged Scholarship and Equity through a Global Network of Refugee Scholars." *Scholarly and Research Communication Journal* 5, no. 3: 1–16.

International Network for Education in Emergencies (INEE). 2010. *Minimum Standards for Education: Preparedness, Response, Recovery*. New York: INEE.

Jayawardena, Kumari. 1986. *Feminism and Nationalism in the Third World*. London: Zed Books.

Jazeel, Tariq, and Colin McFarlane. 2007. "Responsible Learning: Cultures of Knowledge Production and the North-South Divide." *Antipode* 39, no. 5: 781–9.

Jentsch, Birgit. 2004. "Making Southern Realities Count: Research Agendas and Design in North-South Collaborations." *International Journal of Research Methodology* 7, no. 3: 259–69.

Kaomea, Julie. 2006. "Nā wāhine mana: A Postcolonial Reading of Classroom Discourse on the Imperial Rescue of Oppressed Hawaiian Women." *Pedagogy, Culture and Society* 14, no. 3: 329–48.

Kateb, George. 1977. "Freedom and Worldliness in the Thought of Hannah Arendt." *Political Theory* 5, no. 3: 141–82.

Kirk, Jacqueline. 2009. *Certification Counts: Recognizing the Learning Attainments of Displaced and Refugee Students*. Paris: UNESCO-International Institute for Educational Planning.

Lavia, Jennifer. 2006. "The Practice of Postcoloniality: A Pedagogy of Hope." *Pedagogy, Culture and Society* 14, no. 3: 279–93.

Mezirow, Jack. 1995. "Transformation Theory of Adult Learning." In *Defense of the Lifeworld*, edited by Michael R. Welton. New York: SUNY.

Murphy, Peter, director, producer. 2016. *Borderless Higher Education: Bringing Higher Education to Refugees in Dadaab*. http://www.bher.org/bher-videos/.

———. 2012. *Hunger for Education on the Edge of the Planet*. http://www.bher.org/bher-videos/.

Narayan, Uma. 1997. *Dislocating Cultures*. London and New York: Routledge.

Nyerere, Julius. 1968. *Freedom and Socialism (Uhuru na Ujama): A Selection from Writings and Speeches 1965–1967*. Oxford: Oxford University Press.

Ogden, Jessica A., and John D. H. Porter. 2000. "The Politics of Partnership in Tropical Public Health: Researching Tuberculosis Control in India." *Social Policy & Administration* 34, no. 4: 377–91.

Rawlence, Ben. 2016. *City of Thorns: Nine Lives in the World's Largest Refugee Camp.* New York: Picador.

Rizvi, Fazal, Bob Lingard, and Jennifer Lavia. 2006. "Post Colonialism and Education: Negotiating a Contested Terrain." *Pedagogy, Culture and Society* 14, no. 3: 249–62.

Said, Edward. 1993. *Culture and Imperialism.* New York: Vintage Books.

———. 1978. *Orientalism.* New York: Vintage Books.

Scarry, Elaine. 2011. *Thinking in an Emergency.* New York: W. W. Norton.

Sork, Thomas J. 2016. "Planning Frameworks and Their Limitations in Transnational Collaborations: The Case of the Borderless Higher Education for Refugees (BHER) Project." Paper presented at the Comparative and International Education Society (CIES) Annual Conference, Vancouver, BC, March 2016.

Spivak, Gayatri C. 1988. "Can the Subaltern Speak?" In *Marxism and the Interpretation of Culture,* edited by Cary Nelson and Lawrence Grossberg, 271–313. Urbana, IL: University of Illinois Press.

UNHCR. 2017a. *Refugees in the Horn of Africa: Somali Displacement Crisis.* Kenya, Dadaab. 1 Apr. http://data.unhcr.org/horn-of-africa/region.php.

———. 2017b. *UNHCR Dadaab: Camp Population Statistics: By Country of Origin, Sex and Age Group.* 31 Jan 2017.

# Insecure Nation, Insecure Migrant: Postcolonial Echoes from India's Northeast

*Paula Banerjee and Ranabir Samaddar*

## The Problematic of Security/Insecurity

The issue of protection of the victims of forced migration and migrants in general is both a humanitarian and human rights issue (see chapter 2). Yet as soon as protection becomes in the main an institutionalized affair, the humanitarian aspect becomes dominant. The rights of the migrants are overshadowed by the humanist concern for the distress of the victims of forced migration and migrants in general. The louder the humanized descriptions become, the more overwhelming become the practical considerations of the large humanitarian institutions that are looking after the protection of the displaced. Humanized descriptions sit comfortably with practicality, considerations of security, and imperatives of policy-makers to balance concern for the migrants with policy imperatives of the state, dominant communities, multi-national corporations (MNCs), and the security lobby. Rights of migrants are minimized in this way. There is no easy way out of this paradox. However, the least that can be done in the field of research is to try to remove the cobwebs that shroud the insecure world of the migrants. Indeed, migration is the flag of insecurity—the insecure nation and the insecure migrants. How can we dissect the discourse of security/insecurity? This question is important because no other question defines the migrant issue as much as the problematic of security.

The excessively humanized descriptions perhaps serve the function of downplaying the overwhelming factor of conflict and wars that take place because "communities must be defended"—one can say the "permanent condition" in which communities find themselves. On this rereading of the problematic, the questions that crop up are: What are the conditions in which migration becomes a matter of insecurity/security? What is that point, the threshold, where these two issues intersect? What are the patterns of collective politics and collective violence that require study if we are to understand the intersecting worlds of population flow and security? In other words, if we are to understand why human migration becomes a matter of contentious politics and therefore has to be governed by law, administrative practices, customs, and failing all other things, by brutal violence, we have to study the historical conditions of the emergence of migration as a matter of nationalized security, marked all over by collective violence and collective politics (see also chapter 2). As we shall see, these conditions not only make modern politics, in some respects they make modern politics seem exactly like old politics, which was marked by racism and brute physicality.

Yet, if it is true that what we face here is a situation of aporia, that is to say, an unending cycle of production of nativity–linkages–immigration–nationalism–ethnicity–violence–law–immigration–linkages–nativity–nationalism, it is also true that it is contention that pries open the situation again and again. Precisely the collective politics that in its moment of frenzy makes immigration the most contentious issue in the life of a nation, also exhibits factors or aspects that make immigration the occasion for democratization, justice, tolerance, and a dialogue for accommodation, and what can be called "de-securitization" of issues of life and justice, and therefore a different kind of autonomy.

The field of refugee research is complex, requiring the input of multiple disciplines and perspectives to understand the geopolitical contexts within which forced migration takes place. In the current context, we see profound inequalities—particularly between regions described as the global north and global south—and these inequalities contribute to the difficulties of researchers in the global south (as documented, for example,

PAULA BANERJEE AND RANABIR SAMADDAR

in the South African context in chapter 1). While others document the important contribution of working across disciplines using multiple sources of data to advance our understanding of how and when people make the decision to leave (see chapter 6), or argue the value of the field of demography that focuses on the characteristics of people fleeing and can identify the pathways by which forced migrants are integrated into host societies (see chapter 8), this chapter demonstrates the value of critical historical analysis to understanding the roles of states in creating insecurities that influence the movement of people over generations. One of our aims is to investigate how the world of the incipient nation cannot but be a closed one, marked by a hyper sense of insecurity with the arrival of and mixing with "aliens." This chapter expands this point by focusing on the complexity of forced migration across the borders and within the region of India's Northeast.

## The Colonial Background of Identity Politics and Transition to Postcolonial Era

Alien-hood everywhere of course begins with conquest. The modern history of immigration, insecurity, nationalism, ethnicity, and attacks on "foreigners" began almost everywhere, as in the Northeast of India, with conquest. With conquest and annexation of territory and along with it the people inhabiting that territory by the colonial power, the first seeds of racism were sown. Migration as a security problematic began in this way. Conquest, the administrative reorganization that each conquest required, and the new political-legal-administrative identity of a population, all made population flow an issue of security. Thus, issues of resources became matters of immigration, that is to say, a matter of security, which every conquest underlined. Native/immigrant politics became a question of resource politics, race politics, and nationalist politics at the same time. We begin this essay therefore with turning our attention to the early history of migration into Northeast India.

At this juncture, it is important to underscore why we locate our discussions in India's northeast. To understand how differences were made that ultimately racialized and then nationalized histories of partition and graded democracies, one needs to look at colonial administration and the creation of differences as was done in the northeast of India in the eighteenth century. The colonial administration had introduced in that period the notion of "racial difference" between the plains and the hills.

It is perhaps best to begin our narrative with Assam, a state in Northeast India bordered by the countries of Bhutan and Bangladesh and by seven Indian states including West Bengal to the west that is connected to the rest of India via a 22-kilometre strip of land, known as the Siliguri Corridor. In the known history of Northeast India, including in the colonial period and for some time after, Assam constituted the major part of the region. Even today the politics of Assam affect most of Northeast India and perhaps the first agitations against migrations also began in Assam. In the traditional discourse, the influx of people into Northeast India is viewed as a prime security concern, yet from a non-traditional perspective the interesting point is that even Assam's own beginnings are traceable to the migration of different groups of people from East and Southeast Asia. The beginnings are in the colonial time; however, for the purpose of this chapter, we shall touch the colonial phase briefly and then focus on the post-independence period.

There are several accounts by British officials that speak of their experiences in the northeast frontiers. One such account is by George Dunbar, who was stationed in the present territory of Arunachal Pradesh. His reminiscences dealt with frontier people such as the Abors, the Mishimis, the Hill Miris, the Nishis, and some of the Naga tribes. Quite unconsciously, Dunbar recorded at least three types of movements of people in this region. They included movements for official purposes including movements by the army, and for non-official purposes such as movements for trade and movements as pilgrimages. When Dunbar went to the Dihang valley for the Abor expeditions in 1911–12, he found the area "rather densely populated with strangers" (Dunbar, 1984, 193). He also found out that there were robust trade relations between these people, the Tibetans, and people from the south. In one particularly lucid passage he describes how in some villages, "everything that could not be made locally was Tibetan stuff, brought down by traders." He speaks of regions where "trade comes almost equally from north and south. Along the foot-hills, of course, the Abors get all they need to buy from shopkeepers in the Plains" (Dunbar 1984, 212). He speaks of square blue porcelain beads that were used as mediums of exchange. These beads were not made in the region but by "Bori traders [who] brought them down from Tibet" (Dunbar 1984, 219).

Dunbar again speaks of different groups of migrants who had in the recent past migrated to these areas. One of them was the Kebangs, who migrated from Riu and established a powerful village. Another group interestingly enough were the Nepalis, whom he calls the Gorkhas. He speaks of a "hundred thousand Gorkha settlers, who mostly became graziers" (Dunbar 1984, 287). Dunbar is not the only person to speak of Gorkha settlements; others speak of their presence in this region from a much earlier time. The *Gazetteer* of Naga and Manipur Hills, while discussing the state of immigration into these areas, speak of the Nepalese as the main foreign settlers in these regions. It describes the rest of the foreign population as "a few coolies and cartmen from Bengal and the United Provinces, a few artisans from Punjab, and a few traders from Marwar." The *Gazetteer* also mentions that "emigration from the district could not be measured with any degree of accuracy, owing to the changes in boundary that had recently taken place" (Allen 2002, 35). Even though the *Gazetteer* mentions that migrations are few and far between, in another instance it speaks of a total of eighteen shops in Kohima, where thirteen were owned and maintained by Marwari merchants (Allen 2002, 59). In Imphal town, of thirty-six shops Marwaris owned twenty-nine (Allen 2002, 107). It is as if the presence of Marwaris seemed so commonplace that their influx for trade did not seem exceptional enough to deserve a special mention. From the British administrative commentaries, it was also apparent that the frontier as a space was marked as very different from the civilized world. This sense of difference underpinned their attitude towards the frontier people, who were considered less than human and could be treated with contempt. No wonder then that these memoirs are replete with stories of how the frontier people deserved the violent response that was meted out to them. Allen's *Gazetteer* discusses how the British felt that "the Nagas should be taught a lesson," when they refused to submit to British rule. It also reveals that some Naga villages opposed the British advance in the early part of 1880s, so the British officials felt "it was necessary to open fire, and some 50 or 60 of the enemy were killed." It was also remarked that the "punitive expeditions were a regular feature of the administration of the districts, as it was only by this means that independent Nagas could be taught that the lives and property of those who had submitted to us must be respected" (Allen 2002, 23–5). The lives and property of these frontier people were never respected.

In another section of the frontier, there were massive flows of migrant people with diverse consequences. Different hill tribes in Tripura came from upper Burma. There is one school of opinion that the people belonging to the hill tribes of Tipperah were a branch of the Shan tribe of Burma (Ganguly 1983, 2). People from Bengal started moving to Tripura from the sixteenth century. The rulers of Gaur gave the kings of Tripura the title Manikya.[1] "Ratna Manikya patronized the settlement of a good number of Brahmins, Vaidyas and Kayasthas from Bengal in Tripura. This was perhaps the first case of immigration of population into Tripura from the west as against all the earlier flows of immigration being from the east and the northeast," (Ganguly 1983, 3). In the initial period, royal patronage encouraged migration from Bengal. The British Government appointed their political agent in Agartala in 1871. Following this, the rulers of Tripura were encouraged to appoint administrators from Bengal. In the 1911 census, it was estimated that 97,858 people spoke Bengali, forming over one third of the population of 229,613.[2] Migration from Bengal did not mean that other migrations from the east and northeast stopped. In fact, migrations of groups such as the Reangs, Kukis, Lushais, Mags, Chakmas, and Tripuris continued, arriving in search of jhum lands. In some cases, community conflicts might have driven them to Tripura (Ganguly 1983, 4). Another reason for massive migrations into Tripura in the nineteenth century was that until 1880 there was no regular land revenue system in Tripura. In many cases, the Maharajas granted land in perpetuity at a fixed rent and where no grants were made, the usual custom was to farm out collections. In most cases, grantees could get exemptions from paying land revenue by giving free service to the state. After 1880, a number of rules came into force for regulating the land tenure system. Yet fragmentation of holdings, the landlessness of a large part of the rural population, and the illegal transfer of lands from tribals to non-tribals continued (Gan-Chaudhuri 1980, 106–7).

The transition from the imperial form of rule to the national form only accentuated the political problematic of immigration, because while the imperial form of rule in many ways left the borders—in this case the borders in the northeast—undefined and un-demarcated, the national form of state was to be much more territorial. The idea of a nation, which was

PAULA BANERJEE AND RANABIR SAMADDAR

a weapon in the anti-colonial struggle, also implied to the leaders of the nation the inheritance of a bureaucratic-territorial state, and its re-organization on the basis of a territorial-national principle of identification of population groups, which could not be otherwise congruent with each other. The imperial form of rule, at least the colonial rule in India, negotiated the issue of diversity of the society with a graded form of administration in which divide and rule was an extremely important principle. Difference was the organizing norm of the ruling political form. The national state made a switch over from the norm of difference to that of homogeneity (one nation, one state), which meant settlement of the hitherto "unknown" frontier areas into fully administered areas of the national state. The constitutional deliberations in the country of the preceding ten years (about twenty years if we take the Simon Commission as the starting point) of independence (1928–47) bear out that history of transformation of the principles of organizing politics and administration from a "frontier area" to a fully administered part of the country. Yet it is important to note in this connection what changed and what remained through the transition. While principles of administration changed, and national republican rule replaced the colonial territorial entity and new linguistic-ethnic boundaries were drawn, the ideologies of conquest, racism, and security proved to be permanent gifts of the colonial time.

In 1935, legislation by Assam had designated many of the hill districts as excluded areas or partially excluded areas. A special cadre for the frontier area was created in Burma, and India followed suit. However, by the time the Indian constitution came to be framed, political exclusion of the hill areas (including Manipur and Tripura, which had evolved along different historical lines) was out of the question. The main recommendation of the Constituent Assembly's sub-committee on Northeast Frontier Tribal and Excluded Areas was that the future of these areas did not lie in absorption—instead it lay in political and social amalgamation. Thus, distinction (read difference) would remain, but political identity with the Union would also become an accompanying reality. With nationalist pressure, the concept and history of excluded areas were given summary burial. But more than this, the framing of the constitution and subsequent reorganization of the region reflected three major developments: (a) The boundary demarcation between India and Burma was complete with dividing people like the Nagas and the Mizos who by that time had started to think of themselves as belonging to distinct nation-hoods; (b) National rule in India had firmly established its toehold in these areas, ending by and large the graded system of rule; (c) The restructuring of the political-administrative space by creating settled and (hopefully) stable units of political-administrative units in the form of states.

## The Political Economy of Resources and Violence

Now consider the following two sets of facts—one, reflecting the political economy of resources in the region and the other reflecting a security-oriented thinking dominating the space. The immigrant, as we shall see, emerges as a product of these two sets and their relationship.

The issue of resources began with the colonial trade of tea and timber. In addition to the British-owned tea estates, gradually other estates came to be owned by various Indian groups and the Assamese groups; the Assamese bourgeoisie today consists of tea owners, contractors, transporters, traders, and people engaged in the hotel and real estate industries, liquid gas distribution, or timber trade. Thus, while the revenue generating capacity of states in the northeast has been extremely weak, with the entire region lagging behind the rest of the country in industrial growth, power supply, fertilizer consumption, credit flow, communication facilities, and transport network, the political class survives with central aid with which it makes its nation. We have thus an absolutely combustible combination: rentier state, a parasitical political class, massive mass discontent, weak or nil growth, and the absence of any appropriate policy of local development and resource generation and utilization—with immigrants seen as the cause of all miseries of life.

The region has a population of about 40 million, with 90 per cent living in rural areas, agriculture being the primary occupation of 78 per cent; however, about 25 per cent of the total consumed food grain in this region is imported from outside. Agro-sector reform is almost nil while some of the big public-sector enterprises marked as promising global players such as the Indian Oil Corporation, Oil Indian Limited, and Oil and Natural Gas Corporation operate in this region. Yet, notwithstanding the presence of some of the richest public-sector companies in this region, its incapacity to generate revenue is stark. The indicators relating to small-scale industrial units and manufacturing units present an equally dismal picture.[3]

The level of urbanization in the region is quite low—only 14 per cent of the population of the region lives in towns, while population density increased from fifty-seven per square kilometre in 1961 to 123 in 1991. The pressure on land has grown, and the decadal population growth rate in all the states of the region has been higher than the national average, which is 23.50 (1991 census), while non-agricultural productive activity has almost remained at the same level.[4]

At the same time, the mode of shifting cultivation faced a crisis. Shifting cultivation was for a typical subsistence economy, and though this did not preclude trading of other products, it meant collective management of forestland, including allotment of the portion for each family, maintenance of village commons, and no accumulation of surplus for "expanded reproduction." While shifting agriculture has declined, or been made impossible in a market set up, settled cultivation too has not improved. Large numbers of communities practised settled cultivation over the ages in hill areas too including the practice of wet rice cultivation in the form of terrace farming. In short, the principal issue of sustainability of resource use is now in question in the entire region—from the plains of Assam to the hills of Mizoram. Clearly the issue of sustainability of resources, contrary to the popular notion of depending on controlling immigration, is wider and more complicated. It presents a blocked scenario, which is marked by very little formal trade and economic linkages in the east (Burma), south (the Bay), west (Bangladesh), and north (Bhutan and Tibet). Developed basically in recent history as what can be called an economy of "a market along the foothills," which bears the characteristics of an extraction economy around coal and limestone, and a plantation economy around tea and timber, the entire scenario represents today what Dietmar Rothermund (1993) termed "an enclave economy."

It is perhaps wrong to say that politics in the northeast is divided in two segments—the modern parliamentary politics with franchise, votes, institutions, financial agencies, education, developmental policies, etc. on one hand, and ethnicity, politics of identity, gun-running, gun battles, narcotics, xenophobia, and hatred against outsiders on the other. A more circumspect view would tell us of a combined and closed world (enclave economy) of contentious politics marked by a war of resources and attacks against the most immediate "enemy," the most immediate "invader," the most proximate "occupier," and the most immediate "usurper" of land. Security is intensely physical in this milieu, as is its politics, and the by-products of such politics such as neoracism.

This has been apparent in the way in which the 1,879-kilometre-long border with Bangladesh is considered in this security discourse. The border is not a site invoking commonality to share, not an opportunity to link up with others; the border is seen as a threatening factor, changing the demographic complexion of these states. Tripura's Indigenous population is a minority today—about 28 per cent of about 3 million population of the state. The anti-foreigner agitation in Assam from 1979 to 1985 was perhaps one of the largest mass mobilizations in post-independence India. It involved deaths (of about 7000), riots, massacres, forced displacement (of about 2 million), mass boycotts, paralysis of administration, and an upsurge of Assamese nationalism that required the "foreigner" to be identified as the enemy of the surging Assamese nationalism.[5]

As the Assam anti-foreigner movement showed, the issue of migration and citizenship is the link between the so-called parliamentary sphere of politics and the dark sphere of identity politics. Identity has little to do with looks, claims, tongues, destitution, resources, and justice, or to put it more appropriately, in the politics of identity these matters of looks, claims, tongues, and resources appear only as a matter of rights—that is to say justice transmogrified in the mirror of rights, so that justice means now the expropriation of *others* and the vindication of the "politics of homeland." Because it was a matter of *citizenship*, it showed the hierarchical landscape of nationalism: foreigners could be there to keep the wheels of the tea industry running (in 1921 about one-sixth of Assam's population was engaged in tea gardens) for which the London Stock Exchange had gone mad as early as the late nineteenth century. Similarly, they could be there to reclaim marshy lands and help with food production, but citizenship was for the Indigenous, the ethnic, and the nationals.

High population growth in Assam was thus to become an issue. In fifty years (1901–51), the growth was 138 per cent. Crop production had also increased in this period, along with the area under cultivation and tea production; but all this compared to labour growth was a minor phenomenon to the besieged mind—be it farm labour, peasant labour, plantation labour, or labour in petty jobs. Typically, the protest of the native did not arise around the demand for jobs, but around issues of election, electoral rolls, franchise, and citizenship rights—it was a war against aliens. The citizens were prepared to rather remain economically impoverished, sick, and infirm, and survive on the doles handed out by the "centre," which logically should have been an equally alien presence to the natives along with the tea garden owners and timber merchants. But it was time for the citizens to drive out the aliens, in view of the unnatural population growth in the state—by one count nearly 100 per cent growth between 1961 and 1991. The bloody anti-immigrant movement continued for five years; not only foreign immigrants were attacked, even members of the minority communities—particularly Muslims—were targets at times. Riots, torching of houses, looting, paralyzing administration, civil disobedience—the war continued in all forms. War against foreigners became civil war amongst various communities. The State had to combine strong methods and persuasive techniques to administer inter-ethnic relations, and demography became one more area of governmentality, so much so that defining an Assamese—the first task of claiming a nation—became an enterprise beyond cultural articulations: it was bloody, administrative, contentious, exclusive, expelling, and an elect enterprise. From the neat writings of Assam Sahitya Sabha to the killing fields of Nellie (1983)[6] was but a short road. On the surface it was a question of expelling or killing Muslims—at times Bengali Muslims, at times Assamese Muslims. But at the level of the physicality of nationhood it involved the plain tribes, hill tribes, other linguistic groups such as the Nepalese, and people from other states such as Nagaland, Manipur, Tripura, or West Bengal, and Bihar. Many organizations grew up or gathered strength and momentum in this bloody war, the most prominent being the United Minorities Front, which immediately after its formation in 1985 bagged seventeen out of the state's 126 assembly seats in the elections held in December that year. The ceding of Sylhet (in the form of a referendum) years back in the Great Partition, as could be seen now, had done little to make Assam a pure nation,[7] even after it cut off its (East) Bengal links.

In this war cry, legislative acts proved to be of little use in expelling immigrants—the Foreigners Act or the Illegal Migrants Determination Tribunals Act. The figures told the story—in fifteen years after the Assam Accord of 1985, the total number of inquiries initiated against suspected illegal aliens was 302,554, and the number of illegal immigrants expelled was 1,461. Because it was a war, all communities had developed strategic tools of linkages and enmities—plains/hills, valleys/hills, Hindus/

Muslims, Bengalis/Assamese, Bengali Muslims/Bengali Muslims, Assamese Muslims/Bengali Muslims, Bodos/Assamese, Bodos/Muslims, Bodos/Santhals, Assamese/Nagas, Assamese/Kukis, Karbis/Kukis, Karbis/Assamese. It was not a case of sudden ethnic conflict; it reflected rather a condition of generalized war, because the war consisted of several battles and theatres of attrition. Insecurity from migration had created lines of all kinds and had taken clearly military dimensions. But more on that later; first let us see how this condition engulfed areas outside Assam too.

Way back in 1876–77 in Tripura, the Indigenous people were more than two thirds of the total population of 91,759. By 1991, they counted for less than one third of the state's population of 2,757,205. It was again roughly the same story. With the Great Partition began waves of migration in the state, and finally in the eighties Buddhist Chakma refugees entered in sizeable numbers from the Chittagong Hill Tracts in the wake of the conflict and army operations of the Bangladesh State against the rebellion. The Tripura Upajati Juba Samity (TUJS) was formed in 1967; in 1978 it led to the formation of the first militant movement against immigrants, the Tripura National Volunteers, which soon started attacking settlers and symbols of government authority, including at times security forces. The land question became crucial, and with jhum (shifting) cultivation being systematically disturbed and finally destroyed, clashes began to erupt. The June riots of 1980 were the first major signal of the troubled times. It caused enormous displacements. The Dinesh Singh Committee Report, set up by the Ministry of Home Affairs to investigate the massacre of 1980, gave a tentative estimate of 1,300 deaths. However, unofficial sources claimed the figures to be above 8,000. It also estimated that nearly 372,000 persons were affected by the riots, and of them about 150,000 people belonged to Indigenous communities. Nearly 200,000 people had to be sheltered in camps. The number of total relief camps was 141; nearly 35,000 houses were gutted; and the estimated loss of property was about Rs. 21 crores (slightly more than $1 million USD at the time). Later, an estimated 2,614 families were displaced from severely affected areas such as Khowai, Sadar, and Bishalgarh sub-divisions due to clashes. By 2000, the civil-political-military movement of the Indigenous people against the settlers or migrants had become so strong that a ragtag combination of forces called the Indigenous People's Front of Tripura were elected to the twenty-eight-member Tripura Tribal Autonomous District Council. The

1980s were marked with violence, large-scale settler-native killings, army operations, rape of women by security forces and the militants, kidnapping, and increasing communalisation of the scene.[8] The TUJS demanded from the government of India more powers to the Autonomous District Council, barbed wire fencing of the entire length of the 856-kilometre-long boundary with Bangladesh, push back of immigrants who had arrived after 1971, and the introduction of the inner-line permit system to enter the Tribal Council Area.

The situation of a generalized war in the region finds reflection not only in war rhetoric, but also in actual incidents of expulsion. Thus, in many places the Nepalis have been on the run, in others, Bengalis. Expulsion of Nepalis in many places in the Northeast led to an autonomy movement in the Darjeeling Hills. In North Bengal, adjoining the Bodo areas of Assam, a similar process of conflict later began with the killings and expulsion of several Northeast militant groups from Southern Bhutan. Everywhere, the "immigrant"—known as the settler—faces insecurity in the form of the native; likewise, everywhere the native, known as the "Indigenous," faces insecurity appearing in form of the settler. And altogether, the state faces insecurity from the spectre of aliens swamping the land, aliens who in league with their soulmates here are conspiring with foreign countries to secede or at least make the region a hotbed of conspiracies. This led to bitter clashes and bloody internal rivalries, with day-to-day governing becoming a tough business, because an unlikely issue had leapt to the top of the priority list: governing population flow.

In this context, it is no surprise that security becomes a macro-question, population management becomes a matter of governing from the top, and the army becomes the most accredited institution of such management. Indeed, population flow is "geopolitics" to the army. Population flow in this discourse brings borders, not because the flow is always across borders, but because mobile populations are dangerous in terms of governing and administering: they can mobilize support, and support across borders is more difficult to govern. Thus, the Indo-Burma border, first settled in 1826 in the Yandabo Treaty, later confirmed in the Nehru-U Nu agreement of 1953, and hitherto left un-administered, became militarized. Thus, stretching from the Namkia Mountains bordering Arunachal Pradesh, then Patkai Bum bordering Nagaland, to Hamolin bordering Manipur to the Chin Hills bordering Mizoram, the administration of borders became important. Kachins, Shans, Eastern Nagas, Chins, Arakanese, plus Burmese communist rebels—all could claim links across the border to this side; hence population flow could not be allowed to be negotiated at the community level, it was not simply an innocent matter. It can be seen, therefore, how the military discourse, discourse of social insecurity, physical insecurity, and the contentious politics of nationhood all combined in this political exercise of ensuring security against the aliens.

## Trafficked Women as Aliens

When the alien is a woman, a much worse scenario awaits the migrant everywhere; we allude to the situation of the trafficked women and children. Though liberal South Asian constitutions and laws guarantee people's right to be protected from exploitation and thereby prohibits trafficking too, no amount of liberal and humanitarian legislation has been able to stop this form of servitude or semi-servitude of large groups of women. It is not merely a question of more or less governance but a continuance of the erosion of women's physical, economic, and social security by the patriarchal mode of national security that holds sway in the areas under discussion. Violence faced by the trafficked women is the worst form of violence faced perhaps both by women as a social category and by the category of forcefully displaced people. As a group, victims of trafficking reflect the growing insecurity of the vulnerable population groups in a milieu of traditional insecurity.

There are multiple ways in which people are trafficked. We take examples from the sub-region of East and Northeast India and Bangladesh. Often, those who want to cross borders out of desperation contact traffickers, who they think of as smugglers, and offer them a price; sometimes, traffickers kidnap people for harvesting organs. But, for those who want to be "smuggled," deals are sometimes done amicably, with prices clearly spelled out. However, since the journey is fraught with violence, things may go awry and the vulnerable face further abuse as violence overtakes all other considerations. There are also a number of routes through which women and children are trafficked in and out of these regions.

It is impossible to gather definitive data about the number of women trafficked. However, the growing number of brothels in the border areas of India and Bangladesh suggest that this is a thriving business. Women often shift from one brothel to another. If they are apprehended in a brothel, there is a chance they will be repatriated, but if caught moving from one place to another, they are immediately incarcerated. When women from Bangladesh are trafficked to India, they might then be transported to Pakistan or West Asia. Sanlaap's (2002) research in two red-light areas of West Bengal highlighted women's migration from one location to another. Ninety per cent of the red-light areas the women identified as places where they had worked were situated in the states bordering Bangladesh in the Northeast or West Bengal. In Changrabandha, one of the red-light areas identified, 66 per cent of the women said they had come from Bangladesh. In Dinbazar, many of the trafficked sex workers said that their mothers came from Bangladesh. The report states: "The rate of trafficking in Changrabandha is remarkably higher than in Dinbazar. The red-light area of Changrabandha is adjacent to Bangladesh border and women are trafficked through this border like any other commodity" (Sanlaap 2002, 18).

Most of the women in the Sanlaap (2002) study were illiterate and many had entered prostitution as minors. Some were from families of either wage labourers or cultivators, and in other cases, their mothers were trafficked sex workers. The mothers engaged in sex work could offer no alternative for their daughters; their children are stigmatized and face discrimination when they try to enter other fields of work. Deprived of education and a social environment that offered any promise or hope, the trafficked sex workers of Dinbazar and Changrabandha had few options beyond prostitution as a way to earn a living. Trafficked from one centre to another, these women live with insecurity, at the mercy of both criminals and the police. Their location, near the border, means they are often forced to give shelter to criminals from either Bangladesh or India. The police pursue them, but also use them for sex without any payment. To attract customers from among the truckers crossing at zero point, they stand on the roads, where they are extremely vulnerable to violence (Sanlaap 2002, 25). Without any legal documents, they are criminalized if apprehended and jailed, sometimes for periods longer than mandated.

The border itself is a place of poverty and violence against women. Multiple indicators suggest that the trafficking of women and children is on the increase in the Northeast and also within and from Bengal. The Northeast has been torn apart by multiple levels of conflict, making women and children more vulnerable. For example, attacks on women's land rights and social position, especially in the Khasi and Garo Hills, have compounded women's susceptibility to traffickers. In Meghalaya, the situation is further complicated by the ban on the felling of trees for timber. Such moves on the part of the government are commendable from an environmental point of view, but they rob the rural poor of a chance to earn their livelihood (see chapter 11 for discussion of the complex relationship between conservation and displacement). With few alternatives for earning a living, people are forced to migrate. Many women migrating to urban centres end up in brothels (*Meghalaya Guardian* 2004). Newspaper reports have registered the concern of NGOs: "Non-governmental agencies fighting against the malaise of trafficking of women and children have expressed grave concern that the evil is growing with increasing numbers of women and children from Meghalaya and other North-eastern states being lured and deceived into the flesh trade in the metropolitan cities in the country" (*Assam Tribune* 2004). The case of West Bengal is more complex. Globalization, monetization, and increasing communalization have all added to devaluing or differential valuing of women. West Bengal has acted as a destination point for trafficked women for some time now, but women from rural areas of Bengal are now increasingly being trafficked to other regions. Numerous cases reported in newspapers show the apathy of the police to consider either trafficking or rape as a serious crime especially when the woman is of a minority group. This apathy towards minorities who can be wilfully ignored especially in times of political tensions is also an effect of a rigid idea of national security. Indeed, trafficking in women, children, and labour are enmeshed, where policing methods invariably fail, because labour rights are ignored as well as women's own rights to decide their futures.

## The Ultimate Discourse of Security

The military discourse to control migration and thus prevent conflicts sprang not only from the generals' minds, it had roots in the internal discourse of society's security also, on which the military discourse fed. For instance, the Bodo student leader Upendra Brahma, an active member of Assam Agitation, pressed for implementation of Clause 10 of the Assam Accord, which said: "It will be ensured that relevant laws for prevention of encroachment of government lands and lands in tribal belts and blocks are strictly enforced and unauthorised encroachers evicted as laid down under such laws." Upendra Brahma demanded the eviction of the Indigenous population from Tamalpur and the "immigrants" from the char areas of Brahmaputra. This was certainly the signal for attacks on the Santhal population (not considered as "tribe" in Assam) in Bodo areas. Similarly, the insistence on making Assamese virtually the language of instruction in all parts of the state became a matter of contention with the All Assam Tribal Students Union. The Karbi Autonomous Council Demand Committee complained that the leaders of Assam were taking steps to wipe out other distinct languages and cultures from the state. Specialists started saying that security could be provided now only by deployment of the army. With it began the full-scale security discourse and "securitization" of the social mind. Hereafter tea garden owners could feel secure that the army was there; the people bought security now that they were paying taxes to government and the rebels both; and men of property had bought security with private guards and militias. The true significance of the army operations "Operation Bajrang" (1990) and "Operation Rhino" (1991) lay there. They signified the rejection of any dialogic approach, casting anyone advocating the release of prisoners or protection of human rights as "soft" and a compromiser—one who did not care about lives of jawans (soldiers in the Indian army).

It is not that the ethnic rebels and other liberationist groups and movements in the region and the army generals think along the same lines of security/insecurity. But to understand why the discourse of physical security can lodge itself at the heart of security concerns of a community, group, population, or state, and be so totalizing, we have to study closely the security practices of solidarities stretching from a group to a state and their interface. The intermix of so many concerns at a material level has produced the inflammable "politics of security"—where national security, community security, Indigenous population's security, developmental security, resource security, land and food security, and military security have converged.

The politics of security is a field. This is the field of governmentality, where all issues become relations between the governors and the governed. In this field, one can notice the presence of legal and civic behaviour, also illegal and warlike behaviour along with the presence of the policies triggered by claims of the state that security can be provided by an overall protection by arms and through development. At the same time, the groups realize that that they can survive only by exercising their own security options, one of which is to claim nationhood, homeland, and to pull up the drawbridges so that outsiders cannot come in. In short, while popular sovereignty still exercises the imagination of groups below the nation-state, this can become a potent political tool of democratization only within a group, which is fixed. But where the group is not fixed, and the people refuse to become a population group, the constitutional framework of autonomy fails. The field of governance and rule, which makes population flow a matter of administration and puts its stamp on the latter with law, administrative measures, violence, and suppression, is then by nature a combination of legality, para-legality, and illegality.

## Notes

1   For more details, see Choudhury and Ranjan 1977.

2   See Burman and Chandra 1933, List of Tables: 5 and 6 (since the introduction has no pagination the page numbers are not given). This is one of the first detailed publications of census in Tripura.

3   See Sikdar and Bhorali 1998, 167–72.

4   All figures relating to human development are taken from Ganguly 1996, 29–53. It is noteworthy that Ganguly does not cite immigration as an obstructing factor in achieving the goal of sustainable human development in the region.

5   These figures are from Hussain 1993, 10.

6   Founded in 1917 the Assam Sahitya Sabha is the premier literary institution of Assam. It aims to promote Assamese culture and literature. It has about one thousand branches all over the state. Its support for a distinct identity of the state during the anti-immigration movement in Assam was pronounced. The Nellie massacre took place in Assam during a six-hour period in the morning of 18 February 1983. The massacre claimed the lives of over 2,000 people (unofficial figures run at nearly 10,000) from fourteen villages in the area. The victims were Bengali immigrant Muslims whose ancestors had relocated in pre-partition British India. Some media personnel were witnesses to the massacre. The violence in Nellie was seen by some as fallout of the decision to hold state elections in 1983 in the midst of the anti-immigrant agitation in Assam. It has been described as one of the worst pogroms in independent India.

7   Indeed, as historical research into the history of the Sylhet referendum of 1947 bears out, the referendum by itself was the reflection of the fault lines within the Assam society. See, for instance, Chakrabarty 2002.

8   Figures cited from Hussain 2003, 138.

# References

Allen, B. C. 2002. *Gazetteer of Naga Hills and Manipur*. New Delhi: Mittal Publication.

Burman, Deb, and Thakur Somendra Chandra. 1933. *Census Descriptions of Tripura in 1340*. Agartala: Tripura State Press.

Chakrabarty, Bidyut. 2002. "The 'Hut' and the 'Axe': The 1947 Sylhet Referendum." *Indian Economic and Social History Review* 39, no. 4: 317–50.

Choudhury, Roy, and Nalini Ranjan. 1977. *Tripura through the Ages: A Short History of Tripura from the Earliest Times to 1947 A.D.* Agartala: Bureau of Research and Publication.

Das, Gurudas. 1998. "Liberalisation and Internal Periphery: Understanding the Implications for India's North-East." In *Liberalisation and India's North East*, edited by Gurudas Das and R. K. Purkayastha, 146–9. New Delhi: Commonwealth Publishers.

Dunbar, George. 1984. *Frontiers*. New Delhi: Omsons Publications.

Gan-Chaudhuri, Jagadis. 1980. "Land Reforms." *In Tripura: The Land and its People*, edited by Jagadis Gan-Chaudhuri, 105–23. Delhi: Leela Devi Publications.

Ganguly, J. B. 1983. *The Benign Hills*. Agartala: Tripura Darpan Prakashani.

———. 1996. *Sustainable Human Development in the North-Eastern Region of India*. New Delhi: Regency Publications.

Hazarika, Sanjay. 1994. *Strangers in the Mist*. New Delhi: Penguin.

Hussain, Manirul. 1993. *The Assam Movement: Class, Ideology and Identity*. New Delhi: Manak Publications.

Hussain, Wasbir. 2003. "Bangladeshi Migrants in India: Towards a Practical Solution—A View from the North-Eastern Frontier." In *Missing Boundaries: Refugees, Migrants, Stateless and Internally Displaced Persons in South Asia*, edited by P. R. Chari, Mallika Joseph, and Suba Chandran, 125–50. Delhi: Manohar.

Rothermund, Dietmar. 1993. *An Economic History of India: From Pre-Colonial Times to 1991*. New York: Routledge.

Sanlaap India. 2002. "A Situational Analysis on Trafficking and Prostitution in Dinbazaar(Jalpaiguri) and Changrabandha (Cooch Behar)." Unpublished report. Kolkata: Sanlaap India.

Sikdar, Sujit, and Devadas Bhorali. 1998. "Resource Mobilisation, Distribution Effect and Economic Development of the North-Eastern Region." In *Liberalisation and India's North East*, edited by Gurudas Das and R. K. Purkayastha, 167–72. New Delhi: Commonwealth Publishers.

# Emerging and Developing Research Approaches and Tools

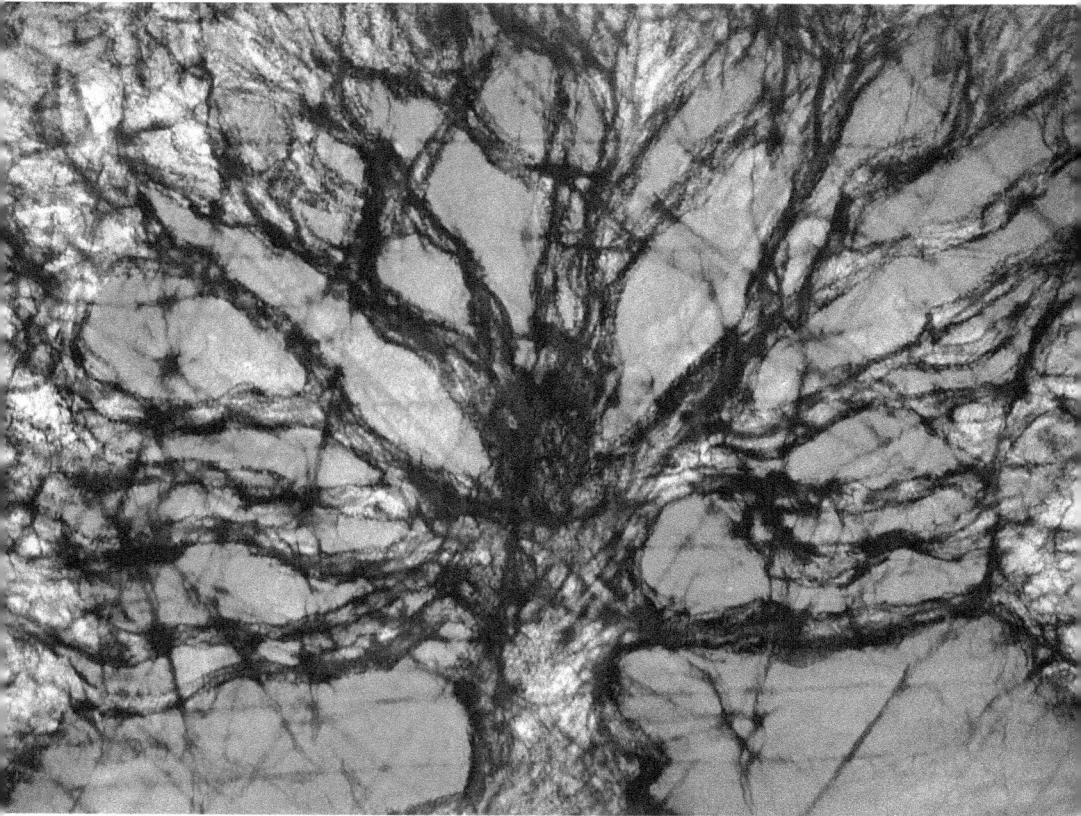

# Big Data and Early Warning of Displacement

*Susan F. Martin and Lisa Singh*

## Introduction

In recent years, the global population of people forcibly displaced by conflict and persecution has reached levels unprecedented since the Second World War: 68.5 million in 2017 (UNHCR 2018b). Acute natural hazards also lead to large-scale movement of people, some temporarily and others permanently. Between 2008 and 2016, the number of disaster-displaced populations averaged 21.5 million each year (IDMC 2016). In many cases, both human-made and natural factors precipitate large-scale displacement, as witnessed by recurrent famines in Somalia caused by the confluence of drought, conflict, and political instability that impede access to food relief.

Because much forced migration is unexpected, communities can be overwhelmed by refugees and displaced persons if they have insufficient warning. Even relatively wealthy countries may fall victim. The massive movements in 2015 of Syrian, Afghan, Iraqi, and other asylum seekers into Greece (with the hope of moving onwards to the rest of Europe) is a clear example of such chaos. In 2017, the concurrent outbreak of famine in northern Nigeria, Yemen, Somalia, and South Sudan also seriously challenged capacities to respond to both the mass starvation and mass displacement that resulted, despite persistent drought and famine warnings.

Given the unprecedented levels of forced displacement, and recurrent problems in addressing large-scale movements, an urgent need exists to develop an evidence-based early warning system that can enable governments and international organizations to formulate contingency plans, establish appropriate policies, and pre-position shelter, food, medicines, and other supplies in areas that are likely to receive large numbers of refugees and displaced persons. This need for early warning, as part of comprehensive contingency planning, has been recognized in the recently adopted Global Compact on Refugees (2018a).

With the wealth of data available via social media, search engines, and more traditional data sources (see chapter 8), it is natural to begin discussing how this information can be used to make progress toward identifying and forecasting forced migration. The precedent is in place to forecast many of the drivers of displacement. For example, in recent decades, early warning systems alert the international community as well as national and local actors of impending humanitarian crises. Tsunami and famine early warning systems monitor and analyze data relevant in anticipating acute and slow onset crises, respectively, relying on scientific, technological, economic, social, and other indicators (see FEWS Net and NOAA National Tsunami Warning Center). Predicting crises in other domains, such as conflict and violence, has proven more difficult but organizations such as the International Crisis Group put out regular alerts of worsening conditions and ACLED, the Armed Conflict Location and Event Dataset, codes the actions of rebels, governments, and militias within unstable states, specifying the exact location and date of battle events, transfers of military control, headquarter establishment, civilian violence, and rioting.

Forecasting displacement during these situations, particularly when a complex mix of drivers are at work, as seen in places facing prolonged drought and conflict, has proven more elusive. This chapter identifies novel big data sources, methodologies, and challenges that need to be addressed in order to develop more robust, timely, and reliable evidence-based systems for detecting and forecasting forced migration in the context of humanitarian crises. The chapter also recognizes the immense challenges and barriers to establishing more reliable forecasting capabilities. Despite the availability of data, patterns of forced migration in anticipation of, during, and following conflict and acute natural hazards are notoriously difficult to predict. What appear to be very similar pre-existing stressors and triggering events and processes can result in significantly different levels, forms, and destinations of displacement. The warning signs of displacement or significant changes in the nature of movement are often present but difficult to piece together in a coherent fashion.

Our research into these systems has identified a number of problems that must be solved to improve the effectiveness of early warning systems, particularly as they apply to displacement: 1) identifying and collecting masses of timely, reliable data on the complex factors that affect flight; 2) developing analytic capability to discover indicators of movement—specifically, leading indicators that displacement will occur rather than trailing indicators that confirm that movement has already taken place; 3) instituting mechanisms to allow policymakers and practitioners to test out scenarios to determine if actions will have positive or negative consequences in averting displacement or providing better assistance and protection; and 4) building the political will to act on the warnings. New technologies and analytic tools make it more likely that the first three problems can be tackled. The fourth problem is, of course, more difficult to solve but more effective early warning tools might challenge political leaders to act, at least in implementing more timely emergency relief operations. We focus our discussion on the lessons learned during a multi-disciplinary project on early warning of displacement, funded by the US National Science Foundation (NSF), Canadian Social Science and Humanities Research Council (SSHRC), the John D. and Catherine T. MacArthur Foundation, and Georgetown University's Massive Data Institute (MDI).

The next section discusses the value of such a multi-disciplinary approach and describes our efforts to build a community of scholars and practitioners to make progress in this area. The following sections assess the directions of research that are necessary to harness potential benefits of big data for anticipating patterns of forced migration: the development and validation of a theoretical model of forced migration that captures the complexity and dynamism of the phenomenon; the identification and collection of relevant data related to the complex factors that affect flight; the need for methods that take disparate forms of data with varying degrees of reliability and completeness and extract meaningful, timely evidence of movement; and the development of analytic tools that enable policymakers and practitioners to test different scenarios to respond to forecasted movements. Through this discussion, we describe initial efforts to use newspaper and social media data to begin generating direct and indirect indicators of movement. While big data has some important limitations, including the ratio of noise to signal that can distort the accuracy of forecasts and potential biases that exist because of incomplete data, these diverse data can be used by researchers to capture fragments of human behaviour at large scale, in real time; this glimpse into human behavior is not always available using traditional approaches. It is the combination of traditional survey data, available administrative data, and new structured data values extracted from big data sources that make early warning systems for forced migration plausible. While obstacles still exist for early warning tools in this area, the growing number of available sources and the advances in technologies makes this an area where significant progress can be made over the next decade.

## Building the Community of Scholars and Practitioners

Developing an effective early warning system of population displacement requires collaboration and shared learning between subject matter experts who understand the factors that contribute to forced migration and technical experts who understand how to collect, store, mine, and analyze masses of data derived from international, national, and local sources. It also requires a close working relationship between these academic experts and practitioners who understand the intricacies of implementing an early warning system in the real-world context of mass displacement. In 2013, we began assembling such a team with funding from the National Science Foundation (NSF) in the United States. The team grew with additional funding from SSHRC. It has included scholars renowned in their respective fields, from Georgetown (US), York (Canada), Fairfield (US), Fordham (US), Kultur (Turkey), Sussex (UK) Universities, University of Toronto (Canada), and Lawrence Livermore National Laboratory (US). We have drawn on the advice of practitioners from the Jesuit Relief Services, Refugees International, Women's Refugee Commission, the Brookings-LSE Project on Internal Displacement, CARE Canada, Médecins Sans Frontières Canada, and the UN High Commissioner for Refugees (UNHCR).

The interdisciplinary approach has exposed social scientists to new modelling approaches for analyzing their subject matter. At the same time, computer scientists have benefited from domain expertise in the social sciences, enhancing the intellectual merit of our project. This expertise has provided insight for the development of beyond state of the art data mining and machine learning of very large, incomplete, and potentially biased open source databases for topic modelling, event detection, sequential mining, change detection, sentiment analysis, and dynamic graph mining to name a few. As social scientists on the team attempted to explain drivers of forced migration to computer scientists who were attempting to model movement, it became clear that the theoretical models needed improving and that data needed to be collected to test these models. Most theoretical work on migration has focused on labour movements and, to a lesser degree, conflict or environmental migration; relatively little has been done in building theoretical frameworks for understanding complex displacement driven by multiple factors.

The collaboration of researchers and practitioners contributed both to our scholarly knowledge of forced migration as well as to our understanding of the advantages and disadvantages of various potential early warning models. As we wanted the system we planned to develop to be timely, accurate, and user friendly, we determined from our practitioners that a simple alert system would not be particularly welcome in the field. Rather, our practitioners urged us to develop a system that would enable a field user to take the early warning information and explore a range of scenarios and options for response. The collaboration further helped us determine the extent to which information from the field is available and its utility for the purpose of early warning. Our approach to addressing these concerns is discussed in the following sections. See chapters 2, 7, 10 and 13 for further discussion of the benefits of interdisciplinary approaches.

## Development of a Theoretical Model of Forced Migration

Our work on early warning focuses on displacement in the context of humanitarian crises—that is, any situation in which there is a widespread threat to life, physical safety, health, or basic subsistence that is beyond the coping capacity of individuals and the communities in which they reside (Martin et al. 2014). We chose two principal case studies to use in testing our theoretical framework: Somalia (2006–07) and Iraq/Syria (2011–15). These cases were chosen because of the complexity of forces underway in displacing people from their homes as well as the familiarity of the study team with the drivers and their consequences for displacement. They also allowed the team to examine one retrospective though still pertinent case— Somalia—and one escalating and rapidly unfolding case—Iraq and Syria.

Understanding not only why people are displaced but also when, where, and how they move is crucial to the effective prevention of, and response to, mass displacement. Leading indicators of forced migration range from macro-level political, security, economic, social, religious, cultural, and environmental indicators to micro-level material measures that determine whether individual households have the resources and motivation to leave their homes and meso-level factors that interfere with or facilitate movement (Government Office for Science 2011). One of the early efforts to understand underlying drivers of displacement was Schmeidl's (1997) work on root causes, proximate conditions, and intervening factors as potential determinants of refugee migration, with a particular emphasis on the role played by economic underdevelopment, human rights violations, ethnic and civil conflicts, external intervention, and interstate wars. In addition Schmeidl examined the impact of "flight facilitators," including migration networks and geographic proximity, and physical obstacles to movement (such as jungles or deserts). She found that underlying economic underdevelopment and population pressures have minimal impact on predicting displacement but instead it is the level and type of violence that determine the likelihood and size of refugee flows. While Schmeidl (1997) examined refugee flows, Naudé (2010) looked more broadly at patterns of international migration in sub-Saharan Africa and found that violent conflict and GDP growth differentials have the largest impacts on international migration in the region. He concluded that international migration from sub-Saharan Africa is both an adapting and mitigating strategy in the face of conflicts and economic stagnation (Naudé 2010, 350). Moore and Shellman (2004) find that the magnitude of genocide and politicide significantly increase both the likelihood and magnitude of forced migration. Melander and Oberg (2007) found that the intensity of armed conflict is not significantly related to the number of forced migrants. Rather they suggest that "the threat perceived by potential forced migrants is more related to where the fighting is taking place, than to the overall intensity of the fighting" (2007, 157). Salehyan and Gleditsch (2006) find that the probability of violent conflict is more than three times higher in source countries than in receiving ones.

A number of studies have considered the role of intervening factors in explaining refugee flows. Massey (1988) and Moore and Shellman (2004) introduce the idea of migration networks in the destination countries as contributing to forced migration while Clark (1989) identified five intervening factors that may affect refugee outflows, including the existence of alternatives to international flight within the country, obstacles to international flight, expected reception in the asylum countries, patterns of decision-making among potential refugee groups, and seasonal factors. Schmeidl and Jenkins (1996) discuss some of the problems of timing where long-term or root causes may occur years before the exodus, while medium-term (or proximate) causes may occur only months beforehand. They argue that "triggering events are the most difficult to place. Theoretically, they would occur almost simultaneously with, or only days before, flight but most conventional methods are unable to evaluate the close timing of triggering events" (Schmeidl and Jenkins 1996, 6). They underscore the importance of triggering events: "for policy purposes, triggering events are critical in preparing for emergency relief" (Schmeidl and Jenkins 1996, 6). Davenport et al. (2003) posit that forced migrants make their decisions to flee when they observe threats to their personal integrity. Melander and Oberg (2006) look beyond the question of why people move to analyze the impact of forced migration flows on those that remain behind. Rather than finding that the departure of forced migrants leads to increased future flows, they find that the magnitude of flows declines over time (2006, 130).

There are also psychological and emotional reasons for flight. What is commonly referred to as dread threat theory (Slovic 1987, 2000; Slovic, Fischoff, and Lichtenstein 2000; Slovic, Kunruetheer, and White 2000; Starr 1969) identifies a heterogeneous list of "fright factors" to measure people's responses to safety questions. Because forced migration often occurs in situations of persistent threat, we add a dynamic element to dread threat theory—the menacing context that emerges when a dread threat persists and requires a community to reorganize its life to mitigate consequences of threat. The concept of menacing context has evident value in analyzing the determinants of forced migration because it links situational factors to decision-making as well as macro, meso, and micro levels of analysis through local perceptions of, and responses to, dread threat (Collmann et al. 2016).

While these frameworks are useful in explaining the reasons that people stay or go in the context of conflict and other crises, they do not adequately capture the diversity in movements that occur in these situations. More effective early warning of displacement must provide greater perspective on when people move, where they go, with whom they move, what modes of transport they take, and other similar factors that determine mobility patterns in situations of conflict and repression. At this stage, no system of this type exists. One major obstacle has been access to relevant, timely local and regional data that can be incorporated into a flexible model of forced migration.

## Using Big Data to Identify Determinants and Dynamics of Mass Displacement

This project gave us the opportunity to begin analysis of local print and social media, specifically Twitter, to identify the changing dynamics of events and perceptions that may directly or indirectly trigger displacement (see Payne and Millard chapter for other uses of social media). Our case example examined displacement in and from Syria and Iraq since 2011. We used an archive of more than 700 million publicly available open source media articles that has been actively compiled since 2006 (Singh and Pemmaraju 2017). News articles are added to this archive—the Expandable Open Source (EOS) database—at the rate of approximately 100,000 per day by automated scraping of Internet sources in forty-six languages across the globe. We also compiled a database containing over 1.5 billion tweets in English and Arabic from organizations and individuals that regularly post on developments in Iraq and Syria, and on relevant hashtags, including ones related to ISIL. Using newspaper and social media data begins to give us a glimpse into what people are talking about, what their perception of different events and conditions are, and whether commentary and concern about local conditions are increasing or decreasing.

To determine which ideas, types of events, and topics are correlates of movement or correlates to direct indicators that may not be available during different crisis situations, we also used statistics compiled by the United Nations High Commissioner for Refugees, the International Organization for Migration, the Office for the Coordination of Humanitarian Affairs, and the Internal Displacement Monitoring Centre. Demographic data and economic indicators can also be drawn from standard sources, such as the UN Human Development Index and the World Bank. These data can serve as direct and indirect indicators/variables in the context of migration. Therefore, we need to understand the relationship between these known variables and the variables extracted from noisy, partial, open source big data. Are they well correlated or is there a limited relationship between them? We also plan to correlate big data variables to interview data collected in different volatile regions around the world. Because interviewing is not scalable, if we can find strong correlates between big data variables and interview variables we can use them as proxies for traditional interview variables that may be difficult to obtain in certain unstable regions of the world.

So the primary question becomes: how do we identify meaningful forced migration-related variables from big data sources? An important secondary question regards how we assess reliability and bias of output variables generated from noisy, big data streams? In the previous section, we highlighted a number of factors that influence an individual's decision to migrate or not during conflict. Our approach hinges on understanding 1) the changing dynamics of each factor in a particular location, and 2) the importance of each factor within a particular location or community. We measure both of these by analyzing the changing newspaper and social media content related to these factors in different regions. To accomplish this, the process begins by identifying relevant documents using state of the art information retrieval techniques, extracting useful structured data representations, i.e., sketches of the data, and then using these data representations to construct variables for use in a dynamic forced migration model (Wei et al. 2014). For example, creating a vector of words about violence and computing the frequency of these words across newspaper articles each day can be used as the basis for a time series variable that captures the changing dynamics of violence in a particular location. These changing dynamics may be a strong indirect indicator of movement in certain conflict areas. Another type of data sketch may be a semantic graph that contains words and phrases as nodes and relationships based on co-occurrence of these words and phrases in articles or tweets. This type of graph can be useful for identifying frequently occurring groups or clusters of words/discussions of local and regional topics of interest. Finally, a third type of data sketch translates words to a mathematical vector space where the weights in the vector space are based on the context in which words are used. Words that are used in similar ways have similar vectors in this word embedding vector space, i.e., similar relationships to other words in the vector space. Of course, many other types of data sketches exist. We highlight these three because they are particularly well suited for tasks involving textual data of varying lengths and *speech quality*.

While it is also possible to generate administrative variables from these data sketches from big data sources, we believe that researchers need to explore big data in new ways and produce new types of variables to gain insight that differs from values that can be determined in other ways. Here we describe interesting variables that we hypothesize will help our understanding of movement in general, and have found important in the context of our analysis of movement in Iraq (Singh et al. forthcoming).

*Topic Buzz*: Discussions revolve around different themes or topics. Determining the topic(s) being discussed in an article or post is central to understanding how its dynamics are changing through time. Is discussion about political violence increasing or decreasing? Are people talking more or less about weather conditions in a particular town? While different approaches have been proposed for extracting topics from text (Blei et al. 2003; Teh et al. 2006; Wang and McCallum 2006; Blei and Lafferty 2006; Churchill et al., 2018), these models have been designed for longer textual documents that are more coherent than social media, e.g., research articles. New algorithms that adequately handle the noise of social media text streams and the short length of these posts are still in their infancy. Even without automated methods for topic identification, words that are representative of topics can be manually determined by experts. While time consuming, manual annotation is always a reasonable option. If we associate factors of movement to topics of conversation, we can see the prevalence of these topics through time.

*Buzz* represents the amount of interest in a topic through time. Topic buzz may be popular and trending one week, e.g., discussion about violence, and have low values the next week. What is interesting is the variation of buzz strength of a topic over time. This buzz strength is based on the frequency of occurrence of relevant words and word embeddings in articles and social media posts for a particular location. One can imagine using a heat map to see the buzz of different topics (indirect indicators of different factors) in different locations. This can give us immediate insight into the distribution of the factors that may be more relevant in a particular region. This distribution is vital for understanding the specific factors that may be more important in different parts of the world.

Our initial focus was on the topics of *violence* and *migration* for computing buzz variables from newspaper data in both English and Arabic (Hockett et al. 2018; King 2016). While we had some expert seed words, we also wanted to determine if using different strategies for augmenting those words would improve topic quality. After evaluating the strengths and weaknesses of different methods for computing topic buzz, Hockett et al. (2018) found that using expert seed words, their synonyms, and similar words to the seed words from a word embedding space, led to the highest topic quality. Hockett et al. (2018) then correlated buzz values for these two topics from over 1 million newspaper articles related to Iraq in 2016 to data from the United Nations International Organization for Migration (IOM) that tracks the number of internally displaced persons (IDPs) in Iraq. This was done to see whether either of these two topics were indirect indicators of possible movement. The research found there was indeed a high correlation between buzz and movement data (a Pearson correlation of 0.76). This high correlation means that buzz has potential to be a reasonable proxy variable for movement. It is a strong indication that using buzz as a leading indirect indicator with other big data generated variables is an important direction for future research.

*Events*: An *event* is something that happens at a particular time and location, e.g., a bombing in Anbar on 10 January 2015. A targeted event is an event in a particular location that is associated with a particular theme or topic of interest to the user, e.g., politics, violence, football, etc. (Wei et al. 2016). Tracking the frequency of targeted events allows us to compute a time series containing the number of targeted events related to topics correlated to forced migration each day. The frequency of different types of discovered events and the topics associated with these events can themselves also be used as indirect indicators of forced migration. Because of this, we are also interested in mapping the detected events and their topics to different factors associated with forced migration. This approach allows us to integrate knowledge from interviews with knowledge from open source text data—e.g., newspapers (Wei et al. 2016; Zhao et al. 2017; Wei et al. 2018) and Twitter data (Wei and Singh 2017a; Wei and Singh 2017b)—to gain a more accurate picture of the situation.

*Perception*: In order to understand whether people will choose to migrate, it is important to understand their perceptions about relevant direct and indirect indicators, e.g., wages, schools, etc. Perceptions can be measured in different ways. Three that are important in the context of migration are tone (sentiment), stance (position), and emotion. An important research direction is to learn to identify tone, stance, and emotion from social media and newspaper content so that perception can be more accurately captured. While a rich body of literature exists for identifying these variables from text, the accuracies for detection still need improvement. Sentiment or tone indicates a global measure of the overall positivity or negativity associated with *how* a document or tweet is written. Tone can be positive, negative, or neutral (see Ribeiro et al. 2016 for a survey of current methods). Our preliminary work suggests that sentiment related to groups that impact migration—e.g., ISIL—changed as different events occurred. What is also evident is that the sentiment related to a similar topic is not always the same in different languages and/or locations (Singh et al. forthcoming).

A variant of sentiment that provides a different form of perception information is stance. Stance is specific to a topic and describes whether the text contains a negative ("anti") or positive ("pro") position towards that topic. In general, there is no guarantee that tone and stance will be exactly correlated. A positive overall tone does not guarantee a positive stance on all topics in the text, and a positive stance towards some topics does not preclude a negative or pessimistic tone. This is why it is important to capture both forms of perception. Work on determining stance from text is in its infancy. Current methods are very similar to those used to determine sentiment (Sobhani et al. 2016; Mohammad, Sobhani, et al. 2016; Mohammad, Kiritchenko et al. 2016). New methods that are able to compute stance with high accuracy using a very small amount of labelled data are needed for dynamic domains like social media.

Finally, emotion considers whether the tweet or article contains emotional content. Researchers are working on identifying a number of different emotions, including happy, sad, relaxed, stressed, and depressed (Canales et al. 2014; Hasan et al. 2014). Similar to sentiment and stance, lexicons containing emotion words and basic machine learning algorithms are currently considered the state of the art. Our team has been able to capture emotion from newspapers and relate it to movement (Agrawal et al. 2016).

An important future direction is to use perception determined from open source data to further investigate dread threat variables on a broader scale. For example, if other sources of information suggest an increase in dread threat levels in Iraq over time, we can determine if that same increase occurs on Twitter. If we are able to map variable values obtained from other sources to variables extracted from tweets, we may be able to further our understanding of the drivers and triggers of forced migration and see the escalation of dread threat levels before large-scale displacement occurs.

## Tools and Analytics

As mentioned in the introduction, we must have tools to help policymakers understand the impact of not acting in certain situations. Our research has focused on two interconnected tools. The first provides early warning and the second allows policymakers and practitioners to analyze the evidence and simulate scenarios (see chapter 7 for other online networks that are useful for knowledge dissemination).

*Early Warning Tool*: An early warning tool should be capable of using indicators drawn from different data sources (many real time sources) within a dynamic theoretical model to alert decision-makers to likely changes in patterns of displacement. In some cases, the displacement will be new, but in many situations, the alert will mark potential shifts in movements. The alert system should go well beyond the binary decision to move or stay. It should seek to provide information to decision makers on who will move (i.e., what are their demographic and socio-economic characteristics), in what numbers, from where, to where. It should also present policymakers with the evidence used to generate the alert and a way for the policymaker to input the strength, reliability, and timeliness of the evidence, thereby allowing the tool to learn from human analysis of the evidence.

*Simulation Tool*: Simulation tools can provide decision makers the capacity to test responses to patterns of movements under varying scenarios. For example, if displacement is related to increasingly more severe food insecurity, decision makers could test various scenarios involving the delivery of food to at-risk populations—including purchases of food in neighbouring countries, vouchers to enable people to buy available food, shipment of food from more distant countries, food drops, food distribution in camps, etc. We see two purposes for such scenario testing. First, it helps determine the likely results of a humanitarian action, e.g., what if food relief is dropped at a particular location? Second, it gives insight into determining the likely results of a third-party action, e.g., what if the Jordanian government closes its border with Syria?

One type of analytic tool that can be particularly helpful is a computational simulation that gives practitioners an opportunity to posit a scenario via a web user interface, run the simulation, and view the simulated results though a geographic visualization. A simulation could forecast seven to twenty days ahead, based on what is known and what can be inferred. We anticipate that practitioners who had access to such a system would run many such scenarios each day in order to better understand the scope of what is possible.

At Georgetown, we built a prototype of how local perception of threat in the locality drives actions to mitigate that threat, including both planned migration and unplanned flight. The simulation already developed is based on system dynamics, defined as a "computer-aided approach to policy analysis and design" that "applies to dynamic problems arising in complex social, managerial, economic, or ecological systems" (Systems Dynamics Society n.d.). Simulations based on systems dynamics have several advantages, including ease of development and computational tractability, but also come with limitations on modelling the inherent economic and social diversity of human populations. In effect, systems dynamics models do not necessarily capture decision-making at the household and individual level.

By contrast, agent-based simulation of forced migration allows for modelling each individual household, where a household decides whether and when to migrate, based on its unique assets, location, social connections, time-varying perception of threat, and other factors (Edwards 2008; Kniveton et al. 2011; Kuznar and Sedlmeyer 2005; Smith 2012). Often lost in this type of analysis, however, are the systems that may facilitate or impede the household from taking certain actions. Finding ways to leverage both models could be valuable for simulating different types of interactions. To date, no full-scale alert system or simulation platform that incorporates either analytic model exists for forced migration.

## Challenges and Limitations in Using Big Data

For all the benefits of big data, a number of challenges exist. First, most of these data are noisy and partial. The signal to noise ratio for most topics is very low. Second, the reliability of different sources, and even authors of articles/social media posts, is not clear since real and false information can be shared using these mediums. These data may also have significant biases. Systematic bias is very different from random error and may be hard to identify, much less compensate for. In order to effectively use big data, we must develop methods and tools to quantify and adjust for the variability in reliability and the potential high levels of bias. Third, big data population coverage varies considerably in terms of demographic and movement data. As technology continues to get cheaper and more pervasive, the utility of big data will continue to grow. Next, there is a lack of reliable ground truth data to compare algorithm output to. While there is some knowledge about where and when people move, it is inconsistent, noisy, and not timely. In order to calibrate algorithms and understand their strengths and weaknesses, having ground truth data is important. Finally, it is difficult to integrate large numbers of sources of data that have varying temporal and spatial resolutions. Using time and GPS coordinates is the most straightforward way to combine these data, but using semantic similarity is an important future direction. A large public and/or private initiative that promotes standardization and interoperability across different distributed platforms and entities is an important direction for making traction on these large-scale challenges.

Reliable, accurate, detailed data are fundamental to making progress on this problem. We need as granular and dynamic data as possible in order to identify relevant indicators of forced migration. The scale of migration can significantly redistribute a population, within and across borders, in very short periods. As "big" as our data sources are now, they do not include information in all of the language groups needed to forecast displacement, nor are the sources sufficiently local (meaning to the community, and even at the household level) to allow us to get at the meso- and micro-level factors influencing movement, particularly in areas where social media penetration is low. Data availability will be vital for making significant progress in this area. We also need to use these data with care, considering anonymization strategies to ensure privacy and developing guidelines for the ethical uses of these personal data (see chapter 13 for more on the ethical dimensions of research on forced migration). While these data can be used for social good, their availability also allows for disruptive forces (Singh 2016). We are particularly concerned that such information could be used to target people, as was done with census data during the Rwandan genocide, or to deter flight even if it is the only way for people to achieve safety. Efforts need to be undertaken to ensure that does not happen.

## Conclusion

Making progress on understanding the drivers of forced migration, and developing tools to forecast when, where, how, and who will be displaced, will have a potentially profound impact on understanding and coping with future movements. Early warning holds the potential to save lives and to make humanitarian responses more effective. It would improve planning as well as directly aid potential refugees before, during, and after their exodus. Such planning can lead to action to try to avert mass displacement by addressing the causes of movement, help divert forced migrants from risky modes of movement (e.g., via unseaworthy boats or across landmine infested borders), and enable governments and international organizations to pre-position shelter, food, medicines, and other supplies in areas that are likely to receive large numbers of refugees and displaced persons. Although governments will not always act benevolently in the face of early warning of displacement—such warnings can also give governments more time to stop refugees from crossing onto their territory—the alternative is often chaos, with the displaced and the communities they enter left without adequate assistance or protection. Big data, if integrated responsibly and combined with available administrative data, can be the catalyst for a timely, reliable early warning system and a mobility simulation platform that identifies likely movement patterns given different policy options.

It is unlikely that further progress will be made in the absence of the two types of collaborations described in this chapter. First, a multidisciplinary approach is essential to answering the core questions arising in the context of early warning—why are people forced to move (or become trapped), what triggers the actual movements, who is likely to become displaced or trapped, and when, where, and how will those who move arrive at their destinations. These decisions are based on a complex mix of political, social, economic, environmental, psychological, and other factors, necessitating the involvement of multiple social science disciplines. Effective early warning requires that computational scientists work closely with their social science colleagues to mine, analyze, and present the data in a practical way. Ensuring that the resulting system is effective requires the active engagement of practitioners throughout the process. As mass displacement is unlikely to reduce significantly in the near future, it is important for humanitarian agencies, researchers, and governments to work together to improve the situation of those forced to migrate through more effective early warning.

## Note

We are fortunate to have a large team of contributors. We would like to acknowledge the work of Jeff Collmann, especially for his perspectives on dread threat, as well as Lara Kinne, Nili Yossinger, Abbie Taylor, Yifang Wei, and Chris Kirov at Georgetown University and Susan McGrath and her team at York University. This work was supported in part by the National Science Foundation (NSF) Grant SMA-1338507, the Georgetown University Mass Data Institute (MDI), the John D. and Catherine T. MacArthur Foundation, and the Canadian Social Science and Humanities Research Council (SSHRC). Any opinions, findings, conclusions, and recommendations expressed in this work are those of the authors and do not necessarily reflect the views of NSF, MDI, the MacArthur Foundation, or SSHRC.

# References

Agrawal, A., and A. An. 2012. "Unsupervised Emotion Detection from Text Using Semantic and Syntactic Relations." *IEEE/WIC/ACM International Joint Conferences on Web Intelligence and Intelligent Agent Technology*—Vol. 1. IEEE Computer Society, Washington, DC.

Armed Conflict Location and Event Dataset. Available at http://www.acleddata.com/ (10/12/2017).

Blei, D. M., A. Y. Ng, and M. I. Jordan. 2003. "Latent Dirichlet Allocation." *Journal of Machine Learning Research* 3: 993–1022.

Blei, D. M., and J. D. Lafferty. "Dynamic Topic Models." 2006. *IEEE International Conference on Machine Learning (ICML)*.

Canales, Lea, and Patricio Martínez-Barco. 2014. "Emotion Detection from Text: A Survey." In *Processing in the 5th Information Systems Research Working Days* (JISIC), 37–43.

Churchill, R., L. Singh, and C. Kirov. 2018. "A Temporal Topic Model for Noisy Mediums." *Pacific Asian Conference on Knowledge Discovery and Data Mining (PAKDD)*.

Clark, Lance. 1989. *Early Warning of Refugee Flows*. Washington, DC: Refugee Policy Group.

Collmann, Jeff, Jane Blake, David Bridgeland, Lara Kinne, Nili S. Yossinger, Robin Dillon, Susan Martin, and Kai Zou. 2016. "Measuring the Potential for Mass Displacement in Menacing Contexts." *Journal of Refugee Studies* 29, no. 3: 273–94.

Davenport, Christina A., Will H. Moore, and Steven C. Poe. 2003. "Sometimes You Just Have to Leave: Domestic Threats and Forced Migration, 1964–1989." *International Interactions* 29, no. 1: 27–55.

Edwards, Scott. 2008. "Computational Tools in Predicting and Assessing Forced Migration." *Journal of Refugee Studies* 21, no. 3: 347–59.

FEWS Net: Famine Early Warning System. Available at http://www.fews.net/ (10/12/2017).

Frías-Martínez, Enrique, Graham Williamson, and Vanessa Frías-Martínez. 2011. "An Agent-Based Model of Epidemic Spread Using Human Mobility and Social Network Information." *Proceedings of 2011 IEEE Third International Conference on Privacy, Security, Risk and Trust*, 57–64, Boston, MA, Oct 2011.

Government Office for Science. 2011. "Foresight: Migration and Global Environmental Change." Final Project Report. London: Government Office for Science.

Hasan, Maryam, Elke Rundensteiner, and Emmanuel Agu. 2014. "Emotex: Detecting Emotions in Twitter Messages." Paper presented at ASE Big Data/SocialCom/ Cybersecurity Conference, Stanford University, May 2014.

IDMC. 2016. *Global Report on Internal Displacement.* Accessed 12 Oct 2017. http://www.internal-displacement.org/globalreport2016/.

International Crisis Group. Available at https://www.crisisgroup.org/crisiswatch (10/12/2017).

Hockett, J., Y. Lui, Y. Wei, L. Singh, N. Schneider. 2018. "Detecting and Using Buzz from Newspapers to Understand Patterns of Movement."

King, Jordan. 2016. *Methods to Overcome Challenges When Learning Arabic Word Embeddings for Text Mining Tasks.* Undergraduate thesis in computer science, Georgetown University.

Kniveton, Dominic, Chris Smith, and Sheila Wood. 2011. "Agent-Based Model Simulations of Future Changes in Migration Flows for Burkina Faso." Global Environmental Change 21 (Supplement 1): S34–S40.

Kuznar, Lawrence A., and Robert Sedlmeyer. 2005. "Collective Violence in Darfur: An Agent-Based Model." *Mathematical Anthropology and Cultural Theory: An International Journal* 1, no. 4: 1–22.

Martin, Susan, Sanjula Weerasinghe, and Abbie Taylor. 2014. *Migration and Humanitarian Crises: Causes, Consequences and Responses.* New York and London: Routledge.

Massey, Douglas. 1988. "Economic Development and International Migration in Comparative Perspective." *Population and Development Review* 14: 383–413.

Melander, Erik, and Magnus Oberg. 2006. "Time to Go? Duration Dependence in Forced Migration." *International Interactions* 32, no. 2: 129–52.

———. 2007. "The Threat of Violence and Forced Migration: Geographical Scope Trumps Intensity of Fighting." *Civil Wars* 9, no. 2: 156–73.

Menkhaus, Ken. 2010. "Stabilisation and Humanitarian Access in a Collapsed State: The Somali Case." *Disasters* 34: S320–S341.

Mohammad, Saif M., Svetlana Kiritchenko, Parinaz Sobhani, Xiaodan Zhu, and Colin Cherry. 2016. "Semeval-2016 Task 6: Detecting Stance in Tweets." *Proceedings of International Workshop on Semantic Evaluation*, 31–41, San Diego CA, June 2016.

Mohammad, Saif M., Parinaz Sobhani, and Svetlana Kiritchenko. 2016. "Stance and Sentiment in Tweets." ACM Transactions on Embedded Computing Systems, arXiv preprint arXiv:1605.01655.

Moore, Will H., and Stephen M. Shellman. 2004. "Fear of Persecution: A Global Study of Forced Migration, 1952–1995." *Journal of Conflict Resolution* 48, no. 5: 723–45.

Naudé, Wim. 2010. "The Determinants of Migration from Sub-Saharan African Countries." *Journal of African Economies* 19, no. 3: 330–56.

NOAA: National Oceanic and Atmospheric Administration National Tsunami Warning Center. Available at http://ntwc.arh.noaa.gov/ (10/12/2017).

Ribeiro, Filipe N., Matheus Araújo, Pollyanna Gonçalves, Marcos André Gonçalves, and Fabrício Benevenuto. 2016. "SentiBench: A Benchmark Comparison of State-of-the-Practice Sentiment Analysis Methods." *EPJ Data Science* 5, no. 1: 1–29.

Salehyan, Idean, and Kristian S. Gleditsch. 2006. "Refugees and the Spread of Civil War." *International Organization* 60, no. 2: 335–66.

Schmeidl, Susanne, and J. Craig Jenkins. 1996. "Issues in Quantitative Modelling in the Early Warning of Refugee Migration." *Refuge* 15, no. 4: 4–7.

Schmeidl, Susanne. 1997. "Exploring the Causes of Forced Migration: A Pooled Time-Series Analysis, 1971–1990." *Social Science Quarterly* 78, no. 2: 284–308.

Singh, Lisa. 2016. "Data Ethics: Attaining Personal Privacy on the Web." In *Ethical Reasoning in Big Data: An Exploratory Analysis*, edited by Jeff Collmann and Sorin Adam Matei, 81–90. New York: Springer.

Singh, Lisa, and Raghu Pemmaraju. 2017. "EOS: A Multilingual Text Archive of International Newspapers and Blog Articles." IEEE International Conference on Big Data (BigData), 4835–7. Boston, MA.

Slovic, Paul. 1987. "Perception of Risk." *Science* 236 (April): 280–5.

———. 2000. *The Perception of Risk*. Sterling, VA: Earthscan Publications.

Slovic, Paul, Baruch Fischoff, and Sarah Lichtenstein. 2000. "Facts and Fears: Understanding Perceived Risk." In *The Perception of Risk*, edited by Paul Slovic, 137–53. Sterling, VA: Earthscan Publications.

Slovic, Paul, Howard Kunreuther, and Gilbert F. White. 2000. "Decision Processes, Rationality and Adjustment." In *The Perception of Risk*, edited by Paul Slovic, 1–31. Sterling, VA: Earthscan Publications.

Smith, Christopher D. 2012. "Assessing the Impact of Climate Change upon Migration in Burkina Faso: An Agent-Based Modeling Approach." PhD diss., University of Sussex.

Sobhani, Parinaz, Saif M. Mohammad, and Svetlana Kiritchenko. 2016. "Detecting Stance in Tweets and Analyzing Its Interaction with Sentiment." *Proceedings of *SEM 2016: Fifth Joint Conference on Lexical and Computational Semantics*, 159–69, Berlin, Aug 2016.

Starr, Chauncey. 1969. "Social Benefit Versus Technological Risk." *Science* 165: 1232–8.

Systems Dynamic Society. n.d. *Introduction to System Dynamics*. Accessed 12 Oct 2017. http://www.systemdynamics.org/what-is-s/.

Teh, Y. W., Jordan, M. I., Beal, M. J., Blei, D. M. 2006. "Hierarchical Dirichlet Processes." *Journal of the American Statistical Association* 101, no. 476: 1566–81.

United Nations High Commissioner for Refugees (UNHCR). 2017. *Figures at a Glance*. Accessed 12 Oct 2017. http://www.unhcr.org/en-us/figures-at-a-glance.html.

UNHCR. 2018a. Global Compact on Refugees. Geneva: UNHCR

———. 2018b. *Global Trends: Forced Displacement in 2017*. Geneva: UNHCR.

Wang, X. and A. McCallum. 2006. "Topics over Time: A Non-Markov Continuous-time Model of Topical Trends." ACM International Conference on Knowledge Discovery and Data Mining (KDD).

Wei, Yifang, Abbie Taylor, Nili S. Yossinger, Eleanor Swingewood, Christopher Cronbaugh, Dennis Quinn, Lisa Singh, Susan F. Martin, Sidney Berkowitz, Jeff Collmann, and Susan McGrath. 2014. "Using Large-Scale Open Source Data to Identify Potential Forced Migration." Presented at and published for the 2014 KDD Workshop on Data Science for Social Good, University of Chicago, Aug 2014.

Wei, Yifang, Lisa Singh, Brian Gallagher, and David Butler. 2016. "Overlapping Target Event and Storyline Detection of Online Newspaper Articles." IEEE International Conference on Data Science and Advanced Analytics, Montreal.

Wei, Y., L. Singh, B. Gallagher, and D. Butler. 2018. "Using Semantic Graphs to Detect Overlapping Target Events and Story Lines from Newspaper Articles. *International Journal of Data Science and Analytics* 5, no. 1: 41–60.

Wei, Y., and L. Singh. 2017. "Location-Based Event Detection Using Geotagged Semantic Graphs." *ACM International Workshop on Mining and Learning with Graphs (MLG) at KDD*, Nova Scotia, Canada.

———. 2017. "Understanding the Impact of Sampling and Noise on Detecting Events Using Twitter." *IEEE International Conference on Big Data (BigData)*, Boston, MA.

# 7

# Building and Sustaining a Web Platform for Researchers, Teachers, Students, and Practitioners in the Field of Refugee and Forced Migration Studies

*James C. Simeon*

## Introduction

The field of refugee and forced migration studies is continuing to evolve and to develop as a discipline with its own specialized terminology as well as conceptual, methodological, and theoretical frameworks and approaches (Voutira and Dona 2007). The advent of the Internet and digital technology has made knowledge readily available to all those with access to a computer (Kaplanis 2013). It has also ushered in the era of e-learning and online instruction, revolutionizing the way that people, at all levels, acquire an education (Arskavskiy 2017). Moreover, it has revolutionized social interaction and the exchange of opinions on the issues of the day (Brignall and Van Valey 2005). Take, for instance, the tremendous role social media had in mobilizing support for the demonstrations of the Arab Spring, from 2010 to 2012, which resulted in the disintegration of a number of dictatorial regimes in North Africa and the Middle East (Brown, Guskin, and Mitchell 2012), as well as in contemporary movements such as Occupy and Black Lives Matter (Waldram 2011; Shafa 2012). The transformation of social interaction through mobile and digital technologies that make new forms of global social justice movements possible, and that have had such a dramatic effect on their societies, has also transformed the way that people conduct research, learn, and obtain a formal education (Hirtz and Kelly 2011; see also chapter 8). All these transformative shifts in social interaction were the impetus for the development of a new web-based platform for refugee and forced migration studies.

The Canadian Association of Refugee and Forced Migration Studies (CARFMS) is an association that is open to students, academics, lawyers, advocates, policymakers, jurists, and members of the public, including refugees; that is, anyone who might have an interest in refugees and other forced migrants. CARFMS is based at the Centre for Refugee Studies (CRS) at York University, and holds annual conferences where the latest research findings on refugees and forced migration are presented, debated, discussed, and subject to peer review and assessment (see the introduction). The CARFMS Online Research and Teaching Tools and Practitioners Forum (ORTT&PF) is a multi-functional online research tool that is designed for all those who work in the field of refugee and forced migration studies. The web platform is found on the CARFMS website at http://carfms.org/ under ORTT and it is directly accessible at http://rfmsot.apps01.yorku.ca/home/. The web platform has two components: the ORTT, Online Research and Teaching Tools; and, PF, the Practitioners Forum. The first is an open access website that contains information that is directly relevant for all those who work with refugees and other forced migrants. The second is a closed website that is available only to CARFMS members and offers discussion forums for members to engage in conversations and debates, within their occupational and/or disciplinary field or in a general open forum, as well as to share information about their research and publications, etc. Together they provide a set of tools that can be used by CARFMS members and the general public to learn, conduct research, and instruct others on refugees and other forced migrants.[1]

This chapter will outline the emergence and development of the CARFMS ORTT&PF. It will focus principally on how the ORTT&PF was conceptualized, established, and piloted to build a community of researchers, teachers, and students of refugee and forced migration studies within Canada and abroad. It begins by reviewing the underlying rationale for the ORTT&PF by examining how e-learning and e-research have emerged as indomitable forces in the Internet and digital age. It will then provide a detailed overview of the origins and the inherent logic and structure of this web platform. In addition, it will address the critical issue of how a web platform of this nature can be made self-sustaining, which is likely the most difficult challenge for any web platform. The next section will examine the current and ever-escalating refugee crisis that underscores the necessity of a web platform of this nature. The ORTT&PF's potential for knowledge mobilization will then be considered as a mechanism for the dissemination of knowledge and understanding of the field of refugee and forced migration studies and for the advancement of the rights and protection of all forced migrants and especially refugees. It will conclude by reflecting on the possible future of the ORTT&PF within CARFMS and the field of refugee and forced migration studies and its impact on international and national policies for the realization of the human rights and dignity of all those who are forced to migrate due to threats to their life, liberty, and security as human beings (Feller 2001).

## e-Learning in the Digital Age

The transformation of society through information technologies has resulted in significant changes in modern life. As Robert Hassan (2008) has noted in *The Information Society: Cyber Dreams and Digital Nightmares*, "Many prominent theorists have argued it [the information society] to be the most profound and comprehensive transformation of economy, culture and politics since the rise of the industrial way of life in the eighteenth century." Others have emphasized that we now live in a "global information society" characterized by a knowledge economy that provides a new opportunity to harness the massive flows of information. Policymaking and decision-making will be routinely informed by what some have identified as "intelligent development" (Wilson, Kellerman, and Corey 2013, 192). An obvious indication of this profound change is the development of Search Engine Optimization (SEO). With the proliferation of data on the Internet, one concern is how to ensure that search engines find your website. SEO has emerged as a key tool to improve the visibility of websites (Grappone and Couzin 2011).

Web searching has become an everyday activity for people who have access to a computer. As access to information has become easier, the nature of learning and understanding has also adapted to the new circumstances of our interconnected world. As several scholars point out: "Advances in information technology, coupled with the changes in society, are creating new paradigms for education. Participants in this new educational paradigm require rich learning environments supported by well-designed resources" (Reigeluth and Khan 1994). Khan (1997) emphasizes that "the Web, as a medium of learning and instruction, has the potential to support the creation of these well-designed resources." Our ORTT&PF website is very much in keeping with the emergence of the new medium of learning, instruction, and training via the Web. However, we are mindful of the fact that "technology must serve learning needs and not the other way around," yet, at the same time, we are of the opinion that "technology and the Internet are innovative forces that interact with pedagogy in creative ways" (Rudestam and Schoenholtz-Read 2010).

The development of an extensive list of e-learning and e-research materials on refugee and forced migration issues will be a welcomed addition to the online instructional materials for all higher educational instructors who are teaching courses in this field. The potential for the use of the ORTT&PF as a support for conducting research and teaching on refugees and forced migrants is enormous (Markauskaite 2011). It can also have a tremendous benefit for all students—whether they are new to the field, a long-time student in advanced graduate studies, or the experienced and accomplished researcher, as well as all those in-between—in advancing their own work in the emerging field of refugee and forced migration studies.

## The Origins and Ongoing Development of the ORTT&PF

The ORTT&PF was the outcome of discussions that the author had, as the incoming president of CARFMS in 2011, with the previous president of the association, professor Christina Clark-Kazak. The idea for an online research and teaching tool seemed to flow naturally with what other organizations and professional associations were doing or considering doing at the time.[2] It was also consistent with the core mission of CARFMS as set out in its by-laws under mandate and purposes and objectives. Indeed, it could be argued that a web platform would in fact be indispensable for achieving the association's mandate, purposes, and objectives. There was also broad-based consultation with key members of the CARFMS Executive who immediately saw the value of such a website and indicated that they would not only support such a website but also directly participate in its development and launch.

## *The Founding of the ORTT&PF*

One of the traditions of the incoming CARFMS president is to identify an initiative that they would like to work on during their term that would benefit the association as a whole. I suggested that the development of the ORTT&PF would be the project that I would like to implement during my term in office. In the interim, I also approached Sanja Begic, Learning Technology Support Specialist, Faculty of Liberal Arts & Professional Studies (LA&PS) at York University—with whom I had collaborated on several previous research projects—to discuss how the website should be designed, structured, and developed over time. It was agreed that the web platform would be developed in two parts: the ORTT and the PF. The proposal was then presented to the CARFMS executive who fully approved it. A committee to oversee the development of the website was struck and several members of the CARFMS executive agreed to serve on it. The committee met on a monthly basis from 2012 to 2015. During that time, the overall design of the web platform was agreed upon such that the ORTT would be an open access website and the PF would be the CARFMS members-only portion of the website.

This dual design, with open and closed access sites, was agreed to for several reasons. The principal reason was that the ORTT should be free for the public at large and would be an excellent way of profiling CARFMS and the work it was doing and advancing in the way of "promoting and supporting excellence in refugee research and teaching in refugee and forced migration issues" (CARFMS/ACERFM by-laws, article 3.1). The PF would be the site for CARFMS members to engage in discussion and debate on those issues and concerns relevant to the association, to encourage information exchange among the members of the association, and to help to foster research collaborations in the field. One of the concerns of the CARFMS executive at the time was attracting individuals to join CARFMS, a relatively new association, by identifying clear benefits of membership. The ORTT&PF was something that filled this need nicely as the PF was available to CARFMS members in good standing only, that is, those members who had paid their membership fees.

## The Structural Framework of the ORTT&PF

The ORTT is designed specifically to help further research and teaching in refugee and forced migration studies. It is structured around a number of core knowledge systems: the glossary of terms; key concepts; methodological approaches; and theoretical frameworks. Each of these, in turn, is designed along a consistent structural format that includes six elements:

1. Definitions;

2. Examples and/or Illustrations;

3. Other Useful Sources;

4. Bibliography;

5. Case Law;

6. Other Related Terms.[3]

The content for terms under each of the core knowledge systems is slowly being built. It is a labour-intensive exercise that will require considerable time to complete in its entirety. However, it should be noted that in order to maintain the relevance of this website it must be under constant development and revision to keep the information as current as possible. In short, it will require ongoing updating and routine maintenance throughout its existence. This is, of course, inevitable given the constant change and flow of information, new discoveries, and developments in the field of refugee and forced migration studies.

The ORTT also includes several other important categories: organizations; programs and courses; and lesson plans. Each of these categories follows its own format for obvious reasons. However, we consider them to be just as essential for those who wish to be fully apprised of the field of refugee and forced migration studies. While the Organizations and

Programs & Courses provide a listing of some of the key organizations and the university degree programs and courses that are offered, the Lesson Plans is an entirely different category. The Lesson Plans at present includes an experiential education assignment that can be used by those who teach a course(s) on refugee and forced migration in post-secondary institutions in Canada or abroad (CARFMS, ORTT, lesson plans 2017).

## The Experiential Education Assignment

The ORTT experiential education assignment was first developed and piloted by Professors Idil Atak (Department of Criminology, Ryerson University) and Nanette Neuwahl (Faculty of Law, University of Montreal). It was subsequently further refined by Professor Atak for her fourth-year seminar class. Several other professors teaching in the field have now applied the assignment, including me. This is not only an experiential education assignment for students, but also a way of preparing content for the ORTT website. Students are assigned terms from a glossary of terms or concepts to work on using the six-element template outlined above. They are typically assigned two or three terms as part of their assignment for their course. The assignment is graded and returned to the students and those students who wish to make the suggested corrections to their assignment and have it submitted for posting on the ORTT website can do so. All those assignments that are submitted by students are further reviewed, and often amended before being approved.

All those instructors who have used this assignment have reported that students find it to be an interesting and rewarding experience. It gives them an opportunity to explore key terms in the field of refugee and forced migration studies in detail and it also gives them an opportunity to see their work added to the ORTT. It is their contribution to the development of the ORTT&PF web platform and to the development of the field of refugee and forced migration studies. So, in this sense, the students have an opportunity to work on an active and "live" research project.

Students' reactions to this assignment have been overwhelmingly positive. The feedback has been used to refine the experiential education assignment further and to make it as deep a learning experience as possible for the students in the course. Students are not required to submit their work for posting on the ORTT website. This is entirely an optional undertaking by students who may choose not to revise their assignment and submit it for possible posting on the website. We encourage other instructors to join us in adopting this experiential education assignment for their courses to help to build the ORTT.[4]

## Funding Applications

We have attempted to raise funds for the ongoing development of the ORTT&PF through minor and major research grants.[5] Some funding has been raised for this purpose, although major funds have yet to be secured; but we remain hopeful. The need for such an online learning, teaching, and research tool has been amply demonstrated over the last number of years. The formal and informal feedback that we have received from researchers, librarians, and administrators has been uniformly positive. All those who have visited the ORTT website have said that it is intuitive, interesting, and provides a useful resource for students, instructors, practitioners, and researchers alike.

## The Practitioners Forum Dialogue and Posting Rules

The PF is still being piloted and has been much slower to develop for several reasons. There was some reluctance to launch this website until we had developed it further and, most importantly, we had a set of rules for how the website should be used. There are now six rules outlining the expectations of CARFMS members who wish to use the website. The basic principle is summarized as follows: "We fully expect that all CARFMS members will use the Practitioners Forum respectfully, responsibly, fairly, and with the fullest courtesy and thoughtfulness possible to everyone, whether they are members of CARFMS or not" (CARFMS Practitioners Forum 2017). The ORTT&PF collaborators took some time to develop and approve the rules that govern the conduct of CARFMS members' use of the PF. One concern was that the association not incur any liability should a CARFMS member(s) misuse the PF, either intentionally or unintentionally. We are now satisfied that the appropriate approval and monitoring processes are in place. However, we are also mindful of the possibility of human error and are proceeding at a deliberately slow pace to prevent this from occurring. At the last three CARFMS annual conferences we invited members to register for the PF, but the enrolment has been disappointingly low. It is not entirely apparent why this is the case, but we are nonetheless hopeful that CARFMS members will eventually routinely, and by virtue of their

CARFMS membership, be automatically registered for the PF. This would entail the merging of the CARFMS membership list with PF website. It would also entail that a certain portion of the business of CARFMS could be conducted on the PF, such as votes on items between annual general meetings or the discussion of relevant public policy issues of the day as they emerge and evolve in real time. Some of the associational business of CARFMS could then be conducted through the PF, in addition to its more general functions as an occupational and disciplinary forum and a networking site for building research partnerships and projects. In short, the PF would become the CARFMS members' website for conducting the business of the association.

## The Long-Term Sustainability of the ORTT&PF

Several factors are necessary for the long-term sustainability of the ORT-T&PF. The first is obvious: the overall utility of the web platform for the needs of anyone who is working in the field of refugee and forced migration studies. It is important to acknowledge that even if the ORTT&PF obtains a large grant to accelerate the development of the web platform that this will not guarantee its long-term sustainability; the initiative will have to become self-sustaining. This is a general problem for all web platforms (see, for example, chapters 9 and 10).

One way of helping to make the ORTT&PF, or any web platform like it, self-sustaining is to ensure it is based within a viable organization or association. The fact that the ORTT&PF is part of CARFMS helps to ensure its long-term sustainability because it has an organizational foundation from which to draw, as required. Another important factor would be to provide volunteer support. This is the very basis on which Wikipedia and other platforms like it are built. Take, for instance, the experiential education assignment, outlined above, that not only benefits students by providing them with the opportunity to contribute to providing content to the ORTT but, at the same time, allows the student to learn a great deal about the terminology in the field of refugee and forced migration studies. It is a "win-win" situation for all concerned: the ORTT&PF gains new content and the students have an opportunity to learn about the field and work on a "live" research project that is developing research and teaching materials for those working on forced migration and refugee issues. It is not often that undergraduate or graduate students in the social sciences have an opportunity to make a direct contribution to an ongoing research project. In this sense, those who make a voluntary contribution to the ORTT&PF not only benefit directly; their voluntary contribution also benefits the general welfare of the intellectual and research community.

Another way that the ORTT&PF can become self-sustaining is for those who offer degree or diploma programs and courses in the field of refugee and forced migration studies to have their institutions listed in the "Programs & Courses" section. Indeed, with this initiative the more collaborators involved the better. In this regard, the CARFMS ORTT&PF committee must constantly promote the platform at every opportunity in order to attract widespread use of and support for its ongoing development. Sustainability would be achieved through a direct contribution from CARFMS to hire a full-time or part-time ORTT&PF manager to ensure that the web platform is constantly developed and refined.

## The Growing Refugee Crisis and the Field of Refugee and Forced Migration Studies

One of the major chronic crises of our time is that millions of people across the globe have been uprooted from their homes, communities, and countries and forced to seek asylum abroad. In 2017, 68.5 million people were forcibly displaced, the highest number on record (UNHCR 2018). The United Nations High Commissioner for Refugees' (UNHCR) Global Forced Displacement 2014 annual report pointed out that: "The year 2014 has seen continuing dramatic growth in mass displacement from wars and conflict, once again reaching levels unprecedented in recent history. One year ago, UNHCR announced that worldwide forced displacement numbers had reached 51.2 million, a level not previously seen in the post-World War II era. Twelve months later, this figure has grown to a staggering 59.5 million, roughly equaling the population of Italy or the United Kingdom. Persecution, conflict, generalized violence, and human rights violations have formed a 'nation of the displaced' that, if they were a country, would make up the 24th largest in the world" (UNHCR 2014, 5). The situation has not improved in the intervening years: by the end of 2016, there were 65.6 million people of concern to the UNHCR (UNHCR 2017). And, as noted above, the current figure now stands at over 68.5 million forcibly displaced people in the world today (UNHCR 2018). In this context, a digital platform dedicated to the protection and plight of refugees and other forced migrants, through the promotion of research and teaching on all aspects of this phenomenon, would fill an important and growing need.

It is important to acknowledge that this field of study is relatively new. For instance the Centre for Refugee Studies (CRS) at York University, the second oldest research institution dedicated to the study of refugees, was founded in 1988 (CRS 2017). Given the fact that the discipline of refugees and forced migration studies is relatively new, it is still emerging as an academic field of study. However, as in every field of study and practice, there are debates and discussions about the future of the discipline. This is perhaps even truer of refugees and forced migration studies given that the nature of the field itself is so focused on addressing the protection concerns of those who are seeking asylum (Chimni 2009).

It is equally important to note that the field of refugee and forced migration studies is both multidisciplinary and interdisciplinary in nature. It draws upon a vast array of disciplines to analyze the situation of asylum seekers and those persons whose most fundamental human rights and dignity as human beings have been severely breached or violated. As with every field of study, refugee and forced migration studies is no different and requires a clear delineation of its basic parameters and central concerns. The ORTT&PF promises to make an important contribution in this regard as it provides a detailed catalogue of the central terms, concepts, methods, and theoretical frameworks within this field of study (see also chapter 13). The advancement of international protection for the world's refugees should be the underlying concern for those who are working in the field of refugee and forced migration studies (Souter 2013) and the ORTT&PF is one such mechanism to help realize this most worthy objective.

The potential of the ORTT&PF lies not only in the provision of useful and authoritative information that could be used by those who are teaching courses in refugee and forced migration studies but also in the ability to draw on the wide range of expertise within the membership of CARFMS and among those willing to participate in the practitioners forum. The practitioners forum will provide the means by which participants can dialogue with each other on the issues and concerns of the day or to make connections with other researchers who are working on common research questions and problems. The practitioners forum will function essentially as a network of scholars, researchers, teachers, practitioners, policymakers, students, and other professionals who desire to share information, knowledge, and understanding on one of the most important international human rights issues of our time. Further, in this regard the PF would be an ideal complement to the Refugee Research Network (RRN) web platform (see chapter 9).

## Knowledge Mobilization

The ORTT&PF is premised on the construction of a "one-stop" website that is a knowledge mobilization platform *par excellence*. It strives to provide the latest detailed information on the basic terms, concepts, methods, and theories currently extant, along with other essential details regarding refugee and forced migration studies, and most importantly it provides an interactive platform for practitioners within and across disciplines to engage in ongoing discussions on pertinent and relevant matters. Despite the fact that the ORTT&PF is a superb knowledge mobilization device in and of itself, we have also undertaken a number of measures to ensure that it is disseminated as a research and teaching tool with a highly interactive forum that will promote the ongoing sharing of information and best practices amongst the community of scholars and practitioners working in the field—and especially among those who are members of CARFMS and/or the International Association for the Study of Forced Migration (IASFM) (IASFM 2017).

The ORTT&PF has been routinely featured at both CARFMS annual conferences and IASFM biannual conferences. The ORTT&PF tries to stay abreast of the latest developments in the field of cloud computing and web-based platforms for research, teaching, learning, and the dissemination of knowledge on refugee and forced migration studies. The panel sessions and roundtables that have been held at the CARFMS and IASFM conferences have been very helpful in disseminating information about the ORTT&PF and its capabilities to members of these respective associations. It has also proved useful in recruiting those who are interested in contributing to the development of the ORTT&PF as one of the foremost web-based platforms of its kind for the advancement of research, teaching, and learning in the field of refugee and forced migration studies. In addition to presenting annual reports about the initiative, we have considered producing a quarterly e-newsletter on the latest developments and additions and to highlight particularly interesting facts and figures on research and teaching in the field. Going forward, such a project would endeavour to highlight some of the foremost researchers and teachers—at all levels of the educational system—in the field by posting their publications on the ORTT&PF website, along with those of our collaborators including the Emerging Scholars and Practitioners on Migration Issues (ESPMI) network (see chapter 10). We will also strive to develop an academic publication series with a well-respected international publisher based, in part, on a symposium that will examine the most interesting developments in cloud computing and the development of hardware and software that can extend the impact and reach of the ORTT&PF to its principal audiences: the researcher/investigator, educator/instructor, student/learner, public and private policymakers, whether they are local, national, regional, or international, and of course refugees and other forced migrants themselves. We will also seek to publish an edited volume, based on the best papers delivered at our proposed annual symposium and supplemented with other contributions from well-known and respected academics in this field.

All ORTT&PF collaborators will be encouraged to prepare and to submit academic journal articles, on either an individual or a collective basis, on the ORTT&PF and its development and contribution to the field of refugee and forced migration studies. Our goal will be to publish in at least one academic journal article each year. We have already presented our ORTT&PF website at four consecutive CARFMS annual conferences, 2012 to 2015, and at two consecutive IASFM biennial conferences, 2012 and 2014. Finally, we will continue to hold roundtables, panel sessions, and demonstrations of the ORTT&PF at future CARFMS and IASFM conferences.

## Conclusions

The ORTT&PF is a major innovation for the field of refugee and forced migration studies. It is geared to utilizing fully digital and interactive technologies to facilitate e-learning and e-research that can be offered to all those working within this field and to the public commons. Beyond the influence of technology, the growing global refugee crisis underscores the significance of this initiative not only to understand this phenomenon but also to address the human misery and suffering that it entails. The ORTT is an online, open-source platform that is already available and has been tested, in part, by academics, researchers, practitioners, students, and asylum advocates. The PF has been made available to all members in good standing in CARFMS and provides an exemplary opportunity for dialogue, discussion, and debate on the issues that matter the most to those in the field of refugee and forced migration studies. It further provides a superb networking opportunity that promotes collaboration and ideational synergies among all CARFMS members in a closed sheltered and protected environment within the context of fulfilling the mandate and the purposes and objectives of CARFMS in advancing the human rights of all forced migrants, including refugees. Perhaps the platform's greatest potential is its capacity to stimulate research interest and collaborations that could lead to contributions to public policy and the welfare and well-being of refugees and other forced migrants.

The overriding objective of the ORTT&PF is to bring together the broad and diverse field of refugee and forced migration studies and practice in order to address the plight of refugees and other forced migrants, and to protect their rights. To do so, the ORTT&PF must make itself self-sustaining in order to be in a position to develop continually and maintain its relevance and utility to all, whether they are members of CARFMS or not. In order for this to happen it must become fully integrated with CARFMS, so that it is a central feature of the association and is supported by it both in terms of financial as well as material resources.

## Notes

1    For a brief introduction, see: "Online Research and Teaching Tools and Practitioners Forum (ORTT & PF), CARFMS Newsletter 4 (2013): 4, http://carfms.org/wp-content/uploads/2014/11/CARFMS-Newsletter-Spring-2013-Issue-4.pdf. (Accessed 8 July 2017) and James C. Simeon, "CARFMS ORTT & PF Web Platform: Helping to Keep All CARFMS Members Ahead of the Curve," CARFMS Newsletter Winter 2017, no. 8, 8–10. http://carfms.org/wp-content/uploads/2017/03/CARFMS-newsletter-winter-2017.pdf. (Accessed 8 July 2017)

2    There are a number of these websites including the Canadian Association of Programs in Public Policy and Administration's (CAPPA) and the University of Toronto's School of Public Policy and Governance's Public Policy and Governance Portal that is now called the Atlas of Public Management, http://www.atlas101.ca/pm/. See also the Critical Issues in International Refugee Law Workshop, http://www.yorku.ca/

ciirl/2008/, the Critical Issues in International Refugee Law Workshop II, http://www.yorku.ca/ciirl/, and the War Crimes and Refugee Status Conference, http://www.yorku.ca/wcrs/conference/resources.html, Resources pages. I had a direct hand in the design and development of these three websites and a number of others. The Refugee Research Network (RRN) also influenced the design of CARFMS ORTT&PF. (Accessed 12 July 2017)

3     For instance, see the ORTT-CARFMS, Glossary of Terms, "Citizenship," http://rfmsot.apps01.yorku.ca/glossary-of-terms/citizenship/.

4     For anyone who wishes to do so, please notify me at my York University email address, jcsimeon@yorku.ca.

5     ORTT&PF collaborators have submitted applications for major research grants to the Social Sciences and Humanities Research Council of Canada and despite the fact that external assessors gave the grant applications positive reviews they were not funded. Minor internal research grant funding has been provided by York University. YorkU has also supported this project through the provision of technical expertise and hosting the web platform on its servers. We are most grateful to York University for its ongoing support for the development of this web platform.

# References

Anderson, Monica, and Paul Hitlin. 2016. "The Hashtag #BlackLivesMatter Emerges: Social Activism on Twitter." *Pew Research Center*, 15 Aug 2016. http://www.pewinternet.org/2016/08/15/the-hashtag-blacklivesmatter-emerges-social-activism-on-twitter/.

Arskavskiy, Marina, 2017. "eLearning Evolution: The 3 Biggest Changes in 5 Years and How to Adopt to them for Success," *SH!FT: Disruptive eLearning*, March 30, 2017, http://info.shiftelearning.com/blog/elearning-evolution-the-biggest-changes. (Accessed July 4, 2017).

Black, Richard. 2001. "Fifty Years of Refugee Studies: From Theory to Policy." *International Migration Review* 35, no. 1: 57–78.

Banerjee, Preeta M., and Gerald Belson. 2015. "Digital Education 2.0: From Content to Connections." *Deloitte Review* 16, 26 Jan 2015. https://dupress.deloitte.com/dup-us-en/deloitte-review/issue-16/future-digital-education-technology.html.

Brignall III, Thomas W., and Thomas Van Valey. 2005. "The Impact of the Internet on Social Interactions." *Sociological Spectrum* 25, no. 3: 335–48.

Brown, Heather, Emily Guskin, and Amy Mitchell. 2012. "The Role of Social Media in the Arab Uprising." *Pew Research Centre*, 28 Nov 2012. http://www.journalism.org/2012/11/28/role-social-media-arab-uprisings/.

CARFMS/ACERMF. By-laws. Accessed 11 July 2017, http://carfms.org/bylaws/.

CARFMS. ORTT, Lesson Plans, Experiential Education Assignment. Accessed 11 July 2017. http://rfmsot.apps01.yorku.ca/glossary-of-terms/citizenship/.

CARFMS. Practitioners Forum. Accessed 11 July 2017. http://rfmsot.apps01.yorku.ca/
    prc/.

Chimni, B. S. 2009. "The Birth of a 'Discipline': From Refugee to Forced Migration
    Studies." *Journal of Refugee Studies* 22, no. 1: 11–29.

Clark-Kazak, Christina. 2017. "Teaching Forced Migration: Pedagogy in the Context
    of Global Displacement Crises." *Migration Studies* 5, no. 2: 286–7.

Centre for Refugee Studies (CRS). "About Us." Accessed 9 July 2017. http://crs.info.
    yorku.ca/about-us.

Feller, Erika. 2001. "The Evolution of the International Refugee Protection Regime."
    *Journal of Law & Policy* 5: 129–39.

Grappone, Jennifer, and Gradiva Couzin. 2011. *Search Engine Optimization: An Hour
    a Day*. Indianapolis: Wiley Publishing.

Hassan, Robert. 2008. *The Information Society: Cyber Dreams and Digital Nightmares*.
    Cambridge: Polity Press.

Hirtz, Sandy, and Kevin Kelly. 2011. *Education for a Digital World 2.0: Innovations in
    Education*. Vancouver, BC: Open Schools BC.

International Association for the Study of Forced Migration (IASFM). Accessed 12
    July 2017. http://iasfm.org/.

Kaplanis, Dimitris. 2013. "How the Internet Changed the Learning Process." *talent-
    lms*, 13 July 2013. https://www.talentlms.com/blog/how-the-internet-changed-
    the-learning-process/.

Khan, Badrul H. 1997. *Web-Based Instruction*. Englewoods Cliffs: Educational
    Technology Publications.

Markauskaite, Lina. 2011. "Digital Knowledge and Digital Research: What Does
    eResearch Offer Education and Social Policy?" In *Methodological Choice
    and Design: Scholarship, Policy and Practice in Social and Educational
    Research*, edited by Lina Markauskaite, Peter Freebody, and Jude Irwin, 17–35.
    Dordrecht: Springer.

Reigeluth, Charles M., and Badrul H. Khan. 1994. "Do Instructional Systems Design
    (ISD) and Educational Systems Design (ESD) Really Need Each Other?"
    Paper presented at the Annual Meeting of the Association for Educational
    Communications and Technology, Nashville, NT.

Rudestam, Kjell E., and Judith Schoenholtz-Read. 2010. *Handbook of Online Learning*.
    Los Angeles: SAGE.

Shafa, Parisa N. 2012. "The Occupy Movement's Use of Social Media as an Organizing
    Method." *Participedia*, 1 Mar 2012. http://participedia.net/en/methods/
    occupy-movements-use-social-media-organizing-method.

Souter, James. 2013. "Refugee Studies: The Challenge of Translating Hope to Reality."
    *openDemocracy*, 8 Jan 2013. https://www.opendemocracy.net/5050/james-
    souter/refugee-studies-challenge-of-translating-hope-into-reality.

UNHCR. 2015. *World at War: Global Trends: Forced Displacement in 2014*. Geneva: UNHCR. Accessed 17 Nov 2018. http://www.unhcr.org/uk/statistics/ country/556725e69/unhcr-global-trends-2014.html.

———. 2017. Global Trends: Forced Displacement in 2016. Geneva: UNHCR. Accessed 17 Nov 2018. http://www.unhcr.org/uk/statistics/unhcrstats/5943e8a34/global-trends-forced-displacement-2016.html.

———. 2018. Global Trends: Forced Displacement in 2017. Geneva: UNHCR. Accessed 17 Nov 2018. ttp://www.unhcr.org/5b27be547.pdf.

Voutira, Eftihia, and Giorgia Dona. 2007. "Refugee Research Methodologies: Consolidation and Transformation of a Field." *Journal of Refugee Studies* 20, no. 2: 163–71.

Waldram, Hannah. 2011. "Occupy Together: How the Global Movement is Spreading via Social Media." *Guardian*, 14 Oct 2011. https://www.theguardian.com/news/ blog/2011/oct/14/occupy-england-protests-gather-momentum-via-facebook.

Wilson, Mark I., Aharon Kellerman, Kenneth E. Corey. 2013. *Global Information Society: Technology, Knowledge and Mobility*. New York: Rowan & Littlefield.

# 8

# The Promise and Potential of the Demography of Refugee and Forced Migration

*Ellen Percy Kraly and Mohammad Jalal Abbasi-Shavazi*

## Introduction

The first sentences of essays addressing contemporary dimensions of refugee and forced migration and population displacement begin with references to scale and complexity, often using metrics to underscore increases in each characteristic. To be sure, our recent writings addressing the demography of refugee and forced migration are no different (see Hugo, Abbasi-Shavazi, and Kraly 2018; Abbasi-Shavazi and Kraly 2018a, b; Kraly and Abbasi-Shavazi 2018). We cite United Nations High Commissioner for Refugees (UNHCR) statistics on refugees within the context of total persons of concern to the UN refugee agency and refer to the increasing levels in recent years, and changes in the geography of flight and internal displacement. To this demographic complexity is added understanding of the breadth and depth of the causes—both proximate and root—of forced migration and population displacement and the search for human safety and security. The lackluster role of demographers in the scientific study of refugee and forced migration is underscored, tracing the dullness of attention in forced migration studies to deterministic tendencies within the population sciences to modelling and prediction.

The population sciences hold the potential to make significant contributions to the social and policy sciences and the evolving landscape of international migration governance. Structural and cultural turns in social and environmental sciences embrace the predictability of human migration and mobility and demand the study of the under-studied—persons driven from homelands, displaced, trafficked. Momentum has increased within international governance and civil society for globally shared responsibilities regarding refugees and migrants and the rights of migrants and workers. The 2016 New York Declaration for Refugees and Migrants set in motion the development of a global compact for safe, orderly, and regular migration that will be considered by the UN General Assembly in 2018, reflecting a process of consultation with stakeholders within member states, civil society, academia, and migrant communities and groups.[1] In his report "Making Migration Work for All," United Nations Secretary-General António Guterres (2018) argued explicitly that facts rather than myths—knowledge and research—are required to improve management of international mobility in a way that will protect migrants and promote the national and human benefits of migration.

In this chapter we work within this context of global governance initiatives regarding international population movements and refugee and forced migrations. Population scholars must be active participants in these initiatives and fulfill our promise to generate knowledge about contemporary human migration and ultimately fulfill the potential of demography to consider future scenarios of international and forced migrations. In advocating and arguing for amplified contributions of population scientists to the study of forced and refugee migrations we seek to complement the themes of this volume that McGrath and Young express in their introduction (see also Kraly and Abbasi-Shavazi 2018). Accordingly, we outline the requests and requirements for demographic knowledge evolving from recent international dialogue regarding the goals of safe, orderly, and regular migration. We also fully acknowledge the need for continued vigilance regarding the use and potential abuse of population data and analysis in migration and refugee policies (see Asher, Banks, and Scheuren 2008). Third, we document the professional initiatives to foster the demographic study of refugee and forced migration. Fourth, we present recent academic

ELLEN PERCY KRALY AND MOHAMMAD JALAL ABBASI-SHAVAZI

perspectives on the place of demography—both its achievements and its potential—in the study of refugee and forced migration. Here we draw on the contributions of colleagues to the edited volume *The Demography of Refugee and Forced Migration* (Hugo, Abbasi-Shavazi, and Kraly 2018), which addresses critical dimensions of social demographic data, research, and training in relationship to refugee and forced migration. We conclude with reflections on the potential expansion of the role of demography and demographers in global as well as national efforts to promote safe, orderly, and regular human and humane migrations. Throughout this chapter, we have also sought to identify points of intersection between our analysis in other chapters of this volume. We are humbled both by what we have learned and by what we have yet to learn from our fellow contributors.

## Global Demand for Demographic Knowledge of Refugees and Forced Migration

The Millennium Declaration—Resolution 55/2 adopted by the UN General Assembly in September 2000—affirmed the mission and vision of the United Nations for the twenty-first century and established the guiding principles for the Millennium Development Goals for 2015 (UNGA 2000). Regarding international and refugee migration, the signatories resolved to "take measures to ensure respect for and protection of the human rights of migrants, migrant workers and their families, to eliminate the increasing acts of racism and xenophobia in many societies and to promote greater harmony and tolerance in all societies" (UNGA 2000, para. 25). Regarding refugees, the declaration resolved to "strengthen international cooperation, including burden sharing in, and the coordination of humanitarian assistance to, countries hosting refugees and to help all refugees and displaced persons to return voluntarily to their homes, in safety and dignity and to be smoothly reintegrated into their societies" (UNGA 2000, para. 26). Collection, analysis, and communication of social demographic data consistent with these resolutions have been among the activities of the offices and affiliated agencies of the United Nations (UN), notably the UN-HCR, Department of Economic and Social Affairs Population Division, International Labour Organization (ILO) and the International Organization for Migration (IOM), which as of 2016 is the migration agency of the United Nations. Over the past decades, each of these entities has made the case for expansion of the empirical foundation for evidence-based policies regarding international migration and migrants, refugees, internally displaced persons, and other population groups of concern to the United Nations.

Human migration and security has been elevated within UN agendas concerning sustainable development and human rights (see UN Development Programme 2009). The Report of the Secretary General, "In Safety and Dignity: Addressing Large Movements of Refugees and Migrants," laid the foundation for the UN High-level Summit for Refugees and Migrants held in New York, 19 September 2016, and the social, economic, environmental, and humanitarian issues demanding international dialogue and action. The need for data, research, and analysis is made explicit: "To maximize the positive impact of migration, we must analyse trends on the basis of a solid evidence base. I call upon all Member States to invest in data collection, including sex- and age-disaggregated data, as well as information on both regular and irregular flows, the vulnerability of migrants and the economic impact of migration. The data should be analysed to plan for future migration and promote the inclusion of migrants" (UNGA 2016, para. 96).

The vision and voice of the late Mr. Peter Sutherland, former Special Representative to the Secretary-General on Migration, was palpable in the engagement of issues throughout the Summit. The report of the Special Representative on Migration and his colleagues (UNGA 2017) exists as his personal "roadmap for improving the governance of international migration" (UNGA 2017, 1) and includes unequivocal advocacy for data collection, analysis, and demographic inquiry. Mr. Sutherland's argument derives from the essential role of evidence in policy concerning migrants and refugees, not only in the existence of data, but in the revelations deriving from research and analysis concerning the causes and consequences of international population movements. Mining of administrative data as well as data collected through existing international surveys is considered an effective strategy in advancing relevant data collection and analysis. The Sustainable Development Goals (SDGs)—particularly those that are migration-related and international covenants concerning human rights—exist as essential touchstones for policy relevant migration research and analysis.

Louise Arbour, Special Representative to Secretary-General Guterres for International Migration, has reaffirmed these priorities for data collection, research, and communication of results throughout the preparatory process for the 2018 Global Compacts for Refugees and for Migrants. In her remarks to representatives of member states related to the report of the secretary-general, Arbour articulated the need for better data and analysis in order to base sound policy choices on fact rather than assumptions and myths concerning the role of human migration and mobility in sustainable development, state security, and human rights (UNSG 2018). Her observations accord with Canefe's and Banerjee and Samaddar's arguments in this volume. In a recorded presentation to the membership of the International Union for the Scientific Study of Population (IUSSP) participating in the *International Population Conference* in Cape Town, South Africa, October–November 2017, Special Representative Arbour articulated the essential role of population data, research, and training regarding migration, mobility, and population displacement in developing effective global policy and planning for the future.

## The Professions of the Population and Social Sciences in Advancing the Demography of Forced and Refugee Migration

The increasing scale, complexity, and diversity of refugee and forced migration have meant that traditional approaches to the management and solution of refugee and other forced migration situations and protection of refugees have become less appropriate and are being questioned. Demography has an important contribution to make in this space and during times of change (Hugo, Abbasi-Shavazi, and Kraly 2018). And yet while other disciplines (especially anthropology, law, political science, and international relations) have made major contributions to refugee and forced migration studies, and despite the increased momentum within the population sciences to the study of international migration and mobilities, demography has hitherto not contributed very strongly to this topic.

## Groundwork of US National Academy of Sciences

The issue of forced migration within population studies has attracted the attention of scholars in very recent decades. The first scientific attempt for the conceptualization of forced migration was made by Kunz (1973, 1981; see also Huyck and Bouvier 1983 and Gordon 1993), but the first collective and pioneering effort was made by a group of demographers and refugee experts supported by the National Academy of Science in 1997. The Population Committee of the National Research Council of the National Academy of Science in Washington organized a workshop on the demography of forced migration. The purpose of the workshop was "to investigate the ways in which population and other social scientists can produce more useful demographic information about forced migrant populations and how they differ" (Reed, Haaga, and Keely 1998, 3). The workshop focused attention on methods of data collection and methodological shortcomings in relation to forced migration in humanitarian crises. Another roundtable was held on "Mortality Patterns in Complex Emergencies" in Washington, DC in 1999 to explore patterns of mortality in recent crises and consider how these patterns resemble or differ from mortality in previous emergencies (Reed and Keely 2001). Despite these efforts, however, no thorough study or publication became available to more comprehensively strengthen the field of demography of refugee and forced migration.

## Contribution of the Refugee Research Network (RRN)

Funded by the Social Sciences and Humanities Research Council of Canada from 2008–15, the Refugee Research Network (RRN) is a global network of scholars, practitioners, and policymakers that generated and mobilized knowledge to benefit people who have been forcibly displaced. Hosted by the Centre for Refugee Studies (CRS) at York University, the RRN's goal has been to mobilize relevant and responsive knowledge among forced migration scholars and to disseminate it to policy and humanitarian actors at local, national, regional, and global levels. The RRN aimed to strengthen the field of forced migration studies by: a) expanding awareness of the global knowledge regime concerning refugee and forced migration issues, b) improving communication of this knowledge within and between academic, policymaking, and practice sectors within and between the global south and north, and c) building alliances and support for the development of regional and global policy frameworks and humanitarian practices affecting refugees and forced migrants.

To this end, in 2008 various institutions from the global south and north were invited to join the network. Mohammad Jalal Abbasi-Shavazi (University of Tehran) participated as a member of the RRN's Management Committee, and was able to attend a number of meetings and seminars organized by the network at York University in Toronto as well as other conferences organized by the International Association for the Study of Forced Migration (IASFM) in Cyprus, Uganda, and Colombia. In his presentations at these meetings, Abbasi-Shavazi articulated the under-representation of demographers and population experts at the IASFM and other refugee and forced migration scientific gatherings. Furthermore, more dedicated attention to refugee and forced migration is warranted within the International Population Conferences organized by the International Union for the Scientific Study of Population (IUSSP), the primary international professional association of demographers and population scholars, as well as at other regional population conferences.

## IUSSP Panel on the Demography of Forced Migration

Recognizing the increasing scale and complexity of forced migration as well as the need for more research on involuntary migration, the IUSSP set up the Scientific Panel on the Demography of Forced Migration during 2010–14, which was chaired by Abbasi-Shavazi and included four other demographers and forced migration scholars including the late Graeme Hugo, University of Adelaide, Susan McGrath, then-director of the Centre for Refugee Studies (CRS) at York University and Director of the RRN, and Jeff Crisp, UNHCR.[2] The panel aimed to achieve three main objectives during its term: first, to organize an international seminar to discuss forced migration from various perspectives within the discipline of demography; second, to publish an edited volume as a reference book on the demography of refugees that can be used by those who are interested in forced migration; and finally, to mainstream the topic within the discipline of demography. In implementing these objectives, the IUSSP Panel would have greatly benefited from the lessons and experiences concerning network formation and sustenance within Latin America (articulated in chapter 12).

The international seminar *Demographic Perspectives on Refugee and Forced Migration* held in Tehran, Iran, from 13–15 May 2012 was organized by the IUSSP Scientific Panel on Demography of Refugees in collaboration with the University of Tehran's Department of Demography, Population Association of Iran, University of Adelaide, the RRN, and the Australian Demographic and Social Research Institute of the Australian National University. Around twenty distinguished scholars with significant background in the field of refugees, as well as representatives from the UNHCR, Australian Department of Immigration and Citizenship, and Internal Displacement Monitoring Centre attended a two-day seminar and presented their findings on cutting edge issues regarding refugee and forced migration. Participants also discussed how demography can contribute toward developing relevant policy and program recommendations for providing protection for forced migrants, the solution of refugee and other forced migrant problems and maximizing the benefits of such migration to origin and destination areas. The late Charles Keely, who participated and took an active role in the previous (US) National Academy of Sciences (NAS) workshops in the late 1990s, attended the IUSSP international seminar and made a significant contribution to the conceptualization of forced migration.

## Summary of the Process of the Book on Demography of Refugee and Forced Migration

Graeme Hugo and Abbasi-Shavazi initially planned the process of editing selected papers for the publication of a book titled *Demography of Refugees*. However, after Hugo's untimely passing, Ellen Percy Kraly (who participated in the Tehran seminar) joined as an editor to continue the project. Given the complexity of the issues covered in the volume as well as this sudden demise of two pioneering authors (also Charles Keely), the process of compilation of chapters and editing the volume took longer than expected. Moreover, throughout the process it became clear that several topics including irregular migration, internally displaced persons, environmentally forced migration, and repatriation of refugee and forced migration needed to be included in the volume. These challenges notwithstanding we are nonetheless very pleased that the edited volume entitled *Demography of Refugee and Forced Migration* has now been published, and a pre-publication version of the book was launched at the IUSSP conference in Cape Town on 2 November 2017. Three leading demographers—Peter McDonald, ex-president of the IUSSP; John Bongaarts, Population Council; and John Wilmoth, director of UN Population Division—along with several authors and participants at the IUSSP conference attended the launch. Kraly launched the book, on the occasion of the sixteenth Coordination Meeting on International Migration and in light of an upcoming UN Summit on the Global Compacts, on 15 February 2018 at the United Nations Bookshop. In brief, the earlier mission and objectives of the NAS on the demography of forced migration has now been accomplished, and it is interesting to note that five distinguished participants of the NAS workshop in 1997 (Charles Keely, Holly Reed, Susanne Schmeidl, Susan Martin, and Bela Hovy) have contributed to the 2018 edited volume.

*Demography of Refugee and Forced Migration* is the product of collaboration among the editors and authors over the last five years. It seeks to demonstrate the benefit of the scope and method of demography to the study of forced migration and refugees by applying a demographic lens to a range of topics in the field. Participating authors discuss how demography can contribute toward a better understanding of refugees by focusing on levels and trends of refugee and forced migration, characteristics of refugees, and pathways by which refugees and forced migrants are integrated/adapted to host/home societies. The issues of interest include but are not limited to: the conceptualization of forced migration within a wider population mobility framework; the broadening of understanding of forced migration beyond refugees to include other types of forced and mixed migrations; the methodology for measuring forced migration; the relevance of existing migration theory to forced migration situations; the structure, scale, and spatial patterning of contemporary forced movements; the characteristics of forced migrants and internally displaced persons; the drivers of different types of forced movement; the dynamics of forced migration and its interrelationships with fertility, mortality, and family change; as well as the return strategies and adaptation patterns of refugees to their home society. Also discussed are the importance of demographic research for developing relevant policy and program recommendations for providing protection for forced migrants, the solution of refugee and other forced migrant problems, and maximizing the benefits of such migration to origin and destination areas.

The book comprises fifteen chapters. After an introductory chapter on advancing the demography of forced migration and refugees, the subsequent chapters are organized into four main parts. Part I is devoted to the conceptualization and data sources of forced migration. Part II presents demographic perspectives by focusing on the relationship between mortality, fertility, family change, and forced migration. It also examines forced migration through the lens of gender. And Part III discusses patterns and dimensions of forced migration. Changing patterns of internal displacement, environmentally related international displacement, and the nexus between forced and irregular migration have been examined from a demographic perspective. In Part IV, the linkages between migration and security, and the issue of return to home and the reintegration process have been discussed, and international, regional, and national legal norms, policies, organizational roles, and relations, as well as good practices related to refugee and forced migration are presented. Future directions in demographic research on forced migration are then offered in the epilogue, within the unfolding context of multi-lateral efforts to promote international cooperation and shared responsibilities for displaced persons in this century.

With the publication of this volume, the main two objectives of the IUSSP Scientific Panel have been successfully met. In order to mainstream demographic perspectives on forced migration, targeted sessions on the demography of forced migration have been held at the meetings of the IUSSP International Population Conferences including South Korea in 2013 and South Africa in 2017, and the International Association of Studies of Forced Migration in Colombia in 2014. Similar sessions were organized at regional population conferences including the Asian Population Association Conferences in Bangkok in 2012 and in Kuala Lumpur in 2015. It is hoped that the book will serve to encourage the introduction of a course on the demography of forced migration and refugees in various social science disciplines.

In engaging demographic analysis within a range of issues germane to population displacement, our hope is that the book is valuable for demographers and social scientists to understand the relevance of their analytic perspectives and tools for forced and refugee migration studies. We also hope that the collection is relevant to those who are interested in forced and refugee migration at national, regional, and international levels of analysis, and makes a useful reference book for students developing skills in developing research designs and data collection initiatives on forced and refugee migrations and displaced persons, families, and populations. Finally, and this is critically important, we hope that the collection as a whole will benefit the process of policy and program analysis regarding displaced populations and refugees.

One positive outcome would be the demand by policymakers for the inclusion of demographic analysis in the development of evidence-based policies and programs concerning efforts to support and protect persons displaced, in flight, and resettled. These outcomes would be amplified through processes of network and capacity building in both the global south and north to promote inclusion, and equity in the production and use of demographic data. The ideas of several contributors to this volume provide profound and powerful recommendations for promotion of just participatory principles and actions with processes of research, analysis, and communication (see in particular chapters 1, 4, and 13).

## The Need for Demographic Data, Research, and Training

Recurring themes in considerations of the role of demographic data and research in the study and response to refugee and forced migrations include: first, the critical value of counts and characteristics of forced migrants and displaced populations; second, the need for more demographic data and research; and third, the benefits of data that are more comprehensive, reliable, and also flexible for understanding shifting characteristics, causes, and consequences of displacement, flight, and refuge. Each of the themes is considered for different analytic purposes including (i) descriptive analysis in order to implement protection and provision for persons in flight and in locations of first asylum; (ii) determination of the consequences of different phases of forced migration—flight, displacement, settlement, and repatriation—for migrants and communities, both of origin and destinations; (iii) revelation of the proximate and ultimate consequences of forced and refugee migration; and (iv) formation of evidence-based policy for prevention and programs of response.

## Demographic Data

The role of demographic data in emergency response to persons and populations forced to flee from humanitarian and environmental crises forms the original "canon" of scholarship and research on the demography of refugee and forced migration. Fundamentally, counts and characteristics of displaced populations and persons in flight inform the scale, substance, and location of response for the protection and sustenance of human life and welfare. Placing the goal to meet the needs of people and populations in flight and displacement within the context of limited funding, demographic data measure scale, geography, and timing to meet requirements for protection and support. Age and gender often serve as indicators of risk and vulnerability (and ideally, resilience) for the allocation of resources (see for example Reed, Seftel, and Behazin 2018; Kraly 2018). Principles of efficiency, effectiveness, equity, and justice in distribution of emergency and other resources are informed by demographic parameters—population size, spatial distribution, and composition by age, gender, ethnicity, etc. Hovy (2018) presents a forceful argument for the assets of registration data, and administrative and operational data more generally for measure of demographic characteristics of populations of humanitarian concern.

Introductory sections of the *Demography of Refugee and Forced Migration* (2018) review the convenings and research of the National Academy of Sciences (NAS) Committee on Population regarding the analysis of forced migration and mortality. NAS' seminal work on mortality and morbidity within forced migrant populations is updated to consider new analytic approaches within the context of more comprehensive perspectives on human health and welfare including infectious and chronic disease and psychiatric disorders (Reed, Sheftel, and Behazin 2018). Social demographic data on gender roles and fertility is critical for understanding changes and disruptions in the reproductive health of forced migrants (see Agadjanian 2018; Kraly 2018). Martin (2018) emphasizes the demographic parameters relevant to assess levels of security among migrants, and the requirements for protection of people and populations in need of protection and safety. Mohammadi, Abbasi-Shavazi, and Sadeghi (2018) empirically illustrate the impacts of demographic, social, and economic situations of refugees prior to, during, and after return to the homeland on the integration and return migration of refugees and refugee families.

The costs of the *lack* of effective demographic data on forced and irregular migration are high—particularly for informed popular discourse and effective public policy regarding political, economic, and social security (see Koser 2018; McAuliffe 2018).

A strong theme in demography of refugee and forced migration is the critical importance of population data on size, composition, geographic distribution, and sources of change to understand the implications and consequences of forced migration and displacement at all scales—individual, family and household, communities and regions. Longitudinal and comparative data on migration as well as other components of population change, fertility, family formation, mortality, morbidity, and disability, each exist in relationship to prospects for health and security, education, and economic productivity (see Abbasi-Shavazi, Mahmoudian, and Sadeghi 2018; Agadjanian 2018; Kraly 2018). Social survey research holds great potential to generate social demographic data to inform assessment of processes of integration and adaptation of migrants as well as the impacts of processes of out-migration from communities of origin.

Several authors in the volume also demonstrate how demographic data are critical in monitoring causes of population displacement and forced migration, particularly proximate causes and correlates of migration (see chapter 13). In its attention to the nature of "force" in forced migration, Keely and Kraly (2018) underscore the importance of understanding and empirically documenting reasons for migration, as well as conditions of migration and movements in data collection systems. Perhaps most significantly, Adamo (2018) illustrates the role of migrant behaviour and decision-making in relationship to measuring the role of environmental and land use change in population mobility and displacement (see also and compare with chapters 6 and 11).

As discussed above, demographic data inform distribution and allocation of resources for the protection and support of forced migrants and refugees. So, too, the development of ongoing policies, programs, and sustainable response at levels of national and international governance requires data on the characteristics of migrant populations to be served and supported and of communities of reception and settlement. Monitoring and evaluation of policies and programs requires monitoring of social demographic change within populations of concern and in relationship to policy goals and program objectives, relative to specific levels of intervention—for example, targets for refugee health at the clinical and community levels, or household versus municipal and regional environmental hazards.

## Demographic Research

Here emerges the "value added" of demographic data for description of scale, distribution, and relative need within migrant populations and communities; for analysis of causes and consequences of refugee and forced migrations and displaced populations; and for policy analysis and program evaluation vis-à-vis populations and persons of concern to international governance, nations, nongovernmental organizations, and civil society. There are six areas that will enhance demographic research: descriptive and comparative analysis; longitudinal analysis; estimation of incomplete data; modelling and future population scenarios; evaluation of data and data collection systems; and development of research designs for qualitative data collection.

The contributions to the *Demography of Refugee and Forced Migration* identify the critical importance of demographic analysis and research for describing migrant populations in comparison to populations of origin, asylum, and settlement (see for example, Abbasi-Shavazi and Kraly 2018). Reed et al. (2018) demonstrate the importance of measuring mortality and morbidity levels among refugees and forced migrants during and throughout the process of flight, asylum, and settlement and in comparison to resident populations in order to estimate "excess mortality" resulting from displacement. Tracking changes in the experiences of women during processes of forced migration benefit from spatial and temporal analysis at different geographic scales. In each of these cases, the value of a demographic perspective in linking population flows (fertility, mortality, and migration/mobilities) with population stock characteristics (location, age/gender, and household composition) is illustrated to go beyond description to reveal the role of forced migration processes on social, economic, and environmental outcomes.

Demographic analysis is a fundamental component of studies of migrant adaptation and integration at the micro-level of analysis, and of the role of migrants and migration in social and economic change and development at the aggregate level of analysis. Longitudinal analysis—and the specific emphasis on period and cohort effects on the life course—is a particular characteristic of demographic perspective in social research. We urge the integration of longitudinal and life course/historical approaches to our understanding of the consequences of forced migration and displacement for individuals, families, and communities. A demographic perspective is critical in the formulation of hypotheses regarding the dynamic effects of forced migration and displacement on individual and household welfare and development of individuals.

An underutilized strength of the use of demographics in research on refugees and forced migration is the capacity for estimation of population characteristics using incomplete data. One of the most significant analytical traditions within the population sciences is the use of population models to provide a range of possibilities for social demographic characteristics and processes—levels of infant and child mortality and fertility, for example. Less developed is the application of formal demographic techniques to the study and estimation of levels and age patterns of migration, forced or voluntary. McAuliffe (2018) underscores the highly significant—and valuable—role of population estimation, notably the use of residual estimation techniques to the study of irregular migration and migrant populations. Demographic analysis is fundamental to monitoring at-risk populations at the regional level (Schmeidl and Hedditch 2018). Here too, formal demographic analysis has potential—at present largely untapped— to provide estimates, and ranges of likelihoods of the size, composition, and geographic distribution of at-risk or displaced populations. Each of these analytic issues in demographic estimation and modelling resonates with the issues Martin and Singh raise in this volume concerning the use of "big data" and social media sources in identifying early phases of forced displacement and flight.

The logical next step from modelling of current migrant and displaced populations is to consider likely scenarios for future population dynamics. This area of demographic research is well integrated in studies of the role of environmental and climate change on population processes and human mobility specifically. There is great potential to expand the role of demographic research to address the implications of social, economic, and political change and conflict for human mobility and displacement. The research programs of the International Institute for Applied Systems Analysis (IIASA) are illustrative of the analytic potential of demography. Population projections may serve to illustrate possible future scenarios of social and economic development (for example, variations in changing levels of education, as well as environmental change, political conflict, etc.) and ultimately human mobility and migration.

Relatedly, demographic research is invaluable to the evaluation of data coverage and quality. Hovy (2018) underscores the values of demographic accounting for assessment of registration coverage of populations of concern. The UNHCR has documented gaps in the demographic data for different populations of concern—for example, coverage in national data systems for gender and age (Kraly 2018). The analytic "chops" for population modelling and demographic estimation in the population sciences holds great potential for identifying ways of improving information systems related to refugees, forced migrants, and displaced populations.

The importance of qualitative data on the experiences and life course of migrants, and within communities of organization and estimation, must also be emphasized, underscored, and advocated. Increasingly, population scientists appreciate the critical role of ethnographic and smaller-scale research in generating knowledge and grounding social theory regarding forced migrants. There is great opportunity for demographers to work with researchers conducting qualitative migration research to implement research designs and field studies that speak to processes regarding population displacement and the experiences of migrants, and that also effectively support some degree of generalization.

## Training and Capacity Building in Demography

The aspirations for enhancing the contributions of demography to understanding and responding to refugee and forced migration and population displacement through data collection and research rest on human, administrative, and operational resources. Put simply—more demographers must be trained, prepared, and motivated to engage in research on refugees and forced migration; more demographic data and research must be incorporated into operational and administrative processes regarding migrants and internally displaced persons. The Emerging Scholars and Practitioners on Migration Issues (ESPMI) network provides a model, as well as stops and starts, that can inform the development of cohorts of social and formal demographers with expertise in forced and refugee migrations (see chapter 10).

The incorporation of demographic methods of data collection and analysis into registration systems has the added benefit of increasing the administrative capacity of international, national, and local programs of public administration more generally (Hovy 2018; Martin 2018). This benefit applies to the not-for-profit sector and civil society organizations as well. Schmeidl and Hedditch (2018) identify the particular benefit of demographic and population geographic data and analysis in national response to internally displaced population and persons. Scholars and advocates recognize the educational benefit of including women migrants in processes of data collection, analysis, and interpretation in various geographies of displacement and resettlement. There is also an important role of analytic training in enhancing capacity for advocacy on behalf of vulnerable groups of migrants—using scientific data, including population measures, to make a case or promote an appropriate response (McAuliffe 2018; see also chapters 1, 7, 12, and 13).

Finally, professional demography must recognize these opportunities for preparing new generations of population scientists to contribute to the study of refugee and forced migration, and ultimately to respond and act. Graduate education and curricula in the population and social sciences should be reconsidered to include more systematically migration, including forced and irregular migrations, within formal demography, social demography, and population studies. Abbasi-Shavazi and Kraly (2018) state: "training of, and investment in, a new generation of scholars in the study of forced migration will not only lead to the generation of new knowledge, but also to better data collection, increasingly rigorous research methodologies, and more evidence-based interpretation concerning forced migrations at the global and regional levels" (84–5). Ultimately, increased opportunities for professional training in demography will yield more demographic data and research concerning refugee and forced migration.

## Promises to Be Fulfilled: "Projections" of the Demography of Refugee and Forced Migrations

During the final stages of preparing this chapter, the Office of Special Representative of the United Nations Secretary-General for International Migration issued the final draft of the Global Compact for Safe, Orderly and Regular Migration (13 July 2018). Prepared by the co-facilitators to lead the intergovernmental consultations and negotiations during the preparatory process, Ambassadors and Permanent Representatives of Mexico and Switzerland, the final draft presents the guiding principles of the Global Compact, and a "cooperative framework comprising of actionable commitments, implementation, and follow-up and review" (GCM 2018, 4). This document was adopted by member states at the *Intergovernmental Conference to Adopt the Global Compact for Safe, Orderly and Regular Migration*, 10–11 December 2018 in Morocco.

Of the twenty-three objectives to achieve safe, orderly, and regular migration, the first objective is to "collect and utilize accurate and disaggregated data as a basis for evidence-based policies." The Global Compact for Migration specifies the expectations, requirements, and steps to fulfill this general objective for "a robust global evidence base on international migration by improving and investing in the collection, analysis and dissemination of accurate, reliable, comparable data, disaggregated by sex, age and migration status" (GCM 2018, 5). With this statement, the role of the population sciences, social demography, and the broader social sciences is placed in clear and critical relief.

In its final form, the Global Compact for Migration identifies several discrete yet interrelated activities for population and migration analysis and research: develop comparable concepts and statistical measures of dimensions of international migration and mobilities; foster capacity-building within and throughout nations for the analysis of migration processes; develop the means to coordinate, compare, and study international migration and population patterns, trends, and processes; promote the collection of data related to international migration in national censuses and representative surveys; mine and adapt administrative data systems for information on migration; and encourage integration of migration research more generally within national policy development and planning (GCM 2018, 5–6). The Global Compact for Refugees also includes dedicated recommendations addressing the need for data and research concerning the specific category of forced migrations—that is, refugees. Although in much less detail than the Global Compact for Migration, Section 3.3 Data and Evidence outlines the need for harmonized and disaggregated data for solutions, response, and responsibility sharing for refugees (UNCHR 2018, 9).

Demographic data, research, and training provide the analytic and empirical infrastructure for assessing the baseline scale, distribution, and characteristics of international migration—including forced and refugee migration and migrants—in international, national, and regional social and environmental dynamics. Accordingly, the population sciences serve to meet the analytic and evidentiary requirements for the Global Compact for Safe, Orderly and Regular Migration, and its goals for shared responsibilities for refugees. In contemplating long-term goal-setting regarding international migration and crisis migrations and displacement, demographic theory and population modelling hold critical potential for significant analytic contributions to specifying future scenarios of the scale and geography of response and burden-sharing, vulnerabilities, and resiliencies among populations and communities throughout the world.

We have referred to the several "drafts" during the preparatory processes for the Global Compacts for Migration and Refugees; we conclude with reference to an early draft of the chapter prepared by our dear friend and mentor, Charlie Keely, for *Demography of Refugee and Forced Migration*. In reflecting on the relationship between forced migration studies and demography, Charlie offered the following:

> I conclude that the field of forced migration studies will not be helped very much by more detailed parsing of definitions or attempts at neologisms for their particular use. The field will continue to be untidy intellectually. What is required is clarity in research design, operational definition, and measurement techniques. Then perhaps, further advances can be made in theory and explanation. We should not be overly negative. Progress has been made in migration studies. The incorporation of migration into population projection analysis has taught us new things and changes political discussion about immigration, for example. The application of the forced migration label has been useful to opening up discussion to issues of State action, coerced migration and coerced return, and so on. Much of this has had more impact on policy than on demography. But demography continues to have its place in understanding this particular aspect of human behaviour

and for understanding its causes and consequences, both demographically and for societies (Keely 2012, 25).

As usual Charlie was correct. Demography has its place in the study of refugee and forced migrations. We encourage, with our hearts and minds, professional population scientists to use the theoretical and empirical assets of demography to enlighten, reveal, and inform knowledge creation and policy development, and to engage and meet the challenges of international governance concerning human migration—and hence "for societies."

## Notes

1   The United States of America withdrew its participation in the New York Declaration on 3 December 2017.

2   https://iussp.org/en/panel/demography-refugee-and-forced-migration.

## References

Abbasi-Shavazi, Mohammad Jalal, and Ellen Percy Kraly. 2018a. "Asia's Under-Researched Forced and Refugee Migration?" *Asian Population Studies* 14, no. 3: 229–31. DOI:10.1080/17441730.2018.1483472

Abbasi-Shavazi, Mohammad Jalal, and Ellen Percy Kraly. 2018b. "Comparative Demographic Analysis of Forced and Refugee Migrations: An Illustrative Note." In *Demography of Refugee and Forced Migration*, edited by Graeme Hugo, Mohammad Jalal Abbasi-Shavazi, and Ellen Percy Kraly, 57–86. The Netherlands: Springer.

Abbasi-Shavazi, Mohammad Jalal, Hossein Mahmoudian, and Rasoul Sadeghi. 2018. "Family Dynamics in the Context of Forced Migration." In *Demography of Refugee and Forced Migration*, edited by Graeme Hugo, Mohammad Jalal Abbasi-Shavazi, and Ellen Percy Kraly, 155–74. The Netherlands: Springer.

Adamo, Susana B. 2018. "Environmentally Related International Displacement: Following in Graeme Hugo's Footsteps." In *Demography of Refugee and Forced Migration*, edited by Graeme Hugo, Mohammad Jalal Abbasi-Shavazi, and Ellen Percy Kraly, 201–16. The Netherlands: Springer.

Agadjanian, Victor. 2018. "Interrelationships of Forced Migration, Fertility and Reproductive Health." In *Demography of Refugee and Forced Migration*, edited by Graeme Hugo, Mohammad Jalal Abbasi-Shavazi, and Ellen Percy Kraly, 113–24. The Netherlands: Springer.

Asher, Jana, David Banks, and Fritz Scheuren, eds. 2008. *Statistical Methods for Human Rights*. New York: Springer.

Aleinikoff, T. Alexander, and Susan Martin. 2018. "Making the Global Compacts Work: What Future for Refugees and Migrants?" Zolberg Institute on Migration and Mobility, New School for Social Research and Kaldor Centre for International Refugee Law, University of New South Wales, Policy Brief no. 6. April.

Global Compact on Migration. 2018. "Global Compact for Safe, Orderly and Regular Migration: Zero Draft." Permanent Mission of Mexico to the United Nations and Permanent Mission of Switzerland to the United Nations, New York, 5 Feb 2018.

Gordon, L. W. 1993. "The Demography of Refugees." Paper presented at the Annual Meeting of the Population Association of American, Cincinnati, OH, 1 Apr 1993.

Guterres, A. 2018. "Migration Can Benefit the World: This is How We at the UN Plan to Help." *Guardian*, 11 Jan 2018. https://www.theguardian.com/commentisfree/2018/jan/11/migration-benefit-world-un-global-compact.

Hovy, Bela. 2018. "Registration: A Sine Qua Non for Refugee Protection." In *Demography of Refugee and Forced Migration*, edited by Graeme Hugo, Mohammad Jalal Abbasi-Shavazi, and Ellen Percy Kraly, 39–55. The Netherlands: Springer.

Hugo, Graeme, Mohammad Jalal Abbasi-Shavazi, and Ellen Percy Kraly. 2018. *The Demography of Refugee and Forced Migration*. The Netherlands: Springer.

Hugo, Graeme, Mohammad Jalal Abbasi-Shavazi, and Ellen Percy Kraly. 2018. "Introduction: Advancing the Demography of Forced Migration and Refugees." In *Demography of Refugee and Forced Migration*, edited by Graeme Hugo, Mohammad Jalal Abbasi-Shavazi, and Ellen Percy Kraly, 1–17. The Netherlands: Springer.

Huyck, Earl E., and Leon F. Bouvier. 1983. "The Demography of Refugees." *Annals of the American Academy of Political and Social Science* 467, no. 1: 39–61.

Keely, Charles B. 2012. "The Concept of Forced Migration." Unpublished manuscript.

Keely, Charles B., and Ellen Percy Kraly. 2018. "Concepts of Refugee and Forced Migration: Considerations for Demographic Analysis." In *Demography of Refugee and Forced Migration*, edited by Graeme Hugo, Mohammad Jalal Abbasi-Shavazi, and Ellen Percy Kraly, 21–37. The Netherlands: Springer.

Koser, Khalid. 2018. "Migration and Security: Exploding the Myths and Understanding the Realities." In *Demography of Refugee and Forced Migration*, edited by Graeme Hugo, Mohammad Jalal Abbasi-Shavazi, and Ellen Percy Kraly, 235–49. The Netherlands: Springer.

Kraly, Ellen Percy. 2018. "Behind and Beyond Disaggregation by Sex: Forced Migration, Gender and the Place of Demography." In *Demography of Refugee and Forced Migration*, edited by Graeme Hugo, Mohammad Jalal Abbasi-Shavazi, and Ellen Percy Kraly, 125–53. The Netherlands: Springer.

Kraly, Ellen Percy. 2018. *International Migration: Initiatives and Goals*. Paper prepared for the United Nations Expert Group Meeting for the Review and Appraisal of the Programme of Action of the International Conference on Population and Development and Its Contribution to the Follow-up and Review of the 2030 Agenda for Sustainable Development. Population Division, Department of Economic and Social Affairs, United Nations Secretariat New York, 1–2 November 2018.

Kraly, Ellen Percy, and Mohammad Jalal Abbasi-Shavazi. 2018. "Epilogue: Advancing Demographic Analysis of Refugee and Forced Migration." In *Demography of Refugee and Forced Migration*, edited by Graeme Hugo, Mohammad Jalal Abbasi-Shavazi, and Ellen Percy Kraly, 305–7. The Netherlands: Springer.

Kunz, Egon F. 1981. "Exile and Resettlement: Refugee Theory." *International Migration Review* 15: 42–51.

———. 1973. "The Refugee in Flight: Kinetic Models and Forms of Displacement." *International Migration Review* 7, no. 2: 125–46.

Martin, Susan F. 2018. "Forced Migration and Refugee Policy." In *Demography of Refugee and Forced Migration*, edited by Graeme Hugo, Mohammad Jalal Abbasi-Shavazi, and Ellen Percy Kraly, 271–303. The Netherlands: Springer.

McAuliffe, Marie. 2018. "The Nexus between Forced and Irregular Migration: Insights from Demography." In *Demography of Refugee and Forced Migration*, edited by Graeme Hugo, Mohammad Jalal Abbasi-Shavazi, and Ellen Percy Kraly, 217–32. The Netherlands: Springer.

Mohammadi, Abdullah, Mohammad Jalal Abbasi-Shavazi, and Rasoul Sadeghi. 2018. "Return to Home: Reintegration and Sustainability of Return to Post-conflict Contexts." In *Demography of Refugee and Forced Migration*, edited by Graeme Hugo, Mohammad Jalal Abbasi-Shavazi, and Ellen Percy Kraly, 251–70. The Netherlands: Springer.

Reed, Holly E., Mara Getz Sheftel, and Arash Behazin. 2018. "Forced Migration and Patterns of Mortality and Morbidity." In *Demography of Refugee and Forced Migration*, edited by Graeme Hugo, Mohammad Jalal Abbasi-Shavazi, and Ellen Percy Kraly, 89–112. The Netherlands: Springer.

Reed, Holly, John Haaga, and Charles Keely. 1998. *The Demography of Forced Migration: Summary of a Workshop*. Washington, DC: National Academy Press.

Reed, Holly, and Charles Keely. 2001. "Forced Migration and Mortality: Roundtable on the Demography of Forced Migration." Committee on Population. Washington, DC: National Academy Press.

Schmeidl, Susanne, and Kaitlyn Hedditch. 2018. "Changing Patterns of Internal Displacement: The Art of Figure Skating." In *Demography of Refugee and Forced Migration*, edited by Graeme Hugo, Mohammad Jalal Abbasi-Shavazi, and Ellen Percy Kraly, 177–99. The Netherlands: Springer.

United Nations Development Programme (UNDP). 2009. *Human Development Report 2009: Overcoming Barriers—Human Mobility and Development.* New York: Palgrave Macmillan.

United Nations General Assembly (UNGA). 2017. "Report of the Special Representative of the Secretary-General on Migration." Seventy-first session 13 and 117 of the Provisional Agenda on Globalization and Interdependence. A/71/728. New York: UNGA.

———. 2016. "In Safety and Dignity: Addressing Large Movements of Refugees and Migrants." Report of the Secretary General. A/70/59. New York: UNGA.

———. 2000. "Resolution Adopted by the General Assembly: United Nations Millennium Declaration." A/RES/55/2. New York: UNGA.

United High Commissioner for Refugees (UNHCR). 2018. "The Global Compact on Refugees."

United Nations Secretary-General (UNSG). 2018. "Informal Briefing on the Forthcoming Secretary-General's Report 'Making Migration Work for All.'" Office of the Special Representative of the Secretary-General for International Migration, 11 Jan 2018.

# Disseminating Knowledge in the Digital Age: The Case of the Refugee Research Network

*William J. Payne and Michele Millard*

## Introduction

Too often, moments that propel the world towards positive social change are marked by horror. One such moment was the death of Alan Kurdi, a toddler born in Syria amidst a brutal war who, together with his mother and brother, drowned on 2 September 2015 as they attempted to cross a four-kilometre stretch of the Aegean Sea between Turkey and the Greek island of Kos. A photograph taken that day by Turkish press photographer Nilüfer Demir challenged the global polity to pay attention to this loss of life. The dissemination of that image through social media ensured that millions were reminded of the cost of war. In the photograph, Alan appears strangely peaceful, and only the various associated captions and commentaries inform us that the little boy had not survived the crossing. The photojournalist later commented, "I hope that my picture can contribute to changing the way we look at immigration" (Küpeli 2015). Certainly, what we do with such moments determines the dimensions of our collective humanity (see chapter 4).

Scholars note that—at least in the months following its dissemination—this photo shifted the language describing those seeking asylum from "migrant" to "refugee" (Aiken et al. 2017). Aiken et al. (2017, 3, 5) determined that the effectiveness of Demir's image—why it went viral—resulted from its "ideal representation of the innocent, irreproachable body worthy of grief," and because "the positioning of [Alan Kurdi's] body masks a violence done, but now unseen." These authors conclude that Twitter allowed for the global reach that this image achieved because it was picked up early on by specific users with large followings. However, they also argue that this global reach failed to translate into real improvement for refugees because the resultant media attention focused as much on the phenomenon of the circulating image as on the geopolitical events that led to the child's death.

Given this dismal analysis of the impact of social media in a time of crisis, are there ways we can employ these tools to effect real change? This chapter provides a detailed analysis of the Refugee Research Network's (RRN) experience with social media to mobilize research and information concerning refugee and forced migration issues. Our goal is to show how that communication and online networking strategy is working.

## The RRN, Knowledge Mobilization, and Social Media

From its beginning, the RRN has used social media as a tool to disseminate knowledge about refugee and forced migration issues (also see chapters 6, 7, and 10). This work has responded to the RRN's guiding principles, that knowledge should be accessible, open source and open access, and not caught behind academic firewalls (see the introduction). The RRN sees knowledge dissemination through the conceptual framework of Knowledge Mobilization (KMb), defined as "the process of connecting academic . . . research . . . to non-academic decision-makers so that . . . research informs decisions about public policy and professional practice" (Phipps et al. 2012, 180; see also chapter 7). The concept of KMb, popularized by Canada's Social Sciences and Humanities Research Council (SSHRC), provides an emerging frame for the multi-dimensional interactions between society and university-based researchers that can foster the social innovations we need to address problems such as climate change, poverty, forced migration, and so on (Cooper 2014; Phipps et al. 2012). Phipps et

WILLIAM J. PAYNE AND MICHELE MILLARD

al. (2012) emphasize the need to create a "culture of research" rooted in these networked interactions that connects decision-makers to existing and emerging knowledge and leads to solutions to the difficult challenges of our time (see also chapters 3, 6, 10, and 13).

Bennet and Bennet (2007) emphasize that this process is more than just the transfer of knowledge and that KMb creates value through bringing together knowledge, people, and action such that both the creation and the use of knowledge are embedded in communities and organizations (see also chapter 10). Phipps et al. (2012) emphasize that KMb can be thought of as a program comprising several specific processes, that collaboration and learning are key to this program in what is increasingly an uncertain world, and that KMb helps decision-makers in society approach "wicked problems" using an evidence-based approach.

The concept of KMb has emerged in a context in which funders consider universities through the lens of "social relevance" and in which researchers face an increased expectation that they produce knowledge that is seen as "useful" to society (Naidorf 2014). In this register, KMb is "a complex and emergent process that focuses on making what is known ready for value-producing action" (Naidorf 2014, 15). At the same time, scholars and practitioners have amplified their call for evidence-based policy and practice. In this context, "knowledge brokers" and "research brokering organizations" are poised to provide a crucial role in the reinforcement of the relationship between university-based researchers and those contexts where research can have concrete impact (Cooper 2015; Naidorf 2014). At a time when "the field of KMb . . . is still in its infancy" (Cooper 2015, 15), the RRN seeks to play this brokering role as well as to facilitate relationships and communication among researchers from different parts of the world.

In a preliminary study of the functioning of the RRN conducted in 2009, participants in the network identified KMb as a key long-term benefit of their involvement, noting that the "potential impact included influencing policy, increasing the public's awareness of refugees and forced migration issues, and developing long-term relationships with NGOs and INGOs" (Hynie et al. 2014, 10). However, RRN participants also said that communication problems, because of the "tyranny of distance" and other challenges had limited the impact of the network and that "the benefits [of their involvement] needed to be more tangible and relevant to their own agendas" (Hynie et al. 2014, 11). A redoubled focus on KMb through social media is one way that the RRN has sought to address the issues raised in the evaluation. Over the last ten years, the RRN has gained insight into the opportunities and limitations of social media as a forum for engagement within and between multiple sectors.

## Studying Social Media

Social media has fundamentally changed how we create, manage, and share information and knowledge and is itself rapidly evolving. According to Cooper (2015, 8), "KMb efforts . . . are increasingly mediated through online platforms such as websites and online communities as well as through social media outlets such as Twitter and Facebook." A key element of the RRN has been its use of online tools, including a website and a suite of social media platforms (Facebook, YouTube, Twitter, and listservs), to connect with different audiences, including academics, practitioners, policy actors, and refugees themselves (see also chapter 10).

"Social media" has been succinctly defined as "Internet services where the online content is generated by the users of the service" and include tools for communication, collaboration, and sharing of multimedia that have proven useful in every step of the research process including identification, creation, quality assurance, and dissemination of knowledge (Cann et al. 2011, 7). These tools stimulate opinion-sharing and information exchange and include Internet-based applications that allow for the production and circulation of user-generated content (Go and You 2016).

Scholars note that social media also provide people with limited technical knowledge the opportunity of being involved as consumers or even producers of content and as such it has great potential for social and cultural transformation (Panagiotopoulos 2012). While the academic literature on the use of social media is particularly focused on its use in the marketplace, there is a burgeoning interest in the use of social media by non-profits to communicate and build relationships with their publics (Campbell et al. 2014; Lim and Lee-Won 2017), and for activism (Dekker and Engbersen 2012; Panagiotopoulos 2012).

In research concerning social media as part of social justice campaigning, Paek et al. (2013) found that frequency of social media use is related to the civic/political participation of the users and leads to a sense of civic

WILLIAM J. PAYNE AND MICHELE MILLARD

mindedness and inspiration to taking concrete action. However, they also found that the connection between social media use and the desired behavioural outcomes is weak, and conclude that "social media may be a long tail strategy" that is more likely to be successful across larger geographical areas and over longer time periods (Paek et al. 2013, 1578). In a recent meta-analytic study that reviewed the findings of more than a hundred empirical studies about social media, the authors found a positive relationship between social media use and various forms of citizen engagement including constructive impact on levels of social capital, civic engagement, and political participation. Skoric et al. (2016, 1833) conclude that "the Internet could offer new opportunities for citizen networking and open up new venues for political expression, potentially activating those previously disengaged citizens." The rapid growth in social media use coupled with evidence of a linkage between social media and social change underline the importance of these tools in our day (see also chapter 6).

Different social media platforms play distinct roles and Facebook and Twitter are particularly associated with helping behaviour (Paek et al. 2013). Nah and Saxton (2013, 308) found that Facebook and Twitter are "in some ways different tools that can be used for different purposes, and may as a result require different configurations of organizational resources, governance characteristics, and contextual and environmental factors in order to implement and maintain." Researchers have also shown that social media tools vary based on the degree of self-disclosure they require, the level of social presentation they allow, and the extent to which they facilitate two-way symmetrical communications (Go and You 2016).

## Social Media, Scholars, and KMb

According to Phipps et al. (2012, 183), "social media has the potential to support knowledge mobilization and research-based relationships." There is also compelling, if preliminary, evidence that social media promotion of publications, especially when combined with open access to that research, can substantially impact its dissemination. For example, while on maternity leave, Melissa Terras (2012) uploaded open access versions of her own peer-reviewed articles to her home institution's repository, tweeted about each item, and then analyzed the resultant downloading patterns. She saw a significant increase in interest in her research as a result of this Twitter dissemination, as much as an elevenfold increase based on the results of her limited experiment.

However, in a recent investigation of the actual use of social media for KMb, Cooper (2014) found that less than a third of research brokering organizations (RBOs) in Canada used social media. Furthermore, those who did use Facebook and Twitter had only small networks. And while the scale of social media usage and speed of uptake of these tools across the globe suggests the possibility of great potential for their application to KMb, this author also found that much of the social media activity of RBOs to date is not actually focused on mobilizing research knowledge. Consequently, Cooper (2014, 17) insists that "social media must be embedded in larger processes in order to promote higher levels of activity and substantial interaction."

The concept of "research impact" has emerged as a key consideration in the formulation of research projects, though the term itself has come under some scrutiny. For example, Chubb and Watermeyer (2016b) wrote that "academics applying for research funding have expressed their concern at feeling the need to exaggerate and embellish the possible future impact of their work." As the governing rationality of neoliberalism seeks to transform us into self-investing entrepreneurs seeking to increase the value of our "human capital," other measures of quality in universities and research institutions are replaced with, "metrics oriented entirely to return on investment" (Brown 2015, 23). Recent investigation shows that researchers see their scholarly integrity at risk when they are compelled to "sell . . . their research ideas, or . . . the nonacademic impact of these, to research funders" (Chubb and Watermeyer 2016a, 1). Yet those of us engaged with research—and perhaps with a particular urgency when that research relates to human suffering—do nevertheless want our work to make a difference, to matter, in some small way to make the world a better place. The RRN's experience is that social media can be part of this "making a difference."

## Findings, Analysis, and Discussion

The authors of this paper have had direct involvement with the social media presence of the RRN for between two and eleven years. This critical reflection of our experiences builds on the earlier evaluation of the RRN

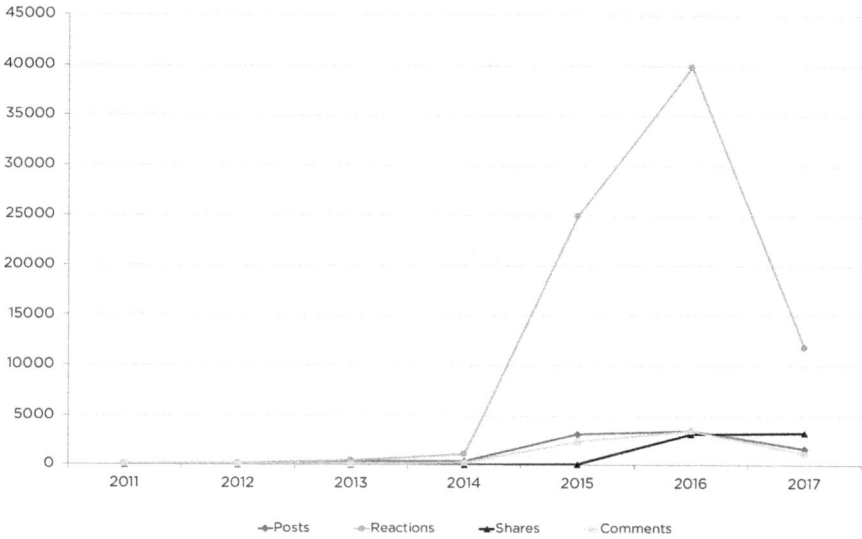

**FIGURE 9.1**
RRN Facebook Group Activity from 6 January 2011 to 29 June 2017. Source: https://
sociograph.io.

and draws on our analysis of our own experience with the RRN social media tools. In addition to our own scrutiny of the use of these social media
tools, we also rely on the free analytics generated by Sociograph.io that
provides a graphic and numerical account of the RRN Facebook group's
activity over time.[1]

In this section, we provide a concise description of the RRN's application of a range of social media tools (including Facebook, Twitter, You-
Tube, and webinars) including how they have been put to use. We stress:
the need to develop an engaged audience prior to significant "trigger"
moments when accelerated social change may be possible, the feedback
relationship between an engaged audience and quality postings, and finally the key roles of moderator and of an associated quality website to
ensure the effectiveness of social media tools. We also provide some preliminary thoughts on the impact of social media in terms of the mobilization of knowledge in the field of refugees and forced migration. Finally, we

comment on what can be known from the RRN's experience regarding the opportunities and limitations of social media as a forum for engagement within and between various constituencies and in particular for academics who seek to make their research accessible and available to all who might benefit from it.

## Reach of the RRN Facebook Group

As of 26 October 2018, the RRN's FB group had 38,813 members. It is an "open" group, which means that anyone can see the group, its members, and their posts, though a staff person of the RRN also moderates it (the RRN's Methodology & Production of Knowledge in Forced Migration Contexts cluster also has its own FB group; see chapter 13). Though the original purpose of the FB group was to mobilize and sustain a Canadian and international network of researchers and research centres committed to the study of refugee and forced migration issues and to finding solutions to the plight of refugees, it has evolved into a loosely connected, much broader network of people interested in these issues through the sharing of information and has also been used as a forum for information exchanges such as refugees looking for directions and advice about safe routes to travel and students looking for educational and practice experiences. In addition to the postings by members of the group, as part of the RRN's communications strategy two staff members also regularly scan sources of relevant information and post resources on the FB group.

There was slow but steady growth from its 2009 FB beginning, but then something started to happen in the last third of 2014 that resulted in significantly higher activity over subsequent months. We suspect that the spike in interest was in response to the increased focus on refugee issues in the news, particularly stories about refugees in boats crossing the Mediterranean (including the tragedy of Alan Kurdi and his family). It may also be that the internal network started working, in the sense that an individual would sign up to be a group member and then their friends would see something of interest and subsequently joined. The RRN connected with other refugee-focused FB groups and was involved in establishing FB groups for the International Association for the Study of Forced Migration (IASFM) and the Canadian Association for Refugee and Forced Migration Studies (CARFMS), so there was some intermingling of the various FB groups, contributing to the greater global reach of the RRN Group (see

WILLIAM J. PAYNE AND MICHELE MILLARD

also chapter 10). The result of this momentum was exponential growth in the membership of the group between 2015 and 2017 such that for a time it was attracting about a thousand new members per month. It has since levelled off to more modest yet steady growth.

## Users of the RRN Facebook Group

In the beginning, the membership of the RRN FB group was primarily North American, though the rapid increase in members mentioned above coincided with a significant globalization of the membership as well, especially from the Middle East. While nearly half of the members use English as their primary language on their own FB pages (43 per cent), about the same number use a different primary language (44 per cent), most notably Arabic, Amharic, Swahili, and Bengali (note that 11 per cent had no posts at all).[2] And while most posts to the RRN FB group are still in English, some people post in other languages, including German, Swedish, Arabic, and Rohingya among others.

To gain additional insight into the range of people joining the RRN Facebook group, we did an analysis of a sample of the group's members by looking at the FB profiles of one hundred people who joined on 16–17 March 2016 and another hundred people who joined on 4–9 July 2017. The results of this analysis indicate that the increased global reach of this FB group continues: the two hundred new members surveyed in two different timeframes live in thirty-six different countries including, in addition to North America and Australia, twelve European countries, ten sub-Saharan African countries, seven countries from the Middle East, and four countries from South Asia. The data also suggest a trend towards a transnational membership (i.e., people who have lived in more than one country), with particular interest in the group by those with university-level education and a preponderance of members who are involved either through employment or volunteer activities in work focused on refugees and migrants.

The RRN FB group moderator, also one of the authors of this chapter, has identified a "90/10 rule" in that most people receive and read content but do not actually post. Over time though, we have also seen a greater use of the "like" button and some more substantive comments being made regarding posts. And while the growth of the RRN FB group may be part of a feedback loop such that people who have something they want to disseminate may be more likely to post on the RRN FB group because of its large audience, a key issue that likely impacts the decision to post here is the quality of the posts that members receive.

There is a normative, even political, function to the RRN FB group. The RRN is about research and intellectual exploration but it is key to remember that the particular grounding and framing of the project is focused on improving the lives of those in forced migration or refugee situations. The group provides a credible venue where research and information can be disseminated, where new scholars can talk to each other and ask for information and advice, and where refugees themselves can gain insight about what is happening at the global level, what policies are in place, and where the movements of people are happening. A few members are clearly communication officers for their respective institutions so there are many postings regarding employment opportunities and educational programs related to forced migration. Other members regularly post information to shine light on under-examined issues or issues that have dropped off the mainstream media radar. With the groundswell of volunteerism in Europe, people are posting key practical information including guides regarding how to navigate the asylum system, tools for asylum seekers who are travelling, and free online language courses among other items. There is also an emerging group of people using the FB group to announce new relevant journal articles, books, and other publications.

While individual members may be focused on particular issues, the collective effort results in an FB group that helps people identify the global phenomenon behind the myriad particulars and to think about the deep-rooted causes and systemic issues that need to be addressed. For example, many posters have added to the conversation regarding how forced migration from Syria and Iraq is tied to climate change, that severe drought during the first decade of this century led to many farmers moving to the cities, thus aggravating social tensions (Kelley et al. 2015). Members respond to particular posts in a variety of ways, including like/ dislike buttons, comments, and sharing posts with their own networks. These tools provide people with a way to respond emotionally to terrible stories such as a shocking account of organ harvesting among Somali forced migrants.

Infographics and memes tend to generate high levels of response because these formats communicate a great deal of substance in a simple image or short video. For example, one meme that said "I'm more afraid of the people who are afraid of refugees than I am of refugees" received a great deal of response. Two hundred and seventy-five people "liked" it and many people also added comments. Stories about the poor behaviour of governments in relation to asylum access and refugee resettlement also generate a great deal of interest and activity. As such, the RRN FB page is contributing to the public discourse. We have seen some indication that academics are starting to recognize the potential for using the RRN FB group as a venue for dissemination of relevant research by sending a link to an open-access version of a journal article or other published research (for example on Academia.edu). Furthermore, people occasionally use the FB group to request specific articles they do not have direct access to because of paywalls, something that is especially relevant in the global south.

Sometimes, refugees themselves post short messages showing fear and anxiety. "I am stuck here . . . We live in this refugee camp and we are desperate, so please help us." Often, there is nothing the RRN can do beyond providing the platform for others to respond, though in a few cases we have managed to connect people in crisis with a local NGO. Occasionally, people ask how to get to a particular country and other members of the group are able to suggest where they might find useful information sources or an NGO that might be able to offer assistance.

While the spikes in activity on the RRN FB group (see Figure 9.1 above) seem to be associated temporally with real-life events, it is notable that the actual number of posts only shows a modest increase—what really changed is the amount of engagement with posted material by people who "like" or comment on a post. For example, during a 24-hour period in July 2017, several items attracted the attention of a segment of the FB group including video about a UNHCR program for economic development for refugees that elicited several shares, a posting for a new IOM program in a refugee camp in Iraq (six "wows"), an announcement about funding for a scholarship for someone to study activism in response to the European refugee crisis (22 "likes") and a link to a new online service called "emergencybnb" designed to connect refugees with potential hosts (22 "shares"). These spikes of activity have likely led to notable increases in people joining the group, which perhaps also reflects the increased global use of social media.

## Role of Moderator of Facebook Group

While geopolitical shifts likely contributed to the increased participation in the RRN FB group over time, institutional support and the particular commitment of specific people has been key to the success of the group. Though the group is open, the RRN does provide oversight to membership and participation in the group. As part of the writing of this paper, the moderator (one of the authors) systematized the guidelines used to moderate the group, both in terms of accepting posts and in excluding individuals from membership as follows:

Dos

1.  Members are free to post content about new research, papers, publications, conferences, workshops, NGO reports, best practices, videos, university programs in forced migration studies, scholarship, internship and job opportunities, and anything else you can think of that is a form of knowledge in refugee and forced migration studies.

2.  Everyone is free to ask questions and carry on discussions around refugee/forced migration issues, programs, practices.

3.  Content must be broadly relevant to refugee and forced migration issues, and overall supportive of refugees. Policies, attitudes, and practices can be critiqued, but not the existence of refugees (i.e., identifying them as bogus) and their right to seek asylum, as well as to enjoy human, civil, social, economic, and political rights.

4.  If posting about non-refugee specific topics (i.e., climate change, gender, employment, migration, human rights), the content should overlap with refugee and forced migration issues. For example, a posting about human rights issues is not sufficient—there should be a connection to refugees and forced migration.

5. Certain campaigns and activities that are strictly advocacy around programs and services are allowed, but on very limited terms—it's not really relevant to the knowledge sharing focus of the group.

Don'ts

1. Advertising commercial services, self-promotion, or posting otherwise inappropriate content (porn, hate, xenophobia) will not be approved.

2. Posting exploitative "death porn"—e.g., raw footage or photos of victims of violence is often put forth without attribution or context and can violate the privacy of the victims and their families. Please refrain.

3. Posting videos or other types of content without some sort of explanation or context is not informative. If you link to a story or video, please make sure there is some sort of explanation or context in the description if the link doesn't have one or if there's no preview.

4. Posting personal funding campaigns (e.g., someone who wants to volunteer in a camp and is raising funding for their travel, or campaigns for individual refugees) is not permitted.

The role of the moderator has been key to the success of this FB group. The moderation of the FB group is a loose form of curation in which the moderator uses the "3-second rule": if it is not quickly clear to the moderator that the post has something to do with human rights, forced displacement, migration and refugee issues, or the human rights of people in danger of displacement, it is not approved. Overall, the moderation seeks to ensure that the content of the FB group reflects the complexity of the relevant issues.

In addition to the vetting role described above, the moderator also posts relevant material, provides commentary on posted material, and responds to the posts and comments of others. The institutional capacity and engagement provided by the moderator, a staff person at the Centre for Refugee Studies, has been key, and the success of the RRN FB group is closely tied to the fact that the moderator makes time to be on the group as part of their daily routine. For the duration of the project, the RRN Co-ordinator has held this role as part of their assigned duties, a time frame that corresponds with the increased level of activity in the group, likely because members are encouraged through this steady institutional engagement. It is essential that an FB group like this be moderated. If a time comes when resources are no longer available to include this role as part of the responsibilities of a staff member, the RRN would need to develop a volunteer moderation role, perhaps shared by several people, though we are skeptical that the quality of the FB group would be maintained without institutional support.

## RRN's Experience with Twitter

Paek et al. (2013) comment that different social media platforms play distinct roles, even in relation to the same campaign or project. Perhaps significant, those who participate in an FB group are called "members" while those who subscribe to a particular Twitter feed are called "followers." Early on, the RRN identified that organizations and individuals involved with forced migration and refugee issues in their professional lives are especially oriented towards using Twitter as a source of relevant information. As the most common platform for microblogging, the RRN uses Twitter to provide short and concise pieces of information, usually with links to items directly related to academic research in the area of forced migration. As of 26 October 2018, the RRN Twitter feed has 3,312 followers, much smaller than the FB group but still significant (for other uses of Twitter in the RRN, see chapters 6 and 10). While the FB group experienced exponential growth during certain periods, subscription to the RRN Twitter account has also grown at a steady pace over the past two years since a graduate student was assigned the duty of regularly posting items to the Twitter feed.

On two occasions (10 May 2016 and 11 July 2017), we conducted an analysis of the profiles of the most recent followers of the RRN Twitter feed. The results showed that nearly two-thirds of the users are individuals and almost another third are organizations or businesses (9 per cent of profiles did not provide the relevant information). Of those profiles for individuals that provided information regarding employment or profession (about half of this subset of profiles), many indicated a connection to academia and/or to work in the area of refugees and forced migration. The geographical spread of the RRN's Twitter followers is concentrated in the UK and Europe (more than a third of followers) and in North America (nearly a fifth of followers), though it seems to be expanding to other parts of the world over time, particularly to Africa.

In their research of the use of Twitter by non-profits, Nah and Saxton (2013) analyzed the tweets posted by one hundred large U.S. organizations over a one-month period based on the primary purpose of the tweets. They identified that these organizations use Twitter for three primary purposes: informational, organizational promotion, and dialogic (i.e., relationship building). Early on, the RRN made the decision to use Twitter only for informational purposes, specifically for the sharing of academic/research related information in the area of forced migration. Our analysis of the followers of the RRN Twitter feed supports our sense that this information is primarily of interest to academics, professionals, and organizations connected to refugee and forced migration issues.

As with Facebook, regular attention to Twitter is crucial to its success. Unlike the Facebook group, only those few people (staff and key graduate students) identified as administrators are able to post items, and it is especially crucial that those who take on this role have the skills to identify relevant material that will be of interest to the RRN Twitter followers and that the organization has sufficient capacity to ensure that this task is completed on a regular basis. Twitter is especially effective in conjunction with a high-quality organizational website that functions as the permanent repository for items that are promoted using the Twitter feed, something we discuss further below.

## YouTube, Listservs, and Webinars

As part of a KMb strategy using social media, the RRN has also made use of YouTube, listservs, and online discussions. For example, the RRN YouTube channel contains several hundred videos. With adequate resources and infrastructure, video is an effective way to mobilize research. The RRN is connected to several listservs including the news list of the Centre for Refugee Studies (CRS) as well as the listservs of CARFMS, IASFM, and the Canadian Council for Refugees (CCR). Each listserv was established with specific criteria regarding its purpose and the sort of material that members should distribute. We estimate the combined reach of these listservs as approximately 10,000 users—a significant number for the mobilization of research, especially in conjunction with the FB group and the Twitter feed. While not always considered a form of social media, listservs do fit the definition of Cann et al. (2011) as an Internet service in which the users generate content.

## RRN Website and Associated Networks

Most social media tools are by nature ephemeral. Tools such as Facebook and Twitter provide feeds for information, communication, and discussion in real time, though neither is especially well designed to function as repositories of materials for later use. Therefore, an organizational website with a searchable database is essential for the storage and organization of materials that are mobilized through social media. Furthermore, well developed Facebook groups and Twitter feeds are themselves excellent sources of materials that can either be uploaded or linked to the website. The RRN originally envisioned its website as a standalone hub, and it has only been through the experience of the past few years that we have recognized how important it is to see the website in a dynamic relationship with the communication tools of social media. And while the RRN did commit significant resources to the development of a website from the beginning, the site was impacted by major technical challenges that have taken time and resources to surmount.[3] We argue that the process of KMb using social media requires the thorough integration of a highly functional website. Given that the funding that has supported the RRN has ended, we are working with institutional partners to ensure that the now functioning RRN website will continue to be supported as an online research clearinghouse. As well, the Emerging Scholars and Practitioners on Migration Issues (ESPMI) Network set up through the RRN has developed its own effective website and social media presence that complement the work discussed in this paper, as do the activities of the various institutes and centres that have been part of the RRN (see chapter 10).

# Conclusion

This chapter has discussed key learnings of the RRN in relation to "doing" KMb by way of social media: it takes time and effort to build credibility and develop a social media audience; you need to be prepared with effective tools when particular trigger events take place; there is a feedback relationship between the development of a social media audience and the mobilization of quality material; and, the use of social media tools should be integrated with a solid website. As such, we have identified key opportunities and limitations of social media as a tool for the mobilization of knowledge related to forced migration and as a form of engagement within and between the multiple sectors that are involved, including academics, practitioners, policy actors, and refugees themselves.

While social media is often rather shallow and broad, it is nevertheless a useful tool for engagement and can be harnessed to bring people together in other venues for sustained, thoughtful discussion and discourse. Social media is important because it creates a community of likeminded individuals who actually do get to know each other. It also gives opportunities for experts to engage with members of the public or refugees themselves, even if it is at a superficial level. Furthermore, it demonstrates that refugees themselves can be heard. Therefore, it is imperative that academics incorporate social media as part of their dissemination program and activities if they want their work to have impact beyond specialized audiences.

## Notes

1  See sociograph.io.

2  The language of the member's most recent post on their own FB page was used as a proxy for their primary posting language.

3  Hindsight taught us that the open source, open access website platform we initially chose was not designed for the complex databases we wanted to include. Also, the university that hosts the RRN did not have the capacity to support the website platform's technical needs.

# References

Aiken, Joshua, Hannes Einsporn, Monica Greco, Rachel Landry, and Angela Navarro Fusillo. 2017. "#AlanKurdi: Presentation and Dissemination of Images of Suffering on Twitter." Working Paper Series of the Refugee Studies Centre, University of Oxford, Oxford.

Bennet, David, and Alex Bennet. 2007. *Knowledge Mobilization in the Social Sciences and Humanities: Moving from Research to Action.* Marlinton, WV: MQI Press.

Brown, Wendy. 2015. *Undoing the Demos: Neoliberalism's Stealth Revolution.* Brooklyn, NY: Zone Books.

Campbell, David A., Kristina T. Lambright, and Christopher J. Wells. 2014. "Looking for Friends, Fans, and Followers? Social Media Use in Public and Nonprofit Human Services." *Public Administration Review* 74, no. 5: 655–63.

Cann, Alan, Konstantia Dimitriou, and Tristram Hooley. 2011. *Social Media: A Guide for Researchers.* London: Research Information Network.

Chubb, Jennifer, and Richard Watermeyer. 2016a. "Artifice or Integrity in the Marketization of Research Impact? Investigating the Moral Economy of (Pathway to) Impact Statements within Research Funding Proposals in the UK and Australia." *Studies in Higher Education* 42, no. 12: 2360–72.

Chubb, Jennifer, and Richard Watermeyer. 2016b. "Academics Admit Feeling Pressure to Embellish Possible Impact of Research." *Conversation*, 16 Mar. http://theconversation.com/academics-admit-feeling-pressure-to-embellish-possible-impact-of-research-56059.

Cooper, Amanda. 2014. "The Use of Online Strategies and Social Media for ResearchDissemination in Education." *Education Policy Analysis Archives* 22, no. 88: 2–27.

Cooper, Amanda. 2015. "A Tool to Assess and Compare Knowledge Mobilization Efforts of Faculties of Education, Research Brokering Organizations, Ministries of Education, and School Districts." *Brock Education Journal* 25, no. 1: 5–18.

Dekker, Rianne, and Godfried Engbersen. 2012. "How Social Media Transform Migrant Networks and Facilitate Migration." The International Migration Institute Working Paper Series No. 64. https://www.imi-n.org/publications/wp-64-12.

Go, Eun, and Kyung Han You. 2016. "But Not All Social Media Are the Same: Analyzing Organizations' Social Media Usage." *Telematics and Informatics* 33: 176–86.

Hynie, Michaela, Susan McGrath, Julie E. E. Young, and Paula Banerjee. 2014. "Negotiations ofEngaged Scholarship and Equity through a Global Network of Refugee Scholars." *Scholarly and Research Communication* 5, no. 3: 1–16.

Kelley, Colin P., Shahrzad Mohtadi, Mark A. Cane, Richard Seager, and Yochanan Kushnir. 2015. "Climate Change in the Fertile Crescent and Implications of the Recent Syrian Drought." *Proceedings of the National Academy of Sciences of the United States of America* 112, no. 11: 3241–6.

Küpeli, Ismael. 2015. "We Spoke to the Photographer behind the Picture of the Drowned Syrian Boy." *Vice*, 4 Sept 2015. https://www.vice.com/en_ca/article/zngqpx/nilfer-demir-interview-876.

Lim, Young-shin, and Roselyn J. Lee-Won. 2017. "When Retweets Persuade: The Persuasive Effects of Dialogic Retweeting and the Role of Social Presence in Organizations' Twitter-Based Communication." *Telematics and Informatics* 34, no. 5: 422–33.

Nah, Seungahn, and Gregory D. Saxton. 2013. "Modeling the Adoption and Use of Social Media by Nonprofit Organizations. *New Media & Society* 15, no. 2: 294–313.

Naidorf, Judith C. 2014. "Knowledge Utility: From Social Relevance to Knowledge Mobilization. *Education Policy Analysis Archives* 22, no. 89. http://dx.doi.org/10.14507/epaa.v22n89.2014.

Paek, Hye-Jin, Thomas Hove, and Richard T. Cole. 2013. "A Multimethod Approach to Evaluating Social Media Campaign Effectiveness." *46th Hawaii International Conference on System Sciences*, 1570–9.

Panagiotopoulos, Panagiotis. 2012. "Towards Unions 2.0: Rethinking the Audience of Social Media Engagement." *New Technology, Work and Employment* 27, no. 3: 178–92.

Phipps, David J., Krista E. Jensen, and J. Gary Meyers. 2012. "Applying Social Sciences Research for Public Benefit Using Knowledge Mobilization and Social Media." In *Theoretical and Methodological Approaches to Social Sciences and Knowledge Management*, edited by Asunción López-Varela, 179–208. London: InTech Open.

Skoric, Marko M., QinFeng Zhu, Debbie Goh, and Natalie Pang. 2016. "Social Media and Citizen Engagement: A Meta-Analytical Review." *New Media & Society* 18, no 9: 1817–39.

Terras, Melissa. 2012. "The Impact of Social Media on the Dissemination of Research: Results of an Experiment." *Journal of Digital Humanities* 1, no. 3. http://journalofdigitalhumanities.org/1-3/the-impact-of-social-media-on-the-dissemination-of-research-by-melissa-terras/.

# SECTION 3

## *Knowledge Production and the Ethics of Network Formation*

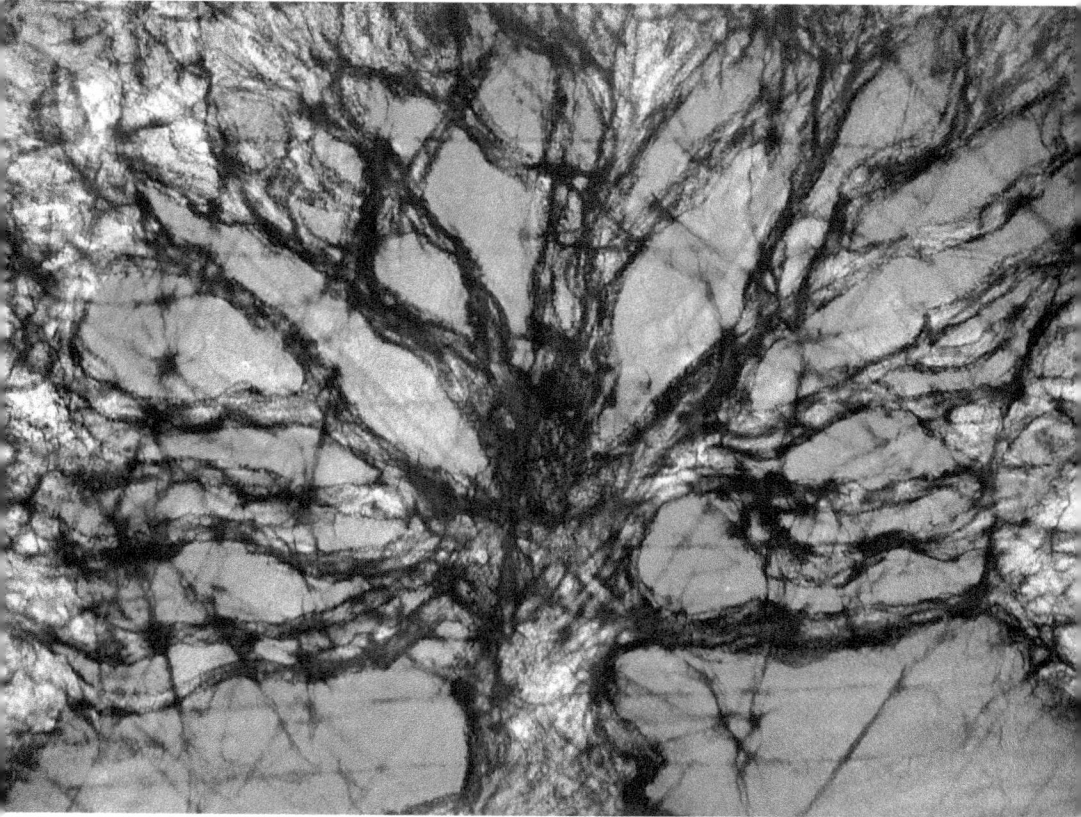

# New, Emerging, Emerged? Navigating Agency, Technology, and Organization in Developing the Emerging Scholars and Practitioners on Migration Issues (ESPMI) Network

*Brittany Lauren Wheeler and Petra Molnar*

## Introduction: How Did We Get Here, and Where Is Here?

Toronto, Canada. Kampala, Uganda. Kolkata, India. Bogotá, Colombia. Poznan, Poland. These are the cities in which the International Association of the Study of Forced Migration (IASFM) and the Refugee Research Network (RRN) met over the past decade. For what would become the ESPMI Network, they were especially crucial, collaborative spaces. These nexus points, complemented by hosts of emails and Skype conversations, gave rise to an international project that now connects hundreds of people across the world who are keen to contribute to the critical study of forced migration, and wish to engage in a realistic discussion about practice. The Emerging Scholars and Practitioners on Migration Issues (ESPMI) Network[1] also connects policymakers, journalists, artists, and others involved with and affected by forced migration. Through identifying project-based work, establishing a network of professional connections, and developing the opportunity to publish and access research and initiatives, ESPMI has charted a largely grassroots course toward creating a space for scholarly and professional support. It has not been easy.

ESPMI emerged from within the international RRN, an initiative born of a SSHRC grant. Primary among the RRN's desired platform of ideas and initiatives were those that encouraged intergenerational, interdisciplinary, and other cross-boundary engagements. ESPMI was a proactive response to these desires, where junior members could develop a meaningful place to contribute to conversations on migration issues. At present, the ESPMI Network is composed of an executive committee in charge of various sub-committees and projects and is generally coordinated by one or two individuals. The coordinator is responsible for communicating and building the vision of the network in collaboration with the executive committee, delegating tasks to specific sub-committees, and liaising with the committee dedicated to the production of the *Refugee Review*, ESPMI's peer reviewed online journal.

This chapter will provide an overview of ESPMI's trajectory as a working group and network. It documents the challenges and successes accompanying the interweaving of in-person and social media-based engagement, in identifying and critiquing the network's mission from within, in weighing the utility of institutional support and traditional funding sources, and in maintaining momentum in endeavours reliant upon the contributions of a network of volunteers. It also acknowledges the ongoing questions that permeated the work of ESPMI, including: what methodologies strike the balance between rigour and inclusive collaboration when creating a peer-reviewed journal? Between the benefits of independent work and the pitfalls of lacking institutional power and attendant funding? Between timely knowledge production and the many practical reformulations required to create a space for that meaningful knowledge?

To answer these questions honestly, the ESPMI team prioritized three working principles: 1) Work tirelessly via personal communication and networking to broaden the network's potential participants and executive leaders, and continuously consider how these participants are represented in/by the network; 2) Embrace the uncertainty inherent in forging ahead while still forming the identity of the group. Ultimately, the ESPMI team organized around the task of creating a new peer-reviewed journal, honing the network's identity and aspirations in large part through undertaking this; 3) Transparently apply the simple method of try-and-try again, and ask-and-ask-again, whether in adopting project ideas, revamping previous attempts at outreach in hopes of striking upon more fertile ground, or in seeking collaborators and advice among established scholars and practitioners.

## Where We Went, and with Whom

### Broad Strokes: From Early Days to Changing Ways

The ESPMI Network, formerly known as the New Scholars Network (NSN), was formed when a small group of graduate students at the Centre for Refugee Studies at York University in Toronto, Canada, created a "new scholars" working group within the RRN in 2010. By 2012, the group had been formalized within the RRN structure and the new executive committee asked what unique role such a network might play when young scholars have other professional associations through their universities. They began to answer this question through actions such as maintaining a listserv for initial members, dedicated to circulating opportunities in the field, and building a basic website and blog to further build capacity and test the boundaries of cost-free options for networking. During 2012, a small volunteer team began the difficult process of drafting an initial call for submissions for the first edition of the journal, *Refugee Review*, settling on the theme of refugees and social movements, and concurrently encouraging the group's contacts to act as peer reviewers (this process is detailed below). As a way to catalyze transnational conversations, in January 2013 the executive committee attended the IASFM Conference in Kolkata, India, and scheduled a small lunch meeting for new scholars to meet. New members were brought on board and the first volume of *Refugee Review* was released in the summer of 2013.[2] Following time spent further building the network, the executive committee attended the IASFM Conference in Bogotá, Colombia in 2014—solidifying their connections, hosting a larger meeting, and later releasing a second volume of the *Refugee Review* in July 2015. In summer 2016, the executive committee travelled to Poznan, Poland for another IASFM conference, and during a

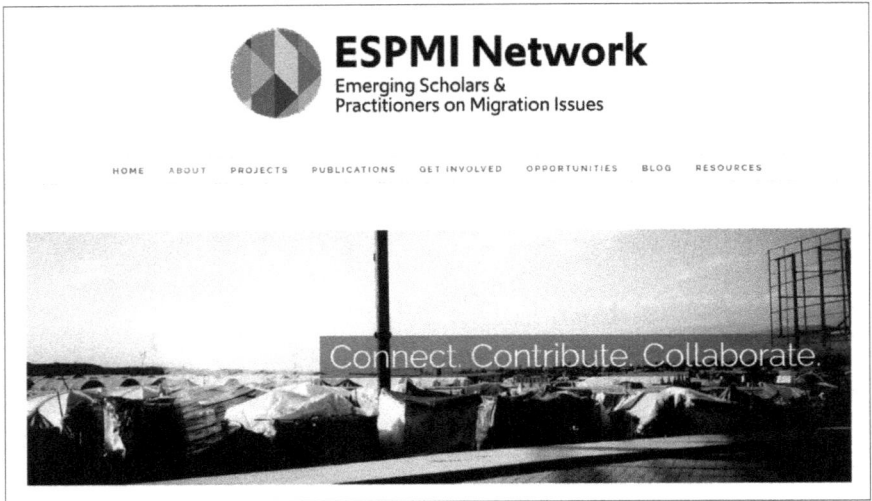

**FIGURE 10.1**
Banner of the ESPMI Network's Website with ESPMI Statement (2016). Source: Accessed
June 21, 2017. https://espminetwork.com.

meeting with emerging scholars, marked the transition in leadership from
a small, long-standing work group to an expanded committee taking the
network in expansive directions.

## A Necessary Name Change

In 2015 the executive committee decided to formally change the New
Scholars Network to the Emerging Scholars and Practitioners on Migration Issues (ESPMI) network. The executive committee felt that in order to
be as inclusive as possible both within and beyond traditional academia,
and to represent the multiple academic-practitioner alliances many members held, focusing on "scholars" alone was neither representative nor sufficient. The adjective "new" became less relevant as well, as deliverables were
completed and partnerships expanded. After providing an update on the
network in an executive meeting with the RRN in 2015, professor Susan
Kneebone from the University of Melbourne suggested that, as a whole,
the group sounded as though it represented those who were *emerging* in
the field. Following conversations with senior members of the RRN and

BRITTANY LAUREN WHEELER AND PETRA MOLNAR

within the executive committee, ESPMI was reborn, represented by a new logo and website that acted as a more integrated and dynamic platform for the network and the *Refugee Review*. These changes were introduced to coincide with the release of the second volume of the journal.

## Rallying around the Refugee Review: How to Begin a Journal and Make It Sing

When the network formed and took initial steps to begin operating internationally, one of the objectives listed by the initial leadership was to create and publish a peer-reviewed journal. The legacy of this desire, however, did not provide many tools for achieving such a goal, including neither funding nor personnel. The grassroots nature of ESPMI was perhaps never more evident than in the production of the first volume of the *Refugee Review*, published in 2013.

The small executive team found that they had to decide on a theme broad enough—yet specific and rigorous enough—to engage the current leadership, attract attention in response to a new and unknown journal, and confidently carry the weight of its subject. Further, long before the network's name was to change the team decided that they wanted this publishing platform to be not only a space for quality academic pieces, but also practitioner reports, interviews, a discussion series (on a question related to the journal's theme), and opinion pieces. With the decision to expand the call to all these types of submission, a high level of clarity regarding the journal's objectives was imperative within and beyond the call. We also both solicited new work from contacts and received new pieces through our network. This process did not happen on a neat timetable, but concurrently with peer review.

The peer review process also required building. Utilizing the core executive team and individuals from our broader network, we embarked on a process that involved multiple rounds of edits over the course of nearly a year for some submissions. In this, its first iteration, it resembled a peer-reviewed workshopping process, improving preliminarily accepted work of varying levels of readiness with the authors, while concurrently building the structure for publishing the results. This required a delicate balance of communication and transparency about our newness to the process and our commitment to creating something deliverable in a reasonable amount of time. It also required dedicating an enormous amount of time, with the belief that a slower version of peer review would create the solid foundation and quality of content with which we wanted to greet our readership. Ultimately, we did balance this process, and it resulted in ESPMI's singular vision of peer review. The process has since been streamlined, but retains a generous and personal review process for emerging scholars and practitioners, many of whom have not seen their work brought together in such a publication before.

The resulting first edition of the journal featured the work of twenty-six authors and interviewees, eight editors/peer reviewers, the original photography of the authors. It was largely compiled by three executive members. Several members of the executive built a free WordPress site on which to host the journal. The ESPMI Network decided to pursue an open access platform using the Creative Commons standards of attribution and citation to ensure that the journal was widely accessible internationally. The journal remains online, as a website and a downloadable and printable pdf, and copies were also distributed at meetings in the following year.

The second volume of the journal, published in 2015, marked a quantifiable increase in engagement in terms of submissions, editorial review, and reception. The works of more than forty emerging scholars and practitioners were featured, this time rallying around the theme of reconceptualizing refugees and forced migration in the twenty-first century. Another free WordPress site was created utilizing the benefits of the expansion of professional, free templates, and was accompanied, as with the last journal, by a pdf version. The executive team refined the workshopping format of its peer-to-peer-review process, with each submission anonymized and assessed by two peer reviewers to ascertain whether it could be taken forward. This was followed by review by the managing editors and select peer reviewers who would then workshop the piece with the author as needed. Following this second round of peer review, the co-coordinators of ESPMI created guiding documents to formalize the style and editing guidelines for future issues of the journal. The final product, the second volume of the *Refugee Review*, has drawn more than 10,000 unique visitors and accrued almost 20,000 total views at the time of writing.[3] It is also encouraging to note that online engagement remained at a similar level in both 2015 (the year of publication) and 2016 (the year following), and unique visitors to

**FIGURE 10.2**
Screenshot from the online version of *Refugee Review* Volume II, published in 2015, hosted on the current ESPMI website.

the site in 2017 still register at about half of the viewership level of the year of the journal's release.[4]

The *Refugee Review* exemplifies the network's commitment to the presentation of research that held allegiance less to particular institutions or geographies, and more to the lessons drawn from the collective merit of the many institutions, non-profit organizations, projects, and personal involvements that our authors contributed to in their daily lives. The *Refugee Review*, as it continued into its second and third volumes, increasingly brought emerging scholars and practitioners into conversation with early and mid-career faculty, lawyers, and post-doctoral researchers also published within the journal. We believe that the working, and now more established, methodology of our journal complements the multidisciplinary, multi-locative nature of forced migration, and underlines the need for a diverse submission invitation, a rigorous but collaborative peer-review process, and a platform of open presentation. The *Refugee Review* has begun to act as a platform for bringing multiple disciplines and perspectives into closer proximity for those that seek to know more about forced migration. It is too often that we are stymied by disciplinary boundaries, lack of funding, and lack of knowledge about how to come together, and thus it is practical, ethical, and imperative to engage with one another in critical discussion in order to consider not only the reconceptualization of forced migration, but a new paradigm for action. The *Refugee Review* is an ongoing form of such action.

## Making a Home on the World Wide Web: Simple Tools, Large(r) Impact

### The ESPMI Website

The ESPMI Network managed a WordPress website in a blog format, which linked to a Twitter account, a Facebook page, and two separate websites for each edition of the *Refugee Review*. The network's website became the primary way for people to access the content that the network shares on a daily basis, both original and re-blogged posts from other sources. The following chart depicts increased usage of the ESPMI website from its inception in 2012. The network received its highest visit rate to date with over 2.7K visitors in September 2016.[5]

The website was also recently redesigned by the new executive committee. Since the new design went live in March 2017, site activity has continued to increase.

The automatic recording of demographics and visitors has proven to be one of the most rewarding experiences of running the ESPMI website, tracking the expansion of ESPMI's reach in real time. The website and both journal sub-pages have had visitors from all over the world, including Vatican City, Vanuatu, and Central African Republic. However, although the ESPMI website receives a global range of visitors from over 200 countries, the United States, Canada, and the UK currently remain the most represented in site visits.[6]

### Innovative Social Media Highlight: The Guest Twitter Project

The use of social media was paramount in the ESPMI Network's success in reaching a wide and diverse audience, though it was not implemented

## All Time Views

| | Months and Years | | | | | | Average per Day | | | | | |
|------|-----|-----|-----|-----|-----|-----|-----|-----|-----|-----|-----|-----|
| | JAN | FEB | MAR | APR | MAY | JUN | JUL | AUG | SEP | OCT | NOV | DEC |
| 2012 | | 179 | 731 | 397 | 449 | 276 | 415 | 311 | 209 | 165 | 197 | 127 |
| 2013 | 109 | 244 | 125 | 108 | 179 | 958 | 239 | 190 | 341 | 205 | 147 | 146 |
| 2014 | 298 | 503 | 310 | 494 | 431 | 1.0K | 882 | 888 | 1.7K | 428 | 440 | 307 |
| 2015 | 319 | 736 | 622 | 846 | 645 | 717 | 487 | 881 | 986 | 994 | 978 | 717 |
| 2016 | 1.1K | 1.3K | 1.6K | 1.8K | 1.7K | 1.3K | 1.2K | 1.4K | 2.7K | 2.0K | 1.7K | 1.4K |
| 2017 | 1.5K | 1.1K | 108 | 51 | 66 | 51 | 44 | 72 | 82 | 123 | 89 | 24 |
| 2018 | 109 | 27 | 0 | 0 | 0 | 0 | 1 | 0 | 0 | 0 | 0 | 0 |
| 2019 | 0 | 1 | 0 | | | | | | | | | |

FEWER VIEWS ▨▨ ■■■ MORE VIEWS

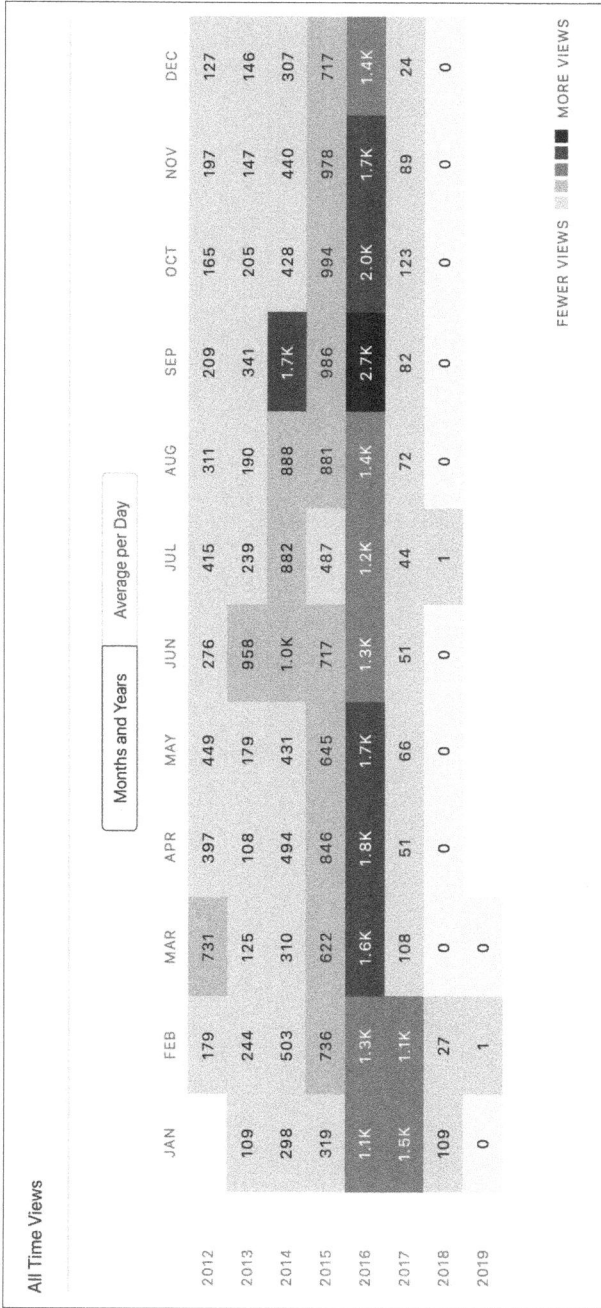

**FIGURE 10.3**
All time views of the ESPMI website, from creation until the website was migrated to its new location. Source: ESPMI Wordpress Insights.

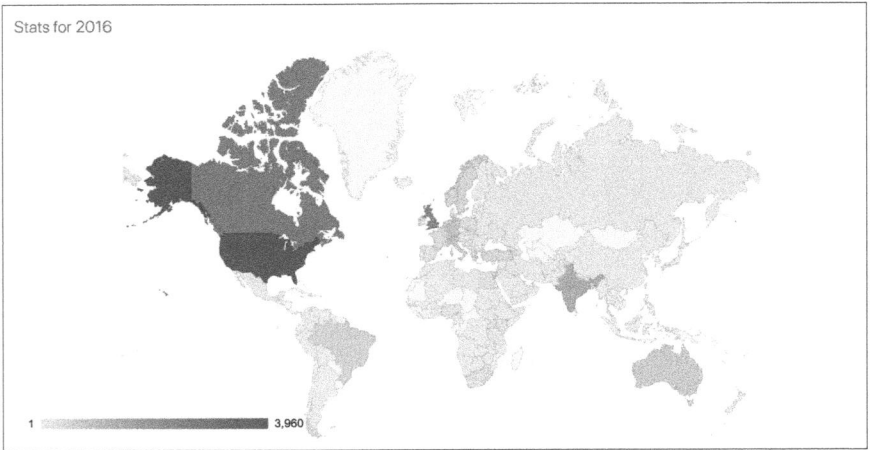

**FIGURE 10.4**
Country-based analytics for the peak year of the ESPMI website, prior to migration (2016). Source: ESPMI Wordpress Traffic.

**ESPMI Network**
@ESPMINetwork

Follow ⌄

Hi @ESPMINetwork! Welcome to the GuestProject. I'm @MarciaVeraE and I will be discussing this week #ForcedMigrationinLatinAmerica Pls join!

1:35 AM - 2 Mar 2015

**ESPMI Network**
@ESPMINetwork

Follow ⌄

Hey all! I'm Cihan Arikan from Malmö, Sweden and I'll be the guest tweeter this week @ESPMINetwork, focusing on #LGBTQ #asylum & #migration

2:06 AM - 9 Mar 2015

**FIGURE 10.5**
Tweets from the *Guest Twitter Project* "Tweeters"
https://twitter.com/ESPMINetwork/status/572329263367647233
https://twitter.com/ESPMINetwork/status/574858755185180672

immediately. As projects such as the website and journal gained momentum, and members were added, additional projects that utilized Twitter, for instance, became more viable. One important vehicle for connecting ESPMI members and Twitter followers via the expertise of those in our network was the *Guest Twitter Project*.

In December 2011, Sweden implemented the project *Curators of Sweden*, where the Twitter handle @sweden allowed a citizen of Sweden to take over the account every week to share insight into their personal lives and the country's wider attributes. (It is interesting to note that though the project used the word "citizen," the project's website clarifies that this means, "someone who is located in Sweden (citizenship irrelevant), or a Swedish citizen abroad.")[7] ESPMI used this model as the inspiration for a similar, friendly takeover. This initiative was meant to take full advantage of a growing network, creating a platform through which to discuss issues that the network's executive group was not familiar with or did not have time to tackle publicly in a meaningful way. The *Guest Twitter Project* proved very successful, with six initial "tweeters" from around the world showcasing their own work and/or expertise for one week each. These varied perspectives also greatly boosted the ESPMI Network's online presence through its @ESPMINetwork handle: tweeting capacity improved by 192 per cent, tweet impressions went up 127 per cent, profile views went up 53 per cent, mentions increased by 42 per cent, and overall followers of ESPMI increased exponentially.[8]

## Other Projects Utilizing Social Media and Networking

The ESPMI Network was also involved with other projects connected to the Refugee Research Network, many of which were advertised or otherwise posted on the ESPMI website or distributed to its members. These projects included participation in several aspects of the Borderless Higher Education for Refugees Project (BHER) supporting tertiary education in Kenya's refugee camps (see chapter 4), the coordination of the review committee for the abstracts submitted to the 2014 International Association for the Study of Forced Migration (IASFM) conference in Bogotá (see chapter 12), and partnering on a SSHRC Connections Grant for the Global Refugee Policy International Workshop at Carleton University in order to provide rapporteurs.

# The Challenges of Funding a Network

Through the years spent developing and promoting the ESPMI Network, multiple funding challenges emerged as we sought to create a platform for knowledge production, information exchange, and interdisciplinary collaboration. These challenges, however, simultaneously heightened many of the strengths of an independent network not explicitly tied to any institution: flexibility, creativity, and problem-solving.

While the ESPMI Network was generously supported by the Refugee Research Network with travel funding for some members of the executive committee to attend IASFM meetings, as well as for the subscription for a slightly more advanced website platform, the independence of the ESPMI Network allowed for freedom in its research trajectories, timelines for deliverables, attempts at collaboration, and in the written material it posted online and in print. The open-access nature of the *Refugee Review*, for example, came largely out of necessity, as the journal was not administered by a post-secondary institution nor funded in any way. However, this openness also allowed for knowledge exchange and the dissemination of ideas among people who may not otherwise have been able to access or afford traditional journal articles and publishing opportunities.

Leading a grassroots organization with no operational funding created many challenges. In particular, the money made available through the RRN SSHRC grant was only earmarked for students. It is important to note that while the executive committee members were almost all, at one point, graduate students, for the majority of our tenure on RRN we were both practitioners in the field of forced migration, and thus not eligible for this type of funding. As such, the work that was done to complete the first two volumes of the journal was entirely unpaid. This type of funding exclusion makes the collaborative, interdisciplinary, and practitioner-academic linked work that ESPMI identified as its goal more difficult to do and is a worthy discussion point for large funding initiatives going forward. While we understand that the funding source originated in academia, with time the questions asked at the beginning of this paper (such as what unique role the network might play when young scholars have other professional associations through their universities) were answered by taking the best of academia and linking it to other critical discussions.

That being said, academic-based funding and the RRN in particular can—and in this case did—provide an enormous amount of moral support and legitimacy to the ESPMI Network. Their advocacy of our work, especially around the promotion of the *Refugee Review*, was sincere and often emphatic. The ability of ESPMI members to travel to conferences in Kolkata, Bogotá, and Poznan allowed us to add enthusiastic students we met to the executive team on numerous occasions, led to the inspiration for re-naming the organization after a particular RRN leadership meeting, and provided a physical space to share print copies of our journal with research centres from around the world. These kinds of support and travel opportunities have bolstered and nurtured the network in very concrete ways and encouraged many projects we have attempted along the way.

## Exploring New Horizons: The Next Chapter for the ESPMI Network[9]

Prior to and during the IASFM Meeting in Poznan, Poland in summer 2016, the executive committee began to advertise the need for new ES-PMI leadership, launching a web-based call for applicants and hosting a well-attended lunchtime session at the conference to discuss current initiatives. For those of us who had worked as part of the executive committee for a number of years, and had attempted ad hoc and formal leadership transitions before, it was rewarding to find a robust response from the international community. This response made it possible to create a larger executive committee than in any previous incarnation of the group, creating roles we had long envisioned,[10] including a general executive, project heads, a head of web, assisting web-based projects posts, and a managing editor, sub-managing editors, and core peer reviewing team for the *Refugee Review*. The new executive committee began their term in the fall of 2016, and we are pleased to highlight some of their key priorities going forward.

1. BROADEN THE GEOGRAPHIC SCOPE OF MEMBERSHIP AND INCREASE MULTI-PERSPECTIVE KNOWLEDGE PRODUCTION[11]

A key priority for the new executive is to broaden ESPMI's geographic scope by further promoting dialogue and collaboration across the global

**FIGURE 10.6**
The New Dissemination
Practices & Public
Engagement in Forced
Migration Research cluster
interrogates current methods
of dissemination and public
engagement utilized by
migration researchers and
practitioners, and discusses
new opportunities for
effective knowledge transfer
(ESPMI Network website,
2019).

*Discussion Question:*

*Share your top dissemination practices! How can scholars be more effective in sharing their research with researched communities, policy actors, and the public?*

New Dissemination Practices and Public Engagement
in Forced Migration Research
#ESPMITALKS

and local divides found so often within research, policy, and practice, which are exacerbated by issues of physical, digital, and other limitations on accessing and sharing information. These efforts will focus on working with a wider range of educational institutions, research centres, and scholarly (and other) networks throughout the global south, and in partnership with scholars and practitioners with lived forced migration experience. The expansion of ESPMI's digital communications platforms will be imperative in order to better reach and engage with colleagues in various cities, countries, and regions, ensuring that ongoing projects, such as the *Refugee Review* and the *Guest Twitter Project* are diverse, multi-perspective forms of knowledge production and information sharing. New potential initiatives include the development of local ESPMI chapters, one-to-one "borderless" scholar matching, developing a referral system, and local events.

## 2. DEVELOP NEW RESEARCH CLUSTERS TO FOSTER CRITICAL REFLECTION AND INNOVATION IN MIGRATION STUDIES

The ESPMI network will continue to confront and interrogate key issues in migration research, dialogue, practice, and policy with the goal of encouraging more reflexive, informed, critical, and innovative responses to migration issues. A strategic priority here is to develop new lines of support for emerging work in the field. The executive has created four new research clusters: Methodological Challenges in Forced Migration Research, New Dissemination Practices and Public Engagement, Bridging Research to Policy and Practice, and Emerging Ideas in Migration Research. These clusters, facilitated by working groups led by ESPMI Executive Committee members, aim to bring together emerging scholars and practitioners to engage in dialogue, generate innovative approaches, drive new dissemination methods, and develop new ways to bridge research with programming and policy. The clusters also provide linkages within the broader ESPMI network, with the intention of developing communities of practice for researchers and practitioners to share literature and ideas, learn about migration issues in different contexts, and cultivate collaborative research projects, papers, and conference panels.

3. *CULTIVATE AND ARCHIVE PATHWAYS TO MIGRATION STUDIES*

The ESPMI Network continues to be committed to developing pathways to migration-related education. Such pathways keep new generations apprised of the historical and contemporary reasons that people have been/ are forced to migrate, ultimately fostering more inclusive and informed local, national, and international responses to migration. The ESPMI Network plans to collaborate and engage in projects that support new migration scholarship in post-secondary education, as well as explore possible projects in elementary and secondary education settings. A key objective here is to develop a directory of migration-related education programs and courses on the ESPMI website. This directory will provide information about a range of courses globally, in person and online, at the college, diploma, undergraduate, Master's, and PhD levels, as well as summer courses. This priority area will also focus on increasing access to a catalogue of scholarships and other funding opportunities.

## Conclusions: A Commitment to Innovative Knowledge Sharing in a Complex World

This chapter has articulated some of the ways that creating, developing, and supporting an interdisciplinary and international network for emerging scholars and practitioners has been hugely rewarding and successful for those involved. It has also touched upon the fact that supporting a grassroots initiative with few resources other than the time the executive committee are willing to voluntarily commit has clear pitfalls.

The ESPMI Network has shown that there is room for collaborative work beyond only the traditional academic dissemination of knowledge. The work of ESPMI shows the importance of interrogating methodologies of collaboration and rigour in innovative publishing, as well as the difficulties with striking the right balance between the benefits of independence and the pitfalls of no institutional affiliation or substantive funding. Creating timely and meaningful knowledge often comes with practical considerations, particularly for innovative, unbounded, transnational initiatives. However, grounded, ambitious innovation is what is needed to push ideas forward, to create platforms for new and diverse voices, and to showcase real commitment to creating space for grappling with the complexities of human migration.

## Notes

1   ESPMI Network, Cluster of the Refugee Research Network, online at: espminetwork. com. Accessed 21 June 2017.

2   *Refugee Review: Social Movements* 1, no. 1: 2013. ESPMI Network—Refugee Research Network. Petra Molnar Diop, Brittany Wheeler, Oana Petrica, Negin Dahya, editors. www.refugeereview.wordpress.org.

3   *Refugee Review: Re-conceptualizing Refugees and Forced Migration in the 21st Century* 2, no. 1: 2015. ESPMI Network—Refugee Research Network. Petra Molnar, Brittany Wheeler, editors. https://refugeereview2.wordpress.com/.

4   Special thanks to Paul Dudman and Claire Ellis, members of the executive committee, for these ESPMI Network analytics, shared with the authors in July 2017.

5   Claire Ellis, Coordinator of ESPMI Network, Internal Report Analytics, provided on 4 May 2017.

6   Claire Ellis, Coordinator of ESPMI Network, Internal Report Analytics, provided on 4 May 2017.

7   See for example The Curators of Sweden, Swedish Institute and VisitSweden, 2011, online at: http://curatorsofsweden.com. See also Sarah Lyall, "Swedes' Twitter Voice: Anyone, Saying (Blush) Almost Anything." *New York Times*, 10 June 2012. Online: http://www.nytimes.com/2012/06/11/world/europe/many-voices-of-sweden-via-twitter. html?_r=1.

8   Supra note 6. ESPMI Network Analytics, ESPMI Network, collected by Brittany Wheeler and Petra Molnar for the use of a presentation: Petra Molnar and Brittany Wheeler, The networking of emerging scholars and practitioners: Value, lessons, and

looking to the future. "Innovations in Forced Migration: Showcasing research from the Refugee Research Network (RRN) and beyond," Toronto, Canada. 15–16 June 2015.

9    Adapted from the 2017 ESPMI Network Report. The authors thank the current Executive Committee for sharing these directions with us for the purpose of this publication.

10   ESPMI Network, "People," online: https://espminetwork.com/people/. Accessed 21 June 2017.

11   This section relies on information provided by Claire Ellis, coordinator of ESPMI, 2016–18.

# What Constitutes Environmental Displacement? Challenges and Opportunities of Exploring Connections across Thematically Diverse Areas

*Pablo Bose and Elizabeth Lunstrum*

## Introduction

As the nascent RRN began to take shape its leadership, including then-director of CRS Susan McGrath, observed a consequential and somewhat surprising gap. While many of the other major thematic areas regarding refugee research—international legal regimes, policy analysis, educational opportunities, and integration initiatives among them—were key thematic areas for the network, environmental issues represented an important new area of both conceptual and practical concern, and largely fell beyond the realm of refugee research proper. As a result, she sought to draw together scholars in this emergent field to help create a new research cluster with an emphasis on networking, interdisciplinarity, and knowledge generation. In this chapter, we explore the successes and challenges of the Environmental Displacement Cluster with a particular focus on four areas—1) the origins and structure of the networking model; 2) making the case for "environmentally induced displacement" as a substantive conceptual field and our main organizing concept; 3) how our cluster enabled other interventions into knowledge production concerning our main organizing concept; and 4) reflections on what has worked in this model and what remain as challenges moving forward.

## Creating the Network

Building the Environmental Displacement Cluster of the RRN initially had as much to do with personal career trajectories as it did with the particularities of the research projects and themes that eventually came to characterize the cluster. York's Centre for Refugee Studies (CRS) had already hosted a multi-year, multi-site study focused on forced migration due to development called the Ethics of Development-Induced Displacement (EDID) Project. Issues related to the environment—including resource extraction and conservation in particular—had played a major role in several of the case studies undertaken by the project, yet the environmental theme remained secondary to the issue of development (understood broadly to include social, economic, political, and environmental aspects). Dr. McGrath brought together the outgoing research coordinator of the EDID project, Pablo Bose (a doctoral student in Environmental Studies at York at the time), with two recently arrived faculty members, Elizabeth (Libby) Lunstrum in Geography and Anna Zalik in Environmental Studies, to discuss shared research interests to ensure the RRN had at least some focus on the environment. The three of us brought together diverse academic backgrounds (geography, development sociology, environmental studies) and seemingly disparate topics of study (conservation, resource extraction, responses to climate change), and we had each conducted fieldwork in different parts of the world (Southern Africa, Nigeria and Mexico, and India). Our initial conversations suggested that there was something important connecting these separate strands of training, research, and regional focus; namely the displacement of populations and livelihoods due to broadly understood environmental factors. We decided therefore to pursue the creation of an "Environmental Displacement Cluster" and to see whether such a network made sense conceptually and practically.

The first question we faced was to ask ourselves whether we would be interested in pursuing the cluster and why. Reflecting on this, our answer is more complex than even we had initially assumed and is tied to a whole host of personal and professional reasons (see chapter 10). We find it telling to walk through some of these reasons in the hope that it might facilitate others in their own development of research clusters.

Let us begin with personal reasons. When Susan McGrath approached us about the possibility, we were intrigued but somewhat uneasy. After all, the three of us focused on very different empirical phenomena, and it was not clear what—if anything—united them (a theme we return to in detail below). We were also already integrated into our own research and activist networks, so how could embarking on a new cluster advance our personal research interests and the particular lines of scholarly inquiry that inspired and shaped our work? But we decided nevertheless to engage in preliminary conversations—primarily via Skype and telephone—to explore this question. Our decision to proceed was partially motivated by the fact that we all liked one another personally, found each other's work compelling, and looked forward to getting to know one another better. We were all recently minted PhDs and new arrivals at our respective institutions. This research cluster therefore offered us the opportunity to broaden our institutional networks as well as our disciplinary ones. For Libby and Anna, it provided the opportunity to become better acquainted with new colleagues at York; for Pablo, the cluster afforded an opportunity to both remain connected to York and to build closer working relationships in geography, a new discipline for him.

In terms of our motivations, apprehensions, and eventually the cluster's outcomes, both concrete and less tangible, it is also important to note that we were all pre-tenure when we began. This made the prospect of developing a cluster somewhat nerve-wracking. It was not clear our efforts would pay out in terms of the main "currency" of tenure these days—that is, scholarly publications—especially since we were not entirely convinced the cluster had a clear focus. But being pre-tenure, and having a very sincere commitment to advancing the study area through collaborative exchange, also motivated us to ensure that the cluster would have concrete results, especially various forms of scholarly dissemination. Looking back at this period of pre-tenure cluster development, one of our core observations is that working on the cluster through development to final outputs put in place the roots of a deep and sincere friendship among the three of us. This is tied, we feel, to the timing of the cluster; precisely that it did unfold over the time we were also going up for tenure. This is not insignificant. The outputs of the cluster, including a workshop and multiple publications, and the connections the cluster made possible were all important elements of our tenure files, but the friendships generated by the cluster also provided a very real sense of moral support for a stressful time in our careers. We mention this to reinforce an important point: the development of research clusters includes benefits that extend well beyond the tight focus of the cluster or even the larger projects of which they are a part. They help develop a moral community based on not only shared interests and political commitments but also recognition, belonging, and friendship (see the introduction and chapter 10).

Our motivation to develop the cluster was, of course, not solely personal. We were also intrigued by the idea of what we could gain by pulling our three diverse areas of scholarship together. Could we gain new insight into the relationship between displacement and environmental factors, logics, and processes? Certainly, there has been substantial literature in each of our individual areas of study, so what fresh understanding might come from bringing them together? Despite some of our previously articulated trepidation, we remained excited to reach for new horizons in our work and decided to take a leap of faith and see where we might end up. What we describe below is where we landed. To perhaps spoil the surprise, we are still not entirely convinced harnessing these diverse phenomena under a broad rubric of environmentally induced displacement leaves us with needed scholarly precision. But, nonetheless, it is in part through the discomfort with this imprecision that we have been able to produce meaningful scholarly interventions in our work as part of this cluster, our work as individual scholars, and in the possibilities opened up to us in the period since we began our collaboration.

Before we arrive there, let us make a few more observations about creating the network, both to chronicle our own history and that of the RRN and, more importantly, to provide insight to others hoping to develop their own research clusters. The first thing to mention is that the cluster came with start-up funds (offered from the larger RRN grant) (see chapter 1). As pre-tenure scholars who did not all have access to research grants just yet, this was vital. The money allowed us to hire a PhD student in geography at York, Ryan Hackett, as our assistant to help us organize the cluster's first scholarly output, which was a workshop. We chose Ryan out of a larger number of qualified applicants because he had the needed logistical skills but also direct research expertise on our topic (his dissertation examined conservation-induced displacement tied to conservation offsets from the Alberta oil sands). It soon became obvious that Ryan was more than merely an assistant; he was shaping the contours of the cluster through his workshop inputs. We realized that he should be asked to join us as a collaborator rather than an assistant. It was he who was central in organizing the workshop, and bringing together our disparate ideas and goals. While we had initially intended to put together a small and mainly locally based workshop, with Ryan's aid we significantly expanded our vision and began to conceive of an international gathering. We applied for and received additional SSHRC funding through the Workshops and Conference Grants program to make the event a reality. The larger budget we now had allowed us to include a wider range of cases, methodological approaches, and participants. As we developed the cluster, moreover, we were careful to invite a range of scholars, from world-renowned experts to mid-career scholars pursuing innovative research, as well as both senior graduate students who presented results from their fieldwork and new graduate students who joined the discussion as participant observers.

We retell this part of our cluster's early days because it highlights two important points. First, the development of clusters—especially those organized by pre-tenure faculty members—is greatly facilitated by seed funding. We strongly doubt our cluster would have taken off without such financial support. In addition, it likely would have proven overwhelming to the cluster leaders had it not been for logistical support offered by York's Centre for Refugee Studies with tasks such as reimbursement for travel and booking accommodation and the workshop venue. This is a reminder that financial and logistical support is not merely appreciated but actually necessary for clusters to succeed—perhaps even more so for a mega-cluster like the RRN.

Secondly, this part of our history also highlights the importance of engaging graduate students from a cluster's inception (see the introduction and chapters 1 and 10). Perhaps selfishly, we had not initially set out to provide opportunities for graduate students as one of our primary aims. It is not that we were against this, it simply was not front and centre on our radar. But we are proud to say that this indeed did become one of our primary contributions. We successfully provided graduate students opportunities for research dissemination and networking with senior scholars and other emerging scholars along with opportunities for logistical training and workshop organization. Hence, learning from our somewhat serendipitous success on this front, we would advocate all networks integrate graduate student training and engagement as a core contribution from the outset.

## Making the Case for Environmental Displacement as a Concept and Research Cluster

Perhaps unlike the other clusters of the RRN, ours faced a challenge from the start regarding our core concept. In short, it was not clear to us where to draw the limits around environmentally induced displacement to determine what it would embrace and what it would leave behind.[1]

Reflecting the particular challenges of our cluster, in both the scholarly world and that of environmental policy, ideas such as "environmental refugees" and "environmental forced migration" have long provoked vigorous debates, not only echoing but indeed surpassing the previous controversies in extending protections to internally displaced persons (IDPs) and other groups not sufficiently addressed by the existing refugee mechanisms (Gemenne and Brücker 2015; Lister 2014; Swyngedouw 2013). We found ourselves confronted with a similar set of challenges. For instance, both conservation and climate change offer clear examples of how environmental processes and logics provoke displacement. But even here there is ambivalence. Displacement linked to climate change is largely "agentless," as it is often environmental processes themselves—albeit ones influenced by human behaviour—that are most immediately inciting forced migration. It is often not a planned or actively orchestrated eviction. With conservation, however, it is most often conservation managers and related government officers who are actively organizing displacement and relocation. And newer trends of climate change related displacement—particularly displacement caused by climate change adaptation and mitigation measures—better fit what is happening with conservation, in the sense that they are active, intentional forms of displacement. Things get even more complicated when we look at resource extraction as a catalyst for environmental displacement. Here it is the desire to access and remove environmental resources that leads to eviction. Depending on the context,

PABLO BOSE AND ELIZABETH LUNSTRUM

these situations may be substantively different than what we see in the cases of climate change and conservation.

Despite these differences, we decided to move forward to develop the cluster and address these three phenomena. Our approach was to allow for connections to emerge, and indeed allow for often-contested understandings of our core concept of environmentally induced displacement, *through* our cluster. In other words, we approached even our core concept as an emergent entity from the beginning, one that was open to much debate both internally within the cluster and externally within our broader scholarly and activist networks. The question that was posed to us time and again is whether the concept itself is valid and whether its application helps in either our understanding of or intervention into the dynamics we are interested in.

If we say something to the effect that "environmentally induced displacement is unethical," does that mean anything? Surely different instances of such displacement are unethical in part because people are dispossessed from their land and livelihoods and separated from their communities, but that is arguably the case for all forms of involuntary relocation. Is there any inherent relation between the diverse "environmental" aspects of displacement and the ethics of that displacement that covers all similar examples of environmentally induced displacement? Arguably there is not, in large part because "the environment" plays such diverse causal roles in each example—sometimes it is the cause of displacement (climate change), sometimes environmental protection is the rationale for displacement (conservation), and other times it is the value of environmental resources that is motivating displacement (resource extraction).

Such imprecision proved challenging at many points. After our workshop, for example, we submitted a proposal for a special issue based on workshop papers to the journal *Geoforum*. We thought *Geoforum* would be a good fit, given that it is a reputable journal well versed in debates on environmental politics/political ecology and displacement. Our anticipation built up to disappointment as our proposal was rejected on the ground that the editors failed to see the "there there"; that is, they failed to grasp the utility of bringing the different cases of displacement induced by climate change, conservation, and mining together under one concept. The upshot, however, is that the challenge posed to us by the journal editors, by participants in our network, and perhaps most of all by ourselves as cluster leaders regarding the usefulness of this research concept and cluster has helped us to refocus and refine the ways in which we theorize the connections between environment and displacement.

In this sense, it was the workshop itself—where we brought what had been a primarily virtual and intermittent network into physical contact and intensive discussion over a focused period—that served as the catalyst for the transformation and continued evolution of the research cluster. To show the utility in our still-emergent concept of environmentally induced displacement and outline the work of the cluster, let us now turn to describing the workshop on the topic we held at York in 2012. It is here that we worked to define the concept and the cluster itself and here that we can locate the roots of our scholarly contributions, which included two peer-reviewed special issues of scholarly journals.

Our workshop proposal and later the workshop—held in 2012 and entitled "Environmental Displacement in a Global Context"—itself began from a set of related observations. From climate change to resource extraction projects, landscapes are being transformed at an unprecedented scale. Conservation efforts are at the same time being instituted to address the loss of habitat and to make urban spaces more sustainable. While seemingly distinct from one another, these share an important feature: they all provoke forms of environmentally induced displacement. As such phenomena have an impact on ever-larger spaces, communities are confronted with the loss of their land and other vital resources. These groups are often vulnerable to begin with, lacking secure rights and access to resources and to formal recourse once these are jeopardized. While scholars have begun to address these kinds of displacements, their conversations tend to focus on particular phenomena, leaving their insights somewhat insulated from one another. There is consequently need for a more comprehensive and systematic understanding of such processes.

This workshop brought together a number of researchers (twenty-one in total) along with an audience of discussants and observers, each with their own expertise in different contexts of environmentally induced displacement. The conversations that resulted were designed to help develop an overarching framework to better grasp the linkages and distinctions between these cases and to chart trends across seemingly disparate contexts. The workshop convened researchers at different points in their careers, and included activists, graduate students, and leading scholars.

Our conversations focused on displacement caused by climate change (including desertification, polar melting, and extreme weather), extractive industries (mineral, forest, and agro-industrial-based extraction), and conservation (in both rural and urban settings). We considered these to be among the most pressing and consequential forms of environmentally induced displacement globally, covering a broad range of practices and contexts.

Our workshop focused on three key questions that cut across these empirical areas.

1. What constitutes environmentally induced displacement? Who or what is being displaced and with what impact? This allowed us to both address and move beyond traditional notions of displacement—that is, dislocation from a particular place—to understand broader causes and impacts. Our discussions examined, for instance, how climate change, extraction, and conservation may prevent groups from accessing natural resources, employment, cultural sites, family connections, and so forth, even in instances where people are not physically removed from the places they inhabit.

2. What practices, discourses, calculations, etc. are employed to rationalize, organize, and undertake environmental displacement? We sought to investigate whether different forms of displacement unfolding in a variety of empirical and geographical contexts are organized and carried out through the deployment of similar practices, calculations, and conceptual frameworks. Furthermore, we examined ways in which these practices and processes may differ from case to case and what impact this may have on groups experiencing forms of dislocation.

3. How do different groups respond to environmentally induced displacement and with what impact? More specifically, how do groups directly impacted by such displacement respond to both actual and potential dislocation? And how do their advocates as well as states and private interests respond? What are the results of such responses? What lessons can be drawn from these experiences in understanding and addressing environmentally induced displacement in a range of contexts?

The backgrounds of those who participated in the workshop and subsequent publications were diverse, as were their approaches, the focus of their respective investigations, and their insights into the three areas of inquiry above. Table 11.1 presents a list of the participants, through whose collaborations and discussions we began to build the case for EID.

Through the workshop we attempted therefore to define environmentally induced displacement as our core, unifying concept. As discussed previously, there was much discussion about definitions and the use of the term environmentally induced displacement to describe our diverse topics and empirical contexts. Several participants raised specific concerns regarding the "fit" of the concept within broader scholarly and policy realms—how would "environmentally induced displacement" relate to established traditions within refugee studies or international development work or the policy debates on environmental refugees within the UNHCR, some asked? There was also significant discussion of the broad application of the term displacement to describe a wide variety of phenomena, many of which did not include forced migration. Several of the workshop presentations conceptualized displacement as processes leading to restricted access to natural resources, employment, cultural sites, or family connections. Others explored the discursive techniques used to rationalize and carry out displacement, while still others dealt with the psycho-social impacts of these varied forms of displacement and connections between place, identity, and belonging. Given the breadth of empirical contexts and topics being discussed under the heading of displacement, several participants suggested that terms such as dispossession, exclusion, or uprootedness might be more appropriate descriptors. Additionally,

PABLO BOSE AND ELIZABETH LUNSTRUM

**TABLE 11.1**: Environmental Displacement Cluster Workshop Participants

| PARTICIPANT | DISCIPLINE | INSTITUTION | SPECIALIZATION |
|---|---|---|---|
| Pablo Bose | Geography | University of Vermont | Climate change, Bangladesh |
| Elizabeth Lunstrum | Geography | York University | Conservation, Southern Africa |
| Anna Zalik | Environmental Studies | York University | Resource extraction, Nigeria, Mexico |
| Ryan Hackett | Geography | York University | Climate change, Canada |
| Andrew Baldwin | Geography | Durham University | Climate change discourse, global |
| Paula Butler | Canadian Studies | Trent University | Resource extraction, Africa |
| Claire Major | Geography | York University | Resource extraction, Canada |
| Jacqueline Medalye, Aaron Saad, and Anders L. Sandberg | Environmental Studies | York University | Climate change discourse, global |
| Amita Baviskar | Sociology | Institute of Economic Growth, Delhi | Development and displacement, India |
| Evans Rubara | Environmental Studies | York University | Resource extraction, Africa |
| Jennifer Hyndman | Geography | York University | Disaster and violence, Sri Lanka, global |
| Andrea Nightingale | Urban and Rural Development | Swedish University for Agricultural Sciences | Climate change, Himalayas |
| James Igoe | Anthropology | University of Virginia | Conservation, global |
| Rachel Hirsch | Social Justice | Brock University | Food security, Arctic |
| Ulrich Oslender | Geography | Florida International University | Resource extraction, Colombia |
| Joyce Barry | Women's Studies | Hamilton College | Resource extraction, United States |
| Robin Roth | Geography | Guelph University | Conservation, Canada |
| Matthew Himley | Geography | Illinois State University | Resource extraction, Peru |
| Roderick Neumann | Geography | Florida International University | Conservation, Africa |

some participants questioned the way in which the term "environmentally induced" was being foregrounded, which suggests that the environment is the driving factor in displacement. Some suggested that eco-genic displacement or environmentally mediated displacement might be a more appropriate label. Others argued the need to think about "environment" as a discursive formation; in other words, that it is not the environment, per se, that induces displacement, but the ways in which discourses regarding the environment—its conservation, utility, and management, for example—are used to enable, justify, and resist displacements.

This, in fact, emerged as one of the key insights of the workshop and of our cluster overall. Despite significant focus on terminology, a definitive answer to these questions was not reached. Participants suggested that while we in our discussions as scholars might autonomously decide what constitutes displacement, the process of defining and categorizing must involve considerations of how people beyond our research cluster might adopt and use specific terminology, and how meaning moves across cultures, languages, and geographic locations. Discussions of appropriate terminology and classifications will likely remain an ongoing and iterative process.

## The (Other) Outcomes of Connecting Disparate Research Interests: Innovative Knowledge Production

It is precisely through the openness of our concept and the diversity of members of our workshop and cluster (in terms of their personal backgrounds, specializations, and empirical cases) that we were able to make important and timely contributions to our understanding of different articulations of environmentally induced displacement. This included not only extending our empirical and theoretical knowledge of displacement tied to climate change, conservation, and resource extraction but also connections across them, including similarities, causal links, and so forth. These contributions are the most important scholarly outputs of our cluster and point to the fact that our main goal from the beginning was knowledge production in a rather classic scholarly sense, reflecting an important goal of the larger RRN (see the introduction). Following the success of the workshop we sought to capitalize on our momentum by organizing a special issue of a journal. We worked closely within the leadership group of the cluster and with our workshop co-organizer Ryan Hackett to craft a proposal for a coherent set of articles based on our discussions. It also became clear that there was substantial interest in two separate aspects of our work as a cluster: a theme that focused on conceptual matters and one that was more concerned with empirical detail and interventions.

Over the next four years, we worked to produce two special journal issues, building on our workshop (and in some cases including participants from that workshop); these are among the major contributions of our cluster. For the journal *Refuge*—an open-access publication that has widespread practitioner as well as scholarly appeal—we chose to focus more on some of the practical debates ongoing in the world of refugee protection (Bose and Lunstrum 2014). These included articles on policy and legal responses to climate change and natural disasters, a discussion of the volume and character of environmentally induced migration, and the specifics of Canadian state policy in this regard. Other contributors took up ethical questions such as the role of social workers in addressing forced migration, the particular context of Indigenous communities in Canada facing displacement, and the need to understand the historical legacies of colonialism and the importance of geographic location in assessing risk and vulnerability of environmentally induced displacement. For our more conceptual special issue, published in *Area*, we focused more specifically on many of the contradictions and debates regarding environmentally induced displacements from a critical geography and political ecology perspective (Lunstrum, Bose, and Zalik 2016). In this issue, we expanded on a number of workshop presentations to explore not only the common ground between conservation, climate change, and resource extraction, but also to examine some of the key contradictions between (and within) each area. Our papers look therefore at particular cases in Bangladesh, Southern Africa, and Mexico and additionally at climate change politics in Canada and eco-tourism and extraction in Latin America.

While the full scope of our conceptual and empirical contributions goes well beyond the themes listed below, we would like to highlight some of the specific interventions that our research cluster has made into our understanding of environmentally induced displacement from both the workshop and resulting publications. We do this to focus not only on these contributions on their own terms, but also to demonstrate the ways in which they were developed by bringing together a diversity of perspectives made possible by the cluster and our open and emergent concept of environmentally induced displacement.

*The Significance of Place, Identity, and Belonging:* A number of participants in their articles and presentations highlighted the important linkages between place and identity, and a sense of belonging. The significance of place and identity takes a variety of forms and influences both displacement and the responses of communities to displacement in a variety of ways. In several empirical contexts, citizenship and rights are linked to place, or more specifically, to place-based identities. Some participants highlighted the contested nature of citizenship in their specific studies, for example by citing highly mobile populations and varied access to political participation and resources. Others called attention to the ways in which various environmental subjectivities—such as Indigenous identities— were mobilized in order to successfully resist displacement, and the dangers that the usage of such strategic essentialism posed for various marginalized groups. The theme of a connection between specific places and the formation or maintenance of social/cultural identity was evident in a number of empirical contexts and often meant that physical displacement entailed threats to cultural identity and in some cases the very existence of particular societies. These linkages between place and identity often dovetailed into discussions within the cluster of the socio-psychological impacts of displacement. Here we saw discussion of affect, emotion, and the sense of "uprootedness" that results from displacement (see chapter 2).

*The Need for Historical Context and Recognition of Multiple Causal Factors:* Several participants argued through their presentations, discussions, and articles that we need to recognize the multiplicity of factors influencing vulnerability to displacement and the need for a focus on the underlying social, political, and economic contexts in which displacement occurs. A number of different issues and constraints may influence a population's vulnerability to displacement and ability to respond. These may include (but are not limited to) existing social or economic inequity, pre-existing or post displacement violence and conflict, colonialism, race and ethnicity, or physical location. Vulnerability and responses to environmentally induced displacement are thus conditioned by multiple factors operating across various scales. A focus on temporality also discourages us from seeing displacement as an isolated or discrete event, instead encouraging critical thinking about causality and not seeing specific cases as discrete events, but rather as complex, multi-staged processes, influenced by a variety of social, economic, and political projects (see also chapter 5). Participants noted that while the growing prominence of environmental risks in global discussions of displacement has increased discussions of "environmental refugees," there is a great deal of danger in adopting a short-term or myopic view of environmentally induced displacement that views it as primarily a new phenomenon.

*Understanding the Role of Coercion*: Many participants suggested that we must distinguish between forced migration and "voluntary" displacement. Forced migration is already recognized as politically unpalatable, but several people discussed more subtle strategies that also serve to involuntarily displace people. This included cases in which people's ability to protect themselves against animal threats in parks were curtailed, or the removal and abandonment of essential infrastructure in specific locations, or the use of environmental pollution as a tool for displacing communities. Several participants also raised the need to consider people's ability to participate in or resist displacement. Some mentioned the ways in which class, race, gender, or other factors play an important role in determining whether a particular community is able to resist projects and processes that might displace them, whether they are able to articulate "authentic" claims to territory or land usage, whether they are recognized by state or other authorities, or whether they have the means as well as motivation to protect themselves and their lands.

*The Importance of Governance Structures in Displacement*: Many of the papers presented during the workshop and subsequently developed into scholarly articles included discussions of the specific governance regimes within various cases of environmentally induced displacement. While participants acknowledged that the role of the state remains important, it is no longer the exclusive centre of discussions on environmental governance and associated displacements. Governance was instead discussed in terms of multiple actors, public and private, operating at a variety of scales to secure norms, legitimacy, rules, and sanctions. These governance networks involve varying roles for states, NGOs and aid agencies, private corporations, and international or supra-national institutions. The ways in which these diverse actors operate and intersect to co-produce specific types of governance has a significant influence on displacement.

Different co-productions of governance may operate to rationalize and facilitate conditions for displacement, while in other instances networked governance structures are employed in strategies to respond to, or resist, displacement.

These themes (and others that developed from our collaborations) lead us to make two observations regarding our cluster and its outputs:

1. Through our discussions in person and through the writing, editing, and revising process, participants helped to greatly expand our understanding of environmentally induced displacement through diverse empirical cases and theoretical frameworks, and

2. It was our open and organic concept of environmentally induced displacement that in part allowed such a complex definition of the concept to arise out of our work together.

## Conclusion: Reflecting on the Cluster . . . Outcomes, Challenges, and New Directions

In many ways, we feel the work of the official cluster on environmental displacement has come to a close. We were successful in organizing a major workshop in 2012, and we also produced those two scholarly special issues, which is precisely what we had envisioned. But the less tangible outcomes are also important (see the introduction). We have developed valuable friendships, trained graduate students, and learned about different articulations of environment and displacement across diverse locations and theoretical frameworks. We should also note here that the question of how active the cluster is remains an open one—we have collaborated intensively through efforts such as the workshop and the subsequent publications, but what sustains our ongoing work is primarily the personal relationships built between participants, rather than a formalized organization or affiliation. Most of the participants in the workshop and/or publications we have referenced previously have gone on to develop their work further either on their own, in continued collaboration with research partners met through the cluster, or in new networks. While most would acknowledge their participation in the cluster events and outputs, it is uncertain whether they would still identify as members of the research cluster now.

As the leaders and organizers of the group, though, we absolutely embrace the outcomes of our cluster and are very grateful to the RRN for facilitating our work along the way. This latter point reminds us of the practical and indeed vital importance of support, both financial and logistical, for clusters to be effective—especially "clusters within clusters," which we see with the RRN model. Despite our many successes, as we have described in this chapter, the issue of defining our concepts remained a significant hurdle. Yet this same challenge has produced one of the key outcomes of our discussion, whether in person and through our writing and research. This has been the notion that there is no single unitary logic to how environmental factors, values, or processes might provoke displacement along starkly different registers, scales, and contexts. There is thus considerable utility and insight to be gained by bringing these diverse examples together, which is precisely what the cluster enabled.

Perhaps one of the most exciting aspects of the cluster is the new possibilities it has generated. We continue to present on its findings in different locations. This includes twice presenting on it at the Centre for Refugee Studies' annual summer school, which draws together a stellar mix of activists, practitioners, and scholars studying the latest trends in forced migration. And the special issue of *Refuge*, in particular, has allowed us to speak to an audience centrally concerned with questions of forced displacement. We have additionally integrated key insights from the cluster into our teaching. This includes units in two of our courses that brought together students from Toronto and the Dadaab Refugee Camp as part of the Borderless Higher Education for Refugees (BHER) Project (see chapter 4). Here we were able to talk about environmental change, including the environmental aspects of displacement, across geographical locations in a way that treated students from the global south and north as equal partners in learning. In Pablo's case, he has been able to develop a new concentration in migration and environment within the Global Studies program he directs and to introduce a new thematic area of focus on migration within the Gund Institute for Environment at the University of Vermont. Moreover, there are important lessons we have learned as scholars and as teachers regarding our approach to collaboration and instruction, especially in terms of modelling ethical practices to student researchers.

We have also used the cluster and its work as a springboard to pursue related projects. For instance, emerging directly from the cluster and funded with seed money from the RRN, Libby and her PhD student Francis Massé have begun a project on the political ecology of international borders. So far, our work has consisted of an annotated bibliography of over 100 sources on the topic (Massé and Lunstrum 2013; see also chapter 13) along with our own empirical work on displacement from Southern Africa's Great Limpopo Transfrontier Conservation Areas (Massé and Lunstrum 2016; Lunstrum 2014). The project foregrounds the question of displacement and, like the cluster, is focused on a broad swathe of environmental practices, processes, logics, and rationales that can lead to displacement at and across international borders. The project is also allowing us to build on a topic broached at the 2012 workshop, and that is the issue of security (see also chapters 3 and 5). Namely, we examine as a core intervention how security concerns articulate with environmental commitments and processes to produce novel rationales for displacement. Similarly, Pablo has built on his work regarding displacements caused through climate change mitigation and adaptation with a more sustained examination of some specific cases in Bangladesh through collaborations with a former student now working as a researcher in Dhaka at the International Centre for Climate Change and Development (Meraz and Bose 2016). The involvement with the cluster also led directly to his involvement with a research consortium based at Leeds and including research partners in France, Norway, and Switzerland to investigate how deltaic societies in Vietnam, Cambodia, Bangladesh, India, the Netherlands, and Tanzania are addressing climate change and displacement; another project on climate change and cashmere farming in Mongolia; and a third on climate change and social impacts in the circumpolar regions. Others involved in our cluster have had similar success expanding upon their work.

The workshop has thus provided participants with opportunities to expand research on environmental displacement in new empirical and theoretical directions by enabling face-to-face collaboration among participants and facilitated the development of a global network of scholars interested in environmental displacement. Given the diverse backgrounds of the participants and geographical diversity of their research sites, the conversation enabled discussion across disciplines and locales. Participants' theoretical and empirical contributions are helping to develop a wider, more comprehensive, yet still organic and emerging conceptualization of environmental displacement—including the varied forms it takes, its diverse impacts, and strategies for addressing if not halting it.

## Note

1   It is useful here to compare our challenges with those faced by other RRN clusters and networks: see in particular the introduction and chapters 10, 12, and 13.

# References

Bose, Pablo, and Elizabeth Lunstrum. 2014. "Introduction: Environmentally Induced Displacement and Forced Migration." *Refuge* 29, no. 2: 5–10.

Gemenne, François, and Pauline Brücker. 2015. "From the Guiding Principles on Internal Displacement to the Nansen Initiative: What the Governance of Environmental Migration Can Learn from the Governance of Internal Displacement." *International Journal of Refugee Law* 27, no. 2: 245–63.

Lister, Matthew. 2014. "Climate Change Refugees." *Critical Review of International Social and Political Philosophy* 17, no. 5: 618–34.

Lunstrum, Elizabeth. 2014. "Green Militarization: Anti-Poaching Efforts and the Spatial Contours of Kruger National Park." *Annals of the Association of American Geographers* 104, no. 4: 816–32.

———. 2015. "Conservation Meets Militarisation in Kruger National Park: Historical Encounters and Complex Legacies." *Conservation and Society* 13, no. 4: 356–69.

Lunstrum, Elizabeth, Pablo Bose, and Anna Zalik. 2016. "Environmental Displacement: The Common Ground of Climate Change, Extraction, and Conservation." *Area* 48, no. 2: 130–3.

Massé, Francis, and Elizabeth Lunstrum. 2016. "Accumulation by Securitization: Commercial Poaching, Neoliberal Conservation, and the Creation of New Wildlife Frontiers." *Geoforum* 69: 227–37.

———. 2013. "Annotated Bibliography on Nature-Society Relations in and of International Borders." Refugee Research Network, Centre for Refugee Studies, York University.

Mostafa, Meraz, and Pablo S. Bose. 2016. "The Narrow Focus on Climate Change in Bangladesh Often Reproduces Exploitation and Vulnerability Rather than Addressing It." *London School of Economics South Asia Blog*, 24 Oct 2016. http://blogs.lse.ac.uk/southasia/2016/10/24/the-narrow-focus-on-climate-change-in-bangladesh-often-reproduces-exploitation-and-vul-nerability-rather-than-addressing-it/.

Swyngedouw, Erik. 2013. "The Non-Political Politics of Climate Change." *ACME: An International E-Journal for Critical Geographies* 12, no. 1: 1–8.

# Bittersweet Symphony: Challenges and Lessons Learned from Network Building in Latin America

*Beatriz Eugenia Sánchez-Mojica*

*It is forbidden to cry without learning.*

Alfredo Cuervo Barrero

## Introduction

Roberto Vidal, a legal scholar at Javeriana University in Bogotá, was a founding partner of the RRN and joined the executive of International Association for the Study of Forced Migration (IASFM) in 2008, becoming president in 2016. He saw the advantages of networking and with the support of the RRN committed to mobilizing a regional network in Latin America. With his colleague Beatriz Eugenia Sánchez-Mojica, a legal scholar at Los Andes University, Vidal began to reach out to academic and NGO colleagues in Colombia and migration scholars in countries in the region. Vidal had worked closely with civil society organizations particularly the *Instituto Latinoamericano para una Sociedad y un*

*Derecho Alternativo* (ILSA). ILSA is a regional network of lawyers' associations, representatives of academic communities, and members of NGOs in Latin America that use a broad human rights approach to promote research and advocacy activities on economic, social, cultural, and environmental rights, and the extension of legal services to excluded populations. Connections were made with academics and practitioners in Argentina, Bolivia, Chile, Colombia, Ecuador, Mexico, Peru, and Venezuela. The administrative staff of Javeriana University and Los Andes University Law School were particularly supportive and agreed to host an organizing conference in November 2010.[1] Funding was secured from the Association of Universities and Colleges Canada (AUCC) and support was also provided by the Jesuit Refugee Service and the National Secretariat of Social Pastoral of Colombia.

At the conference, thirty researchers mapped out the issues related to forced migration including the root causes, the impact of forced migration on Latin American states, the search of durable solutions and the contribution of forced migrants to the process of peace building. They agreed to form the first ever network focused on forced migration in the hemisphere. The Latin American Network for Forced Migration (LANFM)/*Red latino americana de migración forzada* emerged as an attempt to weave bonds between researchers and pre-existing networks from those very diverse origins by promoting knowledge exchange and production, as well partnership building. The intent was to mobilize and exchange knowledge that contributes to alliance building and to inform the development of both national and international policy frameworks and humanitarian practices relevant to refugees and forced migrants in Latin America.

The organizing of LANFM took place in a complex context. In 2010 more than 400,000 people were newly displaced inside their own countries in the region (IDMC 2010, 14). Colombia's internal armed conflict was the major source of forced migration, having produced over 5 million IDPs (IDMC 2010, 16) and more than 324,000 refugees; most had looked for haven in Ecuador, Venezuela, and other countries of the region. Forced displacement was also taking place in Mexico, Guatemala, and Peru; however, their figures were significantly lower (IDMC 2010, 69). States' responses to this phenomenon were extremely diverse. Colombia, for example, recognized IDPs as an issue in the late nineties and developed a sophisticated public policy to deal with it (Sánchez 2009; Vidal 2008). In sharp contrast, neither Guatemala nor Mexico had even considered forced migration as a problem itself and had made no effort to measure its impact or create a public policy to face it (IDMC 2014, 70–1; Rubio 2017).

This chapter meditates on the lights and shadows of the unfinished building process of this network. The Latin American Network for Forced Migration has been a valuable tool for development of new projects, exchange of experiences, and partnership building. It has also faced deep challenges, including the preservation of the network itself. LANFM's main achievements have been in the areas of partnership building and networking, through the organization and hosting of four important workshops and an international conference. The first workshop focused on developing a regional network for research and advocacy. The second drew out connections between trade and investment and forced migration. The third highlighted connections between violence and migration and drew together experiences in Colombia, Mexico, El Salvador, and Guatemala. The last workshop addressed the impacts of extractive industries, such as mining, and brought together academics and NGO representatives from Colombia and Canada. Finally, the international conference was a successful attempt to create ties between the regional network and a global one: the International Association for the Study of Forced Migration (IASFM). However, it was a bittersweet achievement. This event also marked the beginning of the end for LANFM.

The main discussions and contributions of the four workshops and the international conference are highlighted below.

## Forced Migration in Latin America: Creating Regional Networks for Research and Advocacy

Our 2010 conference, entitled *Forced Migration Latin America: Creating Regional Networks for Research and Advocacy*, sought to consolidate existing relationships between academic and NGO researchers and practitioners and to develop a broader regional network (LANFM 2010). Participants in this initial meeting were primarily from institutions and organizations in Colombia and Canada with representatives from Mexico, Peru, Costa Rica, the United States, and Spain.

The conference had two central aspects. Firstly, the overflow of traditional responses to forced migration, including the rights of refugees and protection systems of internal displacement, in the presence of factors such as development, climate change, urban violence, war on drugs, degradation of non-international armed conflicts, and new forms of terrorism, which had increased the number of forced migrants without adequate protection and care. And secondly, the reduced presence in global forums such as IASFM of forced migration processes in Latin America due to a lack of links between academics and practitioners in the region. As a result, the conference focused on the need to consolidate networks to facilitate future multilateral dialogue spaces on forced migration in Latin America and spaces for ongoing communication between regional practitioners and researchers and global networks of forced migration studies.

For this purpose, the methodology developed in the meeting included a closed meeting of international experts on four themes: 1) the forms of forced migration in Latin America; 2) forced migration policies in the region; 3) regional responses; and 4) alternatives to forced migration and the creation of regional research networks as a strategy. The conference was open and included participants from the academic community, organizations, and government entities interested in Colombia in order to present the conclusions and discussions that emerged from previous meetings. This exercise allowed us to advance and question the landscape of forms and solutions to forced migration in Latin America, identifying relevant local and regional trends in the consolidation of specific studies and possible public policy proposals to address and mitigate the adverse effects of these situations.

## Trade and Investment-Induced Population Displacement in Latin America

The second workshop organized by LANFM was held at York University in Toronto, Canada, from 12–14 October 2011 (Ravecca and Payne 2011). It aimed to systematize current knowledge on the connection between trade and investment and forced migration and to establish a common research agenda for LANFM. Understanding and addressing the relevant drivers of forced migration flows is critical to developing new research and policy responses that will improve human rights implementation and human development. A number of trade and investment factors have been linked to forced migration including conflict over resources in the context of "development" activities such as mining, monoculture farming, and petroleum extraction. As well, food insecurity and long-term climate changes that are having negative impacts on the livelihoods of vulnerable communities across the region are seen as related to the phenomenon of forced migration. In this regard the workshop offered innovative perspectives on the problem.

Among other factors explored in the inaugural meeting of the LANFM in 2010, researchers observed that international trading relationships and flows of foreign direct investment have had profound economic, social, and ecological impacts on the region and consequently may contribute to migratory flows, both as push and pull factors. They observed that some of the paths connecting trade and investment to forced migration are direct while others are more indirect and consequently more challenging to assess. Building on these established relationships, the second gathering of the LANFM in Toronto in 2011 was planned in order to: 1) expand our collective understanding of newly emerging or under-studied forms of forced migration; (2) address various policy dimensions including legal standards for businesses engaged in investment and trade that generate population displacements; and (3) identify best policies for supporting those who are displaced.

The aims of this second workshop were to bring together distinct groups of researchers in order to systematize current knowledge on the connection between trade and investment and forced migration, to identify common research agendas for the LANFM, and to put in place capacity building plans to carry out this agenda. Researchers from Latin America and Canada, both academics and researchers from non-governmental organizations including experts on forced migration, investment and trade, gathered for a full day of formal presentations. This was followed by a facilitated second day aimed at identifying research themes for future collaboration. Following the formal sessions of the workshop, a smaller group of scholars met with the directors of CERLAC and CRS for an additional day to explore future joint research initiatives between LANFM, the Refugee Research Network (RRN), and Canadian scholars. The gathering nourished the ground for ongoing alliance building rooted in this mobilization and exchange of knowledge, which was expected to inform the development of policy frameworks and humanitarian practices affecting forced migrants in Latin America and Canada. Through an interactive collective process, three specific areas of focus were identified, and small groups were established to further develop them. These specific focus areas were Law and Regulation, Vulnerability, and Advocacy/Civil Society. Each group clarified their issues, developed relevant research questions, and identified advocacy strategies.

## Migration and Violence: Lessons from Colombia for the Americas

A workshop supported by LANFM focusing on "Migration and Violence: Lessons from Colombia for the Americas" was held in Bogotá on 29–30 June 2012. It was also connected to the Transatlantic Forum on Migration and Integration (TFMI). The workshop explored the issue of drug-violence induced migration in Colombia with a view to lessons learned and research gaps in the Central American context. It focused especially on the migration (both international and internal) resulting from the protracted drug-related conflict in Colombia. A series of panels by Colombian experts in the legal, social science, and public policy fields addressed Colombia's relatively long history in dealing with the internal and international migration consequences of drug-related violence. Each panel discussion also featured a Central American expert as respondent to engage these issues from the Central American context. Central American experts also provided context on how migration and violence in the region and the effects of drug-related violence have impacted international and internal migration patterns.

The main objective of the conference was to foster the development of interdisciplinary academic research in Central America and Mexico regarding the relationship between violence—particularly narco-violence—and migration. The setting in Bogotá was deliberate as the organizers wanted to discuss how lessons learned from Colombia's experience with narco-induced migration could be leveraged for the benefit of Central America and Mexico. With the participation of experts on international cooperation, authorities, university officials, and civil society, the conference highlighted research results and relevant

BEATRIZ EUGENIA SÁNCHEZ-MOJICA

intervention experiences from Colombia, El Salvador, Guatemala, and Mexico. The debate by participants on the forced migration experiences of these four countries allowed the identification of valuable but complex epistemological challenges to understanding the links between violence and human mobility.

Colombia is illustrative of the consequences of forced displacement including the attribution of penal and civil responsibilities. Due to the complexity of the causes that trigger forced mobility, the traditional attribution of culpability to an individual who has caused forced displacement has been proven inadequate. Thus, more systematic approaches to the consequences of crime were introduced. The Colombian approach to dealing with the loss of land by victims of crime is the best example of this trend. This country also faces the challenge of determining whether displacement took place due to political violence or other types of violence, differentiating the infractions of international humanitarian law within the framework of armed internal conflict, mass violations of human rights, generalized violence, and/or of internal strife and unrest. The classical distinctions between political violence and violence due to common organized crime do not appear to function adequately in all cases in order to account for the political nature of local actors such as narcotraffickers, to the extent that it also groups diverse legal actors like officials and businessmen who seek to control political, economic, and social relations that are woven together in a territory. In this sense, the *Ley de Víctimas y Restitución de Tierras* (the Law of Victims and Land Restitution) issued in 2011 in Colombia represents a setback in the recognition of rights of victims of displacement as it reduces justice to only victims of the armed internal conflict, leaving violations of human rights, pervasive violence, disturbances, and interior strife out. Furthermore, the law does not include protection for those who have been displaced due to fumigations, the victims of so-called emerging gangs, the victims who sought refuge abroad,[2] and collective victims such as labour unions, as well as those who are part of social movements and opposing parties. The economic activities in rural areas such as mega-mining and the cultivation of agro-combustibles have raised questions about the financing of non-state armed groups and the creation of new cycles of displacement.

# Extractive Industries and Violence in Latin America

A fourth workshop on *Extractive Industries and Violence in Latin America* was hosted in Bogotá on 7–8 December 2013. This workshop was supported by a broader project led by the Centre for Research on Latin America and the Caribbean (CERLAC) and the Centre for Refugee Studies (CRS) at York University in Canada and funded by the Association of Universities and Colleges of Canada (AUCC). The project aimed to implement a partnership strategy to foster collaborative research and networking among Canadian and Latin American researchers to produce and disseminate new policy-relevant knowledge about the complex determinants of forced migration in the region. The partners organized a two-day workshop in Bogotá with a coordinated session in Toronto. The workshop brought together researchers, NGO practitioners, and graduate students from Colombia, Ecuador, Peru, Bolivia, Mexico, and Canada to: 1) systematize and critically engage with current knowledge on the connection between extractive industries (EIs), violence, and forced migration; 2) establish a common regional research agenda; and 3) put in place capacity-building plans to carry out this agenda (Ibáñez and Vásquez 2014).

The workshop focused on the impact of recent expanding EI development on violence and involuntary displacement of local populations in Latin America. The partners noted that EI activity has expanded rapidly around the globe in recent years in response to the growing demand for minerals and energy from rapidly industrializing countries such as China. This expansion coincided with widespread deregulation and trade liberalization in Latin America, which weakened institutional capacities to regulate the industry and the conflicts it generated. Boom conditions in mining and petroleum producing countries, meanwhile, generated a sharp rise in often violent socio-environmental and political conflicts at the sites of EI operations.

The workshop was exploratory, aiming to foster dialogue, develop future agendas, and to incorporate new researchers into LANFM. The project was built as a research-exchange project and thus no actual research was funded. The workshop methodology was designed to bring together two distinct clusters of researchers from Canadian and Latin American institutions that rarely interact—researchers of extractive industries and researchers of forced migration—in order to foster dialogue across these

areas and to develop a common research agenda. EI researchers presented on their area of specialization and addressed possible intersections
between the processes they study and the production of new vulnerabilities and conflicts that may trigger forced displacement. Researchers
of forced displacement presented their case studies and commented on
possible connections between forced migration processes and the operation of EIs. Presentations were organized around thematic panels that
included researchers from both research clusters, followed by a session
of open questions and discussion. Two days of formal presentations by
experts assessed the state of knowledge on the topic, made connections
between knowledge silos, and identified knowledge gaps in the field. The
presentation of case studies from Colombia, Ecuador, Peru, Bolivia, Guatemala, Haiti, Mexico, and Canada helped ground the discussion in concrete experiences, and permitted participants to identify regional patterns
as well as country-specific conditions. As a result, participants gained a
much richer understanding of the determinants of forced migration in
the region and their relationship with EI development. In organizing the
workshop, partners decided to include case studies from four countries
not originally included in the proposal (Bolivia, Guatemala, Haiti, and
Mexico) because these countries were also experiencing significant EI
development, violence, and displacement and their inclusion could help
broaden the regional coverage of the workshop and of the network.

Knowledge of each other and an open and consensual approach to
decision-making were both essential for the success of the project. The
collaborative approach helped identify themes of relevance to Latin
American partners and their need to broaden the regional coverage of the
network. The networks of the Centre for Research on Latin America and
the Caribbean (CERLAC) were useful to identify non-Colombian participants to be invited and added to the network. The workshop's contribution to development includes enhanced capacity for partner collaboration
through the plan identified above, and the production of policy-relevant
knowledge about the mechanisms that produce vulnerabilities to violence
and forced displacement among communities in relation to EI development. Considering the outcomes and the investment of time, effort, and
funding, the partners' assessment was that the project was extremely valuable, especially in setting the basis for future collaboration.

# IASFM XV Conference: Forced Migration and Peace

In July 2014, Javeriana University, the Pensar Institute (of which Vidal was then director), and Los Andes University organized and held the fifteenth IASFM conference in Bogotá. The complicated relationship between peace and forced migration was the central theme of the event. More than 300 participants from twenty-five countries including academics, activists, members of civil society organizations, officials from international organizations, and forced migrants met and discussed the worldwide situation of forced migration.[3] The topic was examined in the context of two distinct and simultaneous processes: first, the celebration of thirty years of the Cartagena Declaration, an international rights instrument that proved a turning point in managing forced migration in post-conflict situations; and second, the peace talks between the Colombian government, the Revolutionary Armed Forces of Colombia (FARC), and the National Liberation Army (ELN).[4]

The event pursued two main objectives. First, to establish a space for reflection and discussion so that academics, activists, policymakers, and forced migrants could revive the spirit of the Cartagena Declaration, revisiting the lessons that it—and the process it originated from—might offer the Colombian peace process (that was then in progress) and the expected post-conflict period that would follow. The second objective was to deepen the horizontal dialogue between global north and south and to build peer relationships in the study of, debates around, and search for solutions related to the complex phenomenon of forced migration.

The conference delved into six subjects, all linked to the relationship between forced migration and peace. Peace-building and forced exodus was the first subject. It revolved around the idea that any agenda aimed at peacefully resolving conflict must include both management of internal displacement and refugee protection, and compensation for victims. The second topic was justice and forced migration. It focused on the study and analysis of the role of justice systems—at national, regional, and international levels—in recognizing and guaranteeing the rights of forced migrants, including victims of both armed conflicts and situations associated with undemocratic regimes. The discussion around regional responses to forced migration (the third issue) centred on the Cartagena Declaration as an instrument for managing the pressing issue of shelter and forced

BEATRIZ EUGENIA SÁNCHEZ-MOJICA

displacement in the Americas. Lasting and sustainable solutions for overcoming uprooting was the fourth matter of study. It focused on the need to develop sustainable solutions that allow displaced people and refugees to put their uprooting behind them, as well as the need for a critical stance towards existing policies and programs to determine the impact, achievements, and the challenges faced in their implementation. Forced migration in times of peace, the next topic, examined the increasing number of cases of forced migration in situations other than armed conflict. These included environmental disasters, development projects, and violence caused by mafias and criminal groups. Finally, resistance and migration analyzed how displaced people and refugees have shown their ability to create their own spaces and offer resistance to exile and uprooting.

It is important to note that, although this was an IASFM conference, LANFM took a crucial role in it. In fact, I was the conference program chair. Organizing this event in Bogotá was a strategy to weave links between the two networks. Following the conclusions reached at the first workshop in 2010, it was the aim to increase the presence in global forums of forced migration processes in Latin America. Moreover, there was the goal of enabling regional academics and practitioners to meet their peers from other regions, in order to start multilateral and horizontal dialogues. The conference's second objective was crafted to embed the goals set by the Latin American network since the beginning.

The endeavour gave its fruits. *IASFM XIV Conference* was an auspicious space for debate, knowledge sharing, and network building between LANFM's members and the rest of the world. Several projects and collaborations were born there. It must be highlighted that some of the most interesting ideas and proposals emerged from the "south to south" dialogues. It was the case of an exchange initiative for PhD students from Colombia and India, promoted by Universidad del Rosario and the Calcutta Research Group. The attendance of Colombian academics to the *International Conference on Gender, Empowerment and Conflict in South Asia*, held by the Calcutta Research Group in November 2014 was another product of this dialogue. One more was the relationship built with South American Network for Environmental Migration (RESAMA) a pioneering Brazilian and Uruguayan initiative for coordination and mobilization of experts, researchers, and practitioners to include the subject of environmental migration in public agendas in the region. This collaboration, still ongoing, has produced valuable results—such as the book *Refugiados Ambientais*, published in 2018, which contains some articles from the Latin American network members.

Another achievement was the increasing presence of Latin American forced migration issues in the following IASFM conferences: *XVI Conference: Rethinking Forced Migration and Displacement: Theory, Policy, and Praxis*, held in Poznan (Poland) in 2016, included two Latin American panels, with three more for the XVII Conference in Thessaloniki, Greece, in July 2018. Moreover, a permanent working group, formed by former LANFM members and other global south scholars, was created inside IASFM with the purpose of improving the relationship between academia and innovative empirical work for the co-production of knowledge in forced migration.

Paradoxically, and in spite of those achievements, Bogotá's conference was the last event organized by LANFM. Months before the conference, and due to various personal and professional reasons, both Vidal and Sánchez announced their decision to leave their coordination role in the network. That announcement triggered a debate about its future. Finally, a decision was made, including some significant changes to the initiative. It was relaunched by the *II Humanitarian Conference on Forced Migration Issues,* that took place in Bogotá a couple of days before IASFM event, as the *Red sobre Migraciones Forzadas en las Américas* (RMFA)/Network on Forced Migration in the Americas. In a public statement it was announced that RMFA will pursue two objectives. First, it will present an annual report about the institutional responses to forced migration in the region that will be prepared based on research developed by its members. Second, it will hold a biannual conference, where the challenges pointed out by the reports would be studied, and recommendations to lead them will be presented to the region's governments (IICRHMF 2014, 16).

Colombian NGO CODHES[5] agreed to coordinate the network and a group of young scholars and graduate students joined it. Even a Facebook page[6] and a new website were launched. It seemed like a bright new beginning. However, this initiative was short-lived. Less than a year later the network disappeared.

# Bittersweet Symphony: Lessons and Challenges in Building the LANFM

LANFM's birth couldn't have taken place under better omens. The first Latin American network of networks emerged with perfect timing. There was a rising interest for forced migration in the region. The issue was being studied by an increasing number of local scholars, particularly in Colombia (e.g., Ibáñez 2008; Rodríguez 2010; Somohano and Yankelevich 2011). Moreover, international organizations, such as UNHCR and UNPD, were working on it, as well as several NGOs and other organizations from the civil society (e.g., CODHES and Colombian Episcopal Conference 2006). Even states were gradually taking forced migration into consideration. Colombia's sophisticated public policy regarding IDPs is undoubtedly the best known of these state responses (IDMC 2013). But there were other official attempts to manage non-voluntary migration in the region. Peru's Law on internal displacement of 2004[7] and the broad concept of asylum and refuge as a human right in Ecuador's Constitution[8] are perfect examples of those efforts. Therefore, the moment was truly auspicious to start weaving bonds between Latin American academics, practitioners, and even policymakers that were working from different perspectives on non-voluntary exodus issues in the region. There were plenty of experiences, lessons learned, and questions to share and discuss.

Moreover, LANFM's first conference was a success. It gathered a very diverse group of academics, NGO members, practitioners, as well as graduate and undergraduate students—all eager to be part of the network building experience. The quality of the lectures presented back then was outstanding, discussions were intense and fruitful, and multiple ideas for future collaborations between members of the new network were proposed. The event concluded with a statement expressing the participants' strong commitment to continue working together, enlarging and strengthening the newborn community. But only five years later, that community no longer existed. Although LANFM managed to organize three successful workshops as well as a significant international conference, it was unable to sustain itself. How can this be explained? There are four related factors that were not apparent during the network's lifetime.

Only a careful reflection about the context and circumstances of the network has unveiled them.

First of all, despite the multiple ideas that emerged after the first congress and after every workshop, LANFM was unable to transform these ideas into sustainable research projects. Efforts were made, e.g., an application to the Social Sciences and Humanities Research Council of Canada for a Partnership Grant in 2011, but they were not successful. The network's inability to bring funded projects to its membership gradually lowered enthusiasm. If the new community was unable to expand and deepen members' research agendas, there was no point investing time and other resources in it. Thus, little by little, partners stopped presenting initiatives to this forum.

Secondly, there was a lack of strategy for keeping the members in touch between conferences and workshops. The LANFM website, hosted at the RRN website, was launched after the first conference,[9] but it never worked as a true space for conveying and debating ideas, papers, and projects. It just informed members about future events. Absence of continued communication among LANFM's members weakened even more the interest they once shared in the common project. After the IASFM Conference, the Facebook page and website launched by RMFA were not able to keep the community together.

These two factors described above—the network's failed efforts to find funding for its membership projects, as well as its shortcomings on keeping alive the bonds among its members—are linked to a third factor. The network never developed its own administrative structure nor obtained funds to sustain its activities. This means it totally depended on the resources generously given by its partners, in particular York, Javeriana, and Los Andes universities. This kind of arrangement proved adequate for organizing conferences and workshops, but it didn't allow LANFM to go further. Formulating research projects, finding partners, and looking for development funds are all complex activities that demand time as well as human and monetary resources. Building and operating an online platform to connect members equally requires multiple inputs. The network's lack of infrastructure prevented it from performing an ambitious role as an engine for the research agendas of its members and confined it to the position of event host.

Finally, the absence of strong leadership is the fourth element that explains LANFM's short life. As it has been said, this initiative was conceived as a network of networks. The original idea was to build links among pre-existing, well-organized collaborative structures, each one carrying out clear research agendas. This imagined scenario didn't demand a powerful leadership, but a soft one, able to build consensus and developing a coordination strategy among peers. However, the real scenario where the new network had to perform ended up being very different. There weren't networks but universities, NGOs, and people in their personal capacity were the ones who joined LANFM. In other words, there were no groups, only individuals. Thus there wasn't a need to coordinate different collaborative programs; there was a need to design and build one from scratch. But, as previously mentioned, the network didn't have the resources to face such a challenge.

The juncture of these factors led to a weak network. The enthusiasm and goodwill of its members couldn't disguise the fact that there wasn't a solid common ground. There was, of course, a shared matter of interest, but not a project to work on together. People and institutions gathered every time there was a conference or a workshop, but once the event was over conversations among them ceased. When the network stopped organizing events, the silence became absolute.

Moreover, an additional factor should be taken into consideration. LANFM's existence and performance were linked to the leadership provided by the coordinators Sánchez and Vidal. Their professional bond as well as their friendship gave support, energy, and drive to the whole project. This can be a valuable and useful way of working, as demonstrated by Bose and Lustrum's chapter; and in fact, at the beginning it was. But it also implies a risk: it can be a challenge for the new coordinators to maintain a structure built in such a particular way.

The bitterness of the experience has now been exposed, but LANFM also left behind a certain sweetness. Actually, members of the extinct LANFM are still receiving benefits from their past membership. First, it allowed people from diverse backgrounds to meet each other, to share ideas, and even to imagine common projects. It wasn't the first attempt to build a regional network—e.g., *Red Andina de Migraciones*/Andean Network on Migration was founded in 2009,[10] but it was a pioneer joining academic and NGO researchers. Therefore, it was a valuable meeting space to gather people and institutions with a variety of approaches and concerns on forced migration issues. Some of these gatherings have been fruitful. As noted, publications have been written by people connected by this initiative.

Second, it promoted academic exchanges and collaboration among the partner universities. Javeriana and Los Andes have developed an intense relationship regarding forced migration issues that has stood the test of time. Several workshops and seminars have been organized by this tandem, and the collaboration is still going on. In fact, they have recently published the first book on Colombian exiles of the internal armed conflict (Iranzo and Louidor 2018). Following LANFM's spirit, the book brings together works from academics, practitioners, and activists, offering a colourful and multidisciplinary approach. Moreover, a strong relationship between York and Javeriana was built. There has been an intense activity that included exchanges of doctoral students and visiting scholars particularly in refugee law; activities have continued to take place after the network ceased to exist.

Finally, it boosted the presence of scholars and NGO members from Latin America in global forums such as IASFM. It also helped to start building a global south-south dialogue. This last achievement is extremely valuable. There is in Latin America a long tradition of academic dialogue and collaboration with the global north, a complex relationship with plenty of shadow and lights (for an analysis of the global north's dark side and the path to overcoming it, see chapter 1). However, and in spite of the existence of comparable contexts of forced migration, there has been little exchange of knowledge and expertise with countries such as India, Sri Lanka, or Turkey. LANFM opened some paths for this process, throughout collaboration initiatives among the Calcutta Research Group and three Colombian Universities (Javeriana, Los Andes, and Rosario). Those were baby steps but in the right direction and there are chances to enlarge them.

Before ending this chapter, a new question arises. The LANFM experience has had both lights and shadows, but could it be resumed? Would it be worthwhile? The answer is a conditional "yes."

The current context is, perhaps, even more propitious than it was in 2010. The region is facing complex forced migration processes that pose equally complex questions. Each scenario including: Colombian post-conflict processes, Northern Triangle forced displacement caused by criminal gang violence, Venezuela's mass flight due to its political and economic crisis, and Brazil's quest for sustainable solutions to the environmental migration issue, is equally interesting and full of possibilities for academics to work with. Besides, both local academic communities and NGOs have been very active, producing numerous research works on these matters (e.g., Cantor and Rodríguez 2016; Céspedes-Báez and Prieto-Rios 2017; Jubilut et al. 2018). There are also new networks, such as the South American Network for Environmental Migration (RESAMA), developing interesting research agendas. A regional network of networks could be the opportunity for these actors to join forces by promoting knowledge exchange and production, as well as partnership building.

Experience has revealed that a good context and suitable partners are not sufficient to build a regional network. Resuming LANFM will demand learning from past lessons. The new version should have strong leadership and resources to support an infrastructure that can maintain the linkages among network members. It also should have its own defined research agenda, according to the particular Latin American context. This doesn't mean that a new LANFM shouldn't be open to its members' projects and initiatives; however, it must have its own goals and mission if it wants to have a long and independent existence.

## Notes

1 The conference "Forced Migration Latin America: Creating Regional Networks for Research and Advocacy," was hosted at Javeriana University on 17 and 19 November and at Los Andes Law School on 18 November.

2 State's recognition of victims abroad came a few years later with a broad interpretation of 2011 Ley de Víctimas y Restitución de Tierras due, in part, to the demands of Colombian refugee organizations, such as Foro Internacional de Víctimas (see Sánchez 2018).

3 The ESPMI Network performed a relevant role in the conference organization by coordinating the review process of abstracts submitted.

4 Peace talks between Colombian government and FARC reached a successful end in November 2016 with the Acuerdo Final para la Terminación del Conflicto y la Construcción de una Paz Estable y Duradera, signed by the two parties. On the contrary, negotiations with ELN were suspended in January 2018. Resuming this peace process seems unlikely in December 2018.

5 CODHES-Consultoría para los Derechos Humanos y el Desplazamiento is one of the oldest and most well-known Colombian NGOs working on forced migration issues.

6    https://www.facebook.com/Red-sobre-Migraciones-Forzadas-en-las-Am%C3%A9ric
     as-444477895697380/.

7    Peru, Law 28233 of 2004 "Ley de Desplazamientos Internos."

8    Article 41 of 2008's Constitution of the Republic of Ecuador.

9    http://refugeeresearch.net/research-networks/latin-american-network-for-forced-
     migration-lanfm/.

10   This was a sub-regional network, composed by NGOs from the Andean countries.
     During its first years it was very active, but activity has significantly decreased since
     2014.

## References

Cantor, David, and Nicolás Rodríguez Serna. 2016. *The New Refugees: Crime and Forced Displacement in Latin America*. London: Institute of Latin American Studies, University of London.

Céspedes-Báez Lina, and Enrique Prieto-Rios. 2017. *Utopía u oportunidad fallida: Análisis crítico del Acuerdo del Paz*. Bogotá: Editorial Universidad del Rosario.

CODHES and Colombian Episcopal Conference. 2006. *Desafíos para construir nación: El país ante el desplazamiento, el conflicto armado y la crisis humanitaria 1995–2005*. Bogotá: Rubens Impresores. Accessed 4 May 2018. http://www.acnur.org/t3/uploads/media/COI_1264.pdf.

Ibáñez García, María A., and Sergio Vásquez Guzmán. 2014. "Industrias extractivas y violencia en América Latina / Extractive Industries and Violence in Latin America." Workshop report. Universidad de los Andes, Bogotá, 7–8 Dec 2013.

Ibáñez Londoño, A. M. 2008. *El desplazamiento forzoso en Colombia: Un camino sin retorno hacia la pobreza*. Bogotá: Universidad de los Andes.

Internal Displacement Monitoring Centre (IDMC). 2013. "Colombia: Displacement in Brief." 31 Dec 2013. Accessed 4 May 2018. http://www.internal-displacement.org/americas/colombia/summary.

———. 2011. "Internal Displacement Global Overview of Trends and Developments in 2010." March 2011. Geneva: IDMC and Norwegian Refugee Council. Accessed 4 May 2018. http://www.internal-displacement.org/assets/publications/2011/2011-global-overview-2010-global-en.pdf.

IICRHMF. 2014. "II Conferencia Regional Humanitaria sobre Migraciones Forzadas Declaración de Bogotá." 14–15 July 2014. Accessed 4 May 2018. http://www.codhes.org/~codhes/images/Articulos/DeclaracionBogota24092014.pdf.

Iranzo, Dosdad Ángela, and Wooldy E. Louidor. 2018. *Entre la guerra y paz: Los lugares de la diáspora colombiana*. Bogotá: Universidad de los Andes y Pontifica Universidad Javeriana.

Jubilut, Liliana L., Érika Pires Ramos, Carolina de Abreu Batista Claro, and Fernanda de Salles Cavedon-Capdeville. 2018. *Refugiados Ambientais*. Boa Vista: Universidade Federal de Roraima.

LANFM. 2010. "Migración forzada en América Latina: Creando redes para la investigación regional y la incidencia política." Workshop report. Bogotá, Colombia, 16–18 Nov 2010. Accessed 4 May 2018. http://refugeeresearch.net/ rrndev/wp-content/uploads/2015/01/LANFM-Memorias-Primer-Encuentro-Bogota-final-narrative_0.pdf.

Ravecca, Paulo, and William Payne. 2011. "Trade and Investment-Induced Population Displacement in Latin America." Workshop Report, York University, 12–14 Oct 2011. Accessed 4 May 2018. http://refugeeresearch.net/rrndev/wp-content/ uploads/2015/01/Workshop-Report-TIIDLA_0.pdf.

Rodríguez Garavito, César. 2010. *Más allá del desplazamiento: Políticas derechos y superación del desplazamiento forzado en Colombia*. Bogotá: Universidad de los Andes.

Rubio, L. 2017. "Internal Displacement in Mexico: The Debate on Concepts, Statistics and State Responsibility." In *The New Refugees: Crime and Forced Displacement in Latin America*, edited by David Cantor and Nicolás Rodríguez Serna, 47–62. London: Institute of Latin American Studies, University of London.

Sánchez, Beatriz E. 2009. "Cuando los derechos son la jaula: Trasplante rígido del soft law para la gestión del desplazamiento forzado." *Estudios Políticos* 35 (julio-diciembre): 11–32.

———. 2018. "Refugiados colombianos ante la firma de la paz en Colombia: ¿Un retorno no deseado?" In *Entre la guerra y paz: Los lugares de la diáspora colombiana*, edited by Ángela Iranzo Dosdad and Wooldy E. Louidor, 41–74. Bogotá: Universidad de los Andes y Pontifica Universidad Javeriana.

Sánchez, Beatriz E., and René Urueña. 2017. "Colombian Development-Induced Displacement: Considering the Impact of International Law on Domestic Policy." *Groningen Journal of International Law* 5, no. 1: 73–95.

Somohano, Katya, and Pablo Yankelevich. 2011. *El refugio en México: Entre la historia y los desafíos contemporáneos*. México: COMAR-SEGOB.

Vengoechea Barrios, Juliana, Juanita Deperraz, and Marco A. Velásquez Ruiz. 2014. "IASFM 15 Conference Report: Forced Migration and Peace: 30 Years of the Cartagena Declaration on Refugees." Pontifica Universidad Javeriana, Bogotá, July 2014. http://iasfm.org/wp-content/uploads/2014/09/IASFM-FINAL-REPORT.pdf.

Vidal, Roberto. 2008. *Derecho global y desplazamiento interno: Creación, uso y desaparición del desplazamiento forzado por la violencia en el derecho contemporáneo*. Bogotá: Editorial Pontificia Universidad Javeriana.

# Partnering on Research Methodologies in Forced Migration: Challenges, Opportunities, and Lessons Learned

*Christina Clark-Kazak*

## Introduction

In this chapter I explore lessons learned in developing an international network on research methodologies and knowledge production in forced migration. I describe both the successes and challenges of this network, with a view to contributing to more sustainable partnerships in the future. In particular, I highlight the importance of developing specific, concrete initiatives around which network members can rally, and of taking advantage of opportunities that present themselves. This includes adding methodology activities to existing initiatives and events. We also learned about the challenges of funding projects on methodology, in contrast to more traditional, empirically driven research collaborations. Moreover, despite an explicit focus on power and attempts to decolonize forced migration, the network still reflected and reproduced knowledge asymmetries that privileged participation from those in the global north. After these general reflections, the chapter focuses on a specific initiative that had particular success: the development of ethical considerations for research in forced migration contexts. This example provides important insights into community-university partnerships and is analyzed using the interactive and contextual model that Suarez-Balcazar, Harper, and Lewis developed (2005).

## The Need for Partnership on Research Methodologies in Forced Migration

The partnerships described in this chapter have been mobilized in the context of several methodological gaps in the field of forced migration studies. Researchers in forced migration contexts face particular methodological opportunities and challenges (Bakewell 2007; Berriane and de Haas 2012; Temple and Moran 2006). Research with mobile populations, some of whom may not have formal legal status, requires the adaptation of standard sampling methods (Bloch 1999, 2007; Macchiavello 2003; Misago and Landau 2013; Polzer 2013; Singh and Clark 2013). Sampling and data collection are particularly difficult on topics involving clandestine or prohibited activities, such as human trafficking (Brennan 2004; Clawson 2006; Tyldum and Brunovskis 2005; Johnson 2014). Forced migration research has also been prominent in the development of particular methodologies, such as narratives (Bertrand 2000; Clark-Kazak 2009; De Haene, Grietens, and Verschueren 2010; Eastmond 2007; Ghorashi 2008; Powles 2004; Johnson 2012) and participatory action research (Cooper 2005; Doná 2006; Ellis et al. 2007; Guerin and Guerin 2007; Moran, Mohamed, and Lovel 2011; Rodgers 2005; Tang 2008).

While an emerging literature has thus begun to document specific methodological issues in particular cases (Ghelani 2013), important gaps remain. First, the current literature underexplores the methodological implications of disciplinary differences within the field of forced migration and the challenges of interdisciplinary approaches. While scholars in related fields such as international studies have advocated for an "anti-disciplinary" approach that transcends disciplines (Rosow 2003), few similar discussions have occurred within forced migration studies.

On a related second point, there has been little attention to the question of an overarching methodological approach in forced migration studies. Does our field need specific research approaches and methods, or can we piggyback on analogous contexts in the more established fields of international development studies and conflict studies? Are the same methods and theories applicable to the study of both forced and voluntary migration? Our field is only beginning to have serious discussions about what "counts" as data and the appropriateness of certain methods for forced migration research (Bakewell 2008; Jacobsen and Landau 2003; Rodgers 2005; see also chapter 2).

A final area in which there is only an emerging literature relates to particular ethical dilemmas in contexts of forced migration due to vulnerabilities occasioned by structural constraints and unequal power relations (Block, Riggs, and Haslam 2013; Lammers 2007; Samaddar 2001; see also chapter 1). These power inequities require forced migration researchers to pay greater attention to reflexivity (Johnson 2014; Lenette and Boddy 2013), as well as standard ethical principles like voluntary informed consent (Clark-Kazak 2012; Hugman, Bartolomei, and Pittaway 2011) and "do no harm" (Hugman, Pittaway, and Bartolomei 2011; Mackenzie, McDowell, and Pittaway 2007). We should pay more attention (Bradley 2017) to these and related ethical issues, and consider a potential expansion of institution-specific ethical guidelines (Refugee Studies Centre 2007) on research in forced migration situations (Lenning 2001).

## Overview and Description of Activities

The idea for a network on knowledge production and methodologies in forced migration came from a meeting of the Refugee Research Network in 2010 in Toronto. Galya Ben-Arieh (Northwestern University) and Christina Clark-Kazak (York University) agreed to initially co-lead the group, established in 2012. The RRN provided seed money for an annotated bibliography, researched and written by Chizuru Nobe Ghelani (2013). The bibliography provided an important starting point from which to identify the existing literature, as well as the gaps. In particular, Ghelani's analysis revealed specific shortcomings of the literature in relation to: power relations in knowledge production; epistemological differences in what constitutes knowledge and the value attached to knowledge; disciplinary specificities and the opportunities and challenges of interdisciplinary research; as well as the particular methodological and ethical issues related to forced migration studies, in comparison to similar fields like conflict and development studies.

To partially address some of these gaps, in 2014 Clark-Kazak led the development of a Partnership Development Grant (PDG) from SSHRC for a three-year project entitled "Understanding Forced Migration: Methodology, Knowledge Production and Critical Pedagogy." The project aimed to develop research tools, strategies, and approaches adapted to specific contexts of forced migration; to address power inequities in forced knowledge production and mobilization; and to engage in the critical reassessment and design of curriculum to advance teaching practices to respond to the needs and experiences of forced migrants. This initiative was approved by the peer review committee but did not rank high enough to be funded. Ironically, the proposal scored low on methodology.

Shortly after receiving the negative result from this competition Clark-Kazak secured funding for a conference—marking the official end of the RRN grant—that would showcase the many research results of the clusters. A session on methodology was originally slated for this conference but did not materialize due to lack of sufficient papers. However, Anita Fábos (Clark University) and Dianna Shandy (Macalester College) proposed a pre-workshop on narratives, which was added to the two-day RRN conference. Subsequently, Fábos and Shandy received seed money from the International Association for the Study of Forced Migration (IASFM) to host a series of webinars on narrative methodologies (Shandy, Fábos, and Belbas 2016). They also organized linked panels at the IASFM conference in July 2016 in Poland and a panel for the American Anthropological Association conference in 2016 in Minneapolis.

In June 2016, Clark-Kazak responded to a specific call from the Canadian government for research proposals relating to Syrian refugee arrivals. She partnered with the Canadian Council for Refugees (CCR), the United Nations High Commissioner for Refugees (UNHCR), the Canadian Association for Refugee and Forced Migration Studies (CARFMS), and York's Centre for Refugee Studies (CRS) to propose the development of ethical principles for research in contexts of forced migration. As noted above, ethics had been identified as a gap in the literature in the 2013 annotated bibliography, and this had become apparent in practice. For example, while all academic research in Canada is subject to university Ethics Review Board approval, community-based researchers may not require nor benefit from similar reviews. Moreover, established guidelines including the Tri-Council guidelines are general, while the specific realities of refugee research pose particular ethical issues. This ethics initiative was funded, resulting in the development of these guidelines (Clark-Kazak et al. 2017), as well as tools for practitioners and infographics for refugees (Canadian Council for Refugees, n.d.).

## What Worked

Despite modest resources, the network was able to achieve some important results. This section will list some of the strategies that helped to mobilize people and produce tangible results.

First, concrete, realistic activities were important in generating and maintaining momentum. Starting with the annotated bibliography not only provided us with a good sense of the lay of the land and the existing literature; it also produced a clear deliverable that could be shared with network members within the first few months of the creation of the cluster. Disseminating the bibliography also allowed us to attract new members and ideas.

Similarly, the narratives working group organized a series of events and webinars. One of the simple, but effective and sustainable, elements of this work is a Facebook group that emerged from the original pre-conference workshop. The Facebook group now has a membership of more than 700 people that continues to grow (see also chapter 9).

The ethical guidelines are another example of a concrete activity that mobilized new actors around a specific project with clear objectives. As we made progress towards drafting the guidelines within a fairly short timeline, this created positive energy within the group and sparked the interest of others who were not part of the original proposal. Also, while the group was originally conceived in a Canadian context, there is growing interest among international colleagues. This initiative will be the subject of a more detailed analysis below.

A second successful strategy was to move quickly to seize opportunities that presented themselves. For example, hosting the narratives working group on the margins of an already funded event allowed the organizers to capitalize on the knowledge of participants, with very few additional resources. Similarly, responding quickly to the Syria-specific rapid research call with a proposal for ethical guidelines for all contexts of forced migration allowed us to leverage earmarked funds in a creative way.

## Challenges and Lessons Learned

Despite these successes, the network encountered some challenges in mobilizing sustained financial resources and meaningful participation from members in the global south. As mentioned above, the major funding proposal for the network was not successful, and the rejection was based on the evaluators' perception that the proposal lacked a solid methodology. Given that the whole project was about methodology, this was puzzling at first. However, upon reflection it became clear that the project was being evaluated in the same way as a collaborative empirical research project would be assessed. However, the proposal was not framed in this traditional way—with a conceptual framework, data collection methods, etc. We learned that our "methodology" does not resonate with colleagues in the same way as an empirical study on refugees would.

The lessons we drew from this experience were threefold. First, we have oriented our fundraising efforts towards more pedagogically inclined grant opportunities. In other words, it is easier to "sell" the project as a way of learning about forced migration, rather than as a research project per se. Second, for non-academic partners, we present what we are doing in terms of "research and evaluation" instead of "methods." The former frames the issue in more policy-oriented terms, especially in the context of evidence-based policymaking and results-based management. Third, breaking the overarching notion of methodology into more specific methods (e.g., narratives) or issues (e.g., ethics) has tended to resonate more with colleagues and funders.

A second challenge we have encountered relates to the difficulties of engaging in meaningful partnerships with colleagues from the global south and from outside academia who face more severe time and resource pressures (see also chapter 1). Despite the explicit focus on inequalities in knowledge production and the initial enthusiasm from RRN members based in the global south, the PDG proposal, for example, was dominated by co-applicants from universities in the global north. The ethics initiative was focused explicitly on Canada, but on the other hand it did mobilize key contributions from non-governmental organizations and civil society. The next section will examine in more detail the community-university partnerships involved in the ethics project, through the interactive and contextual model developed by Suarez-Balcazar, Harper, and Lewis (2005).

# Ethical Considerations of Research with People in Situations of Forced Migration: A Case Study of Community-University Partnerships

In this section of the chapter, I would like to focus particularly on the development of ethical considerations for research with people in situations of forced migration (Clark-Kazak et al. 2017) to analyze lessons learned from community-university partnerships. Here I draw on the interactive and contextual model developed by Suarez-Balcazar, Harper, and Lewis (2005). As per their definition, this paper will define community-university partnership as "an explicit written or verbal agreement between a community setting . . . and an academic unit to engage in a common project or common goal, which is mutually beneficial for an extended period" (Suarez-Balcazar et al. 2005, 85). In the case of the ethics project, the four partners—York's Centre for Refugee Studies, the Canadian Council for Refugees, the Canadian Association for Refugee and Forced Migration Studies, and the Canadian office of the United Nations High Commissioner for Refugees—first made a written agreement to participate in the project proposal to the funder, on which all had the opportunity to comment. After we received the funding, this formal written agreement was also reinforced by verbal commitments to participate articulated during our first team meetings. The partners agreed that developing ethical guidelines was mutually beneficial to advance a common goal, namely to protect the rights and dignity of refugees and other people in situations of forced migration. This goal was particularly timely given the recent public, media, and research attention to refugees, especially Syrians arriving in Canada through the Canadian government's resettlement plan. While we welcomed the increased profile of forced migration issues, we were collectively concerned with minimizing any potential negative impacts this increased attention could have for individuals in contexts of forced migration. The project was specific—to develop a set of common principles to guide research—and envisaged concrete activities over the timespan of one year. The specificity and practicality of the project facilitated the initial partnership building.

Suarez-Balcazar, Harper, and Lewis (2005, 86) summarize their interactive and contextual model in the following diagram. I will first analyze

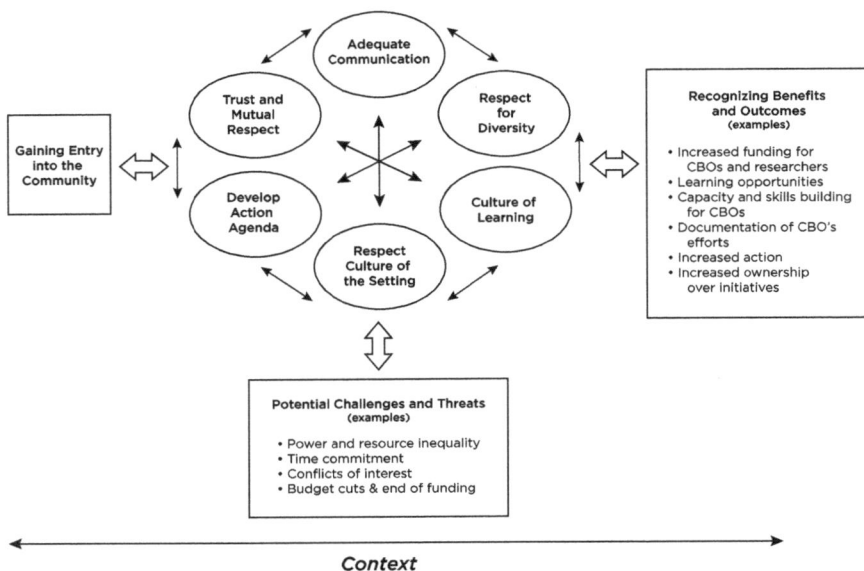

**FIGURE 13.1**
Interactive and Contextual Model of Collaboration: Process of Developing and
Sustaining Community-University Partnerships. Source: Suarez-Balcazar, Harper, and
Lewis (2005, 86), reproduced with permission.

our experiences in relation to each of the elements of the model, and then
turn to the benefits and outcomes, as well as the challenges we encountered.

In this model, "developing and establishing trust and mutual respect
involves taking time to get to know the setting and the different stakeholders" (Suarez-Balcazar et al 2005, 88). In the ethics project this process
was facilitated by pre-existing relationships amongst the partners. It was
then solidified at a workshop on the draft guidelines held at the CCR Fall
Consultation in November 2016, at which CCR members had the opportunity to review the guidelines and make suggestions to edit and improve
them. This workshop was co-facilitated by John Dubé of MOSAIC, a CCR
member organization, and Clark-Kazak, who had drafted the guidelines,
with input from the other members of the project. Other members of the
project served as small group facilitators at the consultations. This activity

CHRISTINA CLARK-KAZAK

allowed us to solidify trust and respect not only amongst the partners involved in the project, but also with other CCR members, who were proactively engaged in the drafting of the guidelines in the early stages of the project. This session yielded concrete suggestions for improvement, such as the addition of more tools, checklists, and practical ways to implement the proposed guidelines. We subsequently reproduced this model of co-facilitation at workshops at the CARFMS conference in May 2017 (co-facilitated by Dubé, Clark-Kazak, and Michaela Hynie) and the North American Refugee Health Conference in June 2017 (co-facilitated by Clark-Kazak and Hynie). Indeed, elements of trust and respect were integrated into the ethical guidelines themselves.

Suarez-Balcazar and colleagues also suggest that adequate communication is an important part of their model. In the ethics project, team meetings were set up at regular intervals. Because of the geographic distance between participants, we relied on GoToMeeting technology, provided by the Canadian Council for Refugees. In between meetings, we used email communications, especially when commenting on the text of the guidelines. Most of these communications involved all members of the project team. However, in cases of specific concerns raised by a particular partner, a telephone conversation involving only those immediately involved was first initiated, followed by reporting back to the team.

The Suarez-Balcazar et al. (2005) model also underscores the importance of respect for differences and a culture of learning as an interactive and reciprocal process. In the ethics project, this was particularly important given the diversity of experiences with research, which was explicitly defined broadly. We were deliberately conscious of the fact that non-academics both engage in research themselves, but also have particular views of research processes (see also chapter 10). The project steering committee included people who served on ethics boards in different capacities, which increased opportunities for sharing knowledge from different real-life perspectives.

Developing an action agenda is also an important part of the Suarez-Balcazar et al. model. In the ethics project, as described above, we had a series of concrete deliverables, to which all members of the team contributed. This included the guidelines, the additional tools available on the CCR website, and the dissemination mechanisms, like workshops and webinars. These collective action items helped to galvanize and mobilize interest.

Indeed, we had many positive outcomes from the community-university partnership on ethics. The project provided specific resources for the project activities that no one partner could have secured. We also all benefited from learning more about ethics and the ways in which our research can be more ethical. In this way, there was also capacity building of the different project leads and for their institutions.

Despite the successes of the ethics project, it was not without its challenges, many of which are identified in the Suarez-Balcazar et al. model. First, there was some inequality in resources and in decision-making processes. As the project was funded by SSHRC and Immigration, Refugees and Citizenship Canada (IRCC) with an academic lead, the academic partner controlled the financial resources of the project and ultimately made decisions. While efforts were made to acknowledge and compensate the contributions of other, non-academic partners, the latter still contributed more than they financially gained from the project.

Second, time commitment to the project was sometimes a challenge during peak activities of the various partners. Because the ethics project had a short funding timeframe, as well as an expectation of delivery of preliminary results within a twelve-month period, the principal applicant had to take the lead in drafting the documents, with input from the rest of the team. Had we had more time, this could have been a more collaborative process.

Finally, a challenge for the future will be the ability to sustain activities, especially dissemination of the guidelines, once the funding stops. While some of the resources developed can continue to be used with little cost—such as the checklists, handouts, and the guidelines themselves, which will all be available electronically on the partners' websites—other dissemination activities like workshops and webinars need continuous resources to be viable (see also chapters 7 and 10).

## Concluding Thoughts

Partnerships on research methodologies in forced migration contexts have produced some notable successes, and we can build on these to broaden and strengthen our field of study. We have made some modest steps forward on producing an annotated bibliography, developing a working group on narratives, and producing ethical guidelines for research with people in situations of forced migration. However, much more remains to be done to do justice to the diverse epistemological and methodological specificities of our field. This chapter has provided some lessons learned. I would like to conclude with some potential next steps.

First, the ethical guidelines, which have been developed within the Canadian context, should be scaled up to include the International Association for the Study of Forced Migration (IASFM) and more awareness of the complexities of research in international contexts of displacement. We have taken a preliminary step towards this through the adoption of an IASFM code of ethics (IASFM 2018). However, the tools that have been developed to date should be translated into more languages and more tools and resources should be developed to reflect the diversity of international migration contexts. In particular, a toolkit could be developed to help community-academic partnerships develop their own tools in different contexts, since the process of tool development in and of itself contributes to the outcome of more ethical, rigorous, and useful research processes.[1]

Second, literature addressing the gaps identified in the annotated bibliography should be compiled into an edited volume and/or special journal issue. This could become an important pedagogical resource in the growing number of courses in forced migration studies. Indeed, more thought should be devoted to the ways in which we teach methodology in our field.

Third, a comprehensive research and evaluation training program should be developed for researchers—university-, community-, and government-based—who undertake research on forced migration. This would be an iterative and collaborative effort to provide researchers with the knowledge and skills they need to advance our understandings of the complexity of forced migration issues.

## Notes

I am grateful for the contributions of Janet Dench, Anita Fábos, Michaela Hynie, and Dianna Shandy to the development of this chapter. We gratefully acknowledge funding from the Social Sciences and Humanities Research Council and Immigration, Refugees and Citizenship Canada for activities mentioned in this paper.

1    I am grateful to Michaela Hynie for contributing this point.

# References

Bakewell, Oliver. 2007. "Editorial Introduction: Researching Refugees: Lessons from the Past, Current Challenges and Future Directions." *Refugee Survey Quarterly* 26, no. 3: 6–14.

———. 2008. "Research beyond the Categories: The Importance of Policy Irrelevant Research into Forced Migration." *Journal of Refugee Studies* 21, no. 4: 432–53.

Berriane, Mohamed, and Hein de Haas. 2012. *African Migrations Research: Innovative Methods and Methodologies*. Trenton, NJ: African World Press.

Bertrand, Didier. 2000. "The Autobiographical Method of Investigating the Psychosocial Wellness of Refugees." In *Psychosocial Wellness of Refugees: Issues in Qualitative and Quantitative Research*, edited by Frederick Ahearn, 88–104. New York and Oxford: Berghahn Books.

Bloch, Alice. 1999. "Carrying out a Survey of Refugees: Some Methodological Considerations and Guidelines." *Journal of Refugee Studies* 12, no. 4: 367–83.

———. 2007. "Methodological Challenges for National and Multi-Sited Comparative Survey Research." *Journal of Refugee Studies* 20, no. 2: 230–47.

Block, Karen, Elisha Riggs, and Nick Haslam. 2013. *Values and Vulnerabilities: The Ethics of Research with Refugees and Asylum Seekers*. Toowong, Australia: Australian Academic Press.

Bradley, Megan. 2007. "Refugee Research Agendas: The Influence of Donors and North-South Partnerships." *Refugee Survey Quarterly* 26, no. 3: 119–35.

———. 2017. "Whose Agenda? Power and Priorities in North-South Research Partnerships." In *Putting Knowledge to Work: Collaborating, Influencing and Learning for International Development*, edited by Luc J. A. Mougeot, 37–70. Ottawa: IDRC.

Brennan, Denise. 2004. "Methodological Challenges in Research with Trafficked Persons: Tales from the Field." *International Migration Review* 43, nos 1–2: 35–54.

Canadian Council for Refugees. N.d. "Ethical Considerations." Accessed 5 Dec 2018. https://ccrweb.ca/en/ethical-considerations-research.

Clark-Kazak, Christina. 2009. "Power and Politics in Migration Narrative Methodology: Research with Young Congolese Migrants in Uganda." *Migration Letters* 6, no. 2: 175–82.

———. 2012. "Research as 'Social Work'? Managing Expectations, Compensation and Relationships in Research with Unassisted, Urban Refugees from the Democratic Republic of Congo." In *Field Research in the Great Lakes Region: The Story Behind the Findings*, edited by An Ansom, Susan Thomson, and Jude Murison, 96–106. Basingstoke: Palgrave Macmillan.

Clark-Kazak, Christina, with CCR, CARFMS, and CRS. 2017. "Ethical Considerations: Research with People in Situations of Forced Migration." *Refuge: Canada's Journal on Refugees* 33, no. 2: 11–17.

Clawson, Heather. 2006. *Estimating Human Trafficking into the United States: Development of a Methodology.* Rockville, MD: ICF International.

Cooper, Elizabeth. 2005. "What Do We Know about Out-of-School Youths? How Participatory Action Research Can Work for Young Refugees in Camps." *Compare: A Journal of Comparative and International Education* 35, no. 4: 463–77.

Doná, Giorgia. 2006. "Children as Research Advisors: Contributions to a 'Methodology of Participation' in Researching Children in Difficult Circumstances." *International Journal of Migration, Health and Social Care* 2, no. 2: 22–34.

———. 2007. "The Microphysics of Participation in Refugee Research." *Journal of Refugee Studies* 20, no. 2: 210–29.

De Haene, Lucia, Hans Grietens, and Karine Verschueren. 2010. "Holding Harm: Narrative Methods in Mental Health Research on Refugee Trauma." *Qualitative Health Research* 20, no. 12: 1664–76.

Eastmond, Marita. 2007. "Stories as Lived Experience: Narratives in Forced Migration Research." *Journal of Refugee Studies* 20, no. 2: 248–64.

Ellis, B. Heidi, Maryam Kia-Keating, Siraad Aden Yusuf, Alisa Lincoln, and Abdirahman Nur. 2007. "Ethical Research in Refugee Communities and the Use of Community Participatory Methods." *Transcultural Psychiatry* 44, no. 3: 459–81.

Ghelani, Chizuru Nobe. 2013. "Annotated Bibliography: Compiled for the Cluster onMethodology and the Knowledge Production in Forced Migration Contexts." Toronto: Centre for Refugee Studies, York University.

Ghorashi, Halleh. 2008. "Giving Silence a Chance: The Importance of Life Stories for Research on Refugees." *Journal of Refugee Studies* 21, no. 1: 118–31.

Guerin, Pauline, and Bernard Guerin. 2007. "Research with Refugee Communities: Going around in Circles with Methodology." *Australian Community Psychologist* 19, no. 1: 150–62.

Hugman, Richard, Linda Bartolomei, and Eileen Pittaway. 2011. "Human Agency and the Meaning of Informed Consent: Reflections on Research with Refugees." *Journal of Refugee Studies* 24, no. 4: 655–71.

Hugman, Richard, Eileen Pittaway, and Linda Bartolomei. 2011. "When 'Do No Harm' is Not Enough: The Ethics of Research with Refugees and Other Vulnerable Groups." *British Journal of Social Work* 41, no. 7: 1271–87.

International Association for the Study of Forced Migration. 2018. Code of Ethics: Critical Reflections on Research Ethics in Situations of Forced Migration. Accessed 5 Dec 2018. http://iasfm.org/blog/2018/11/30/adoption-of-iasfm-research-code-of-ethics/.

Jacobsen, Karen, and Loren Landau. 2003. "The Dual Imperative in Refugee Research: Some Methodological and Ethical Considerations in Social Science Research on Forced Migration." *Disasters* 27, no. 3: 185–206.

Johnson, Heather. 2012. "Listening to Migrant Stories." In *Research Methods in Critical Security Studies: An Introduction*, edited by Mark B. Salter and Can E. Mutlu, 66–71. New York: Routledge.

———. 2014. *Borders, Asylum and Global Non-Citizenship: The Other Side of the Fence.* Cambridge: Cambridge University Press.

Lammers, Ellen. 2007. "Researching Refugees: Preoccupations with Power and Questions of Giving." *Refugee Survey Quarterly* 26, no. 3: 72–81.

Lenette, Caroline, and Jennifer Boddy. 2013. "Visual Ethnography and Refugee Women: Nuanced Understandings of Lived Experiences." *Qualitative Research Journal* 13, no. 1: 72–89.

Lenning, Jennifer. 2001. "Ethics of Research in Refugee Populations." *Lancet* 357: 1432–3.

Macchiavello, M. 2003. *Urban Forced Migrants in Kampala: Methodologies and Ethical and Psychological Issues.* Johannesburg: Forced Migration Studies Programme, University of the Witwatersrand.

Mackenzie, Catriona, Christopher McDowell, and Eileen Pittaway. 2007. "Beyond 'Do No Harm': The Challenge of Constructing Ethical Relationships in Refugee Research." *Journal of Refugee Studies* 20, no. 2: 299–319.

Misago, Jean Pierre, and Loren Landau. 2013. "Gutters, Gates, and Gangs: Collaborative Sampling in 'Post-Violence' Johannesburg." *Journal of Refugee Studies* 26, no. 1: 116–25.

Moran, Rhetta, Zeinab Mohamed, and Hermione Lovel. 2011. "Breaking the Silence: Participatory Research Processes about Health with Somali Refugee People Seeking Asylum." In *Doing Research with Refugees: Issues and Guidelines*, edited by Bogusia Temple and Rhetta Moran, 55–74. Bristol: The Policy Press.

Polzer, Tania. 2013. "Collecting Data on Migrants through Service Provider NGOs: Towards Data Use and Advocacy." *Journal of Refugee Studies* 26, no. 1: 144–54.

Powles, Julia. 2004. "Life History and Personal Narrative: Theoretical and Methodological Issues Relevant to Research and Evaluation in Refugee Contexts." *New Issues in Refugee Research*, Working Paper No. 106. UNHCR: Geneva.

Refugee Studies Centre. 2007. "Ethical Guidelines for Good Research Practice." *Refugee Survey Quarterly* 26, no. 3: 162–72.

Rodgers, Graeme. 2005. "'Hanging Out' with Forced Migrants: Methodological and Ethical Challenges." *Forced Migration Review* 21: 48–9.

Rosow, Stephen J. 2003. "Toward an Anti-disciplinary Global Studies." *International Studies* 4, no. 1: 1–14.

Samaddar, Ranabir. 2001. "Power, Fear, Ethics." *Refugee Watch* 14: 12–20.

Shandy, Dianna, Anita Fábos, and Brad Belbas. 2016. "Reaching a Wider Audience with Webinars." *Anthropology News*, June/July.

Singh, Gayatri, and Benjamin D. Clark. 2013. "Creating a Frame: A Spatial Approach to Random Sampling of Immigrant Households in Inner City Johannesburg." *Journal of Refugee Studies* 26, no. 1: 126–44.

Suarez-Balcazar, Yolanda, Gary W. Harper, and Rhonda Lewis. 2005. "An Interactive and Contextual Model of Community-University Collaborations for Research and Action." *Health Education & Behavior* 32, no. 1: 84–101.

Tang, S. 2008. "Community-Centred Research as Knowledge/Capacity Building in Immigrant and Refugee Communities." In *Engaging Contradictions: Theory, Politics and Methods of Activist Scholarship*, edited by Charles R. Hale, 237–64. Berkeley: University of California Press.

Tyldum, Guri, and Anette Brunovskis. 2005. "Describing the Unobserved: Methodological Challenges in Empirical Studies on Human Trafficking." *International Migration* 43, nos 1/2: 17–34.

# Conclusion: Reflections on Global Refugee Research Networking

*Susan McGrath*

## Introduction

As part of the follow-up to the 2016 New York Declaration, the United Nations High Commissioner for Refugees (UNHCR) proposed a Global Compact on Refugees (GCR) in his annual report to the General Assembly in 2016. Along with the Global Compact for Safe, Orderly and Regular Migration, the GCR was adopted by a UN Intergovernmental Conference in Marrakech, Morocco in December 2018. The GCR calls for the establishment of a "*global academic network* on refugee, forced displacement, and statelessness issues . . . involving universities, academic alliances, and research institutions, together with UNHCR, to facilitate research, training, scholarship opportunities and other initiatives which result in specific deliverables in support of the objectives of the global compact" (UNHCR 2018a, paragraph 43). UNHCR initiated a consultation with researchers led by Professor Pene Mathew of Griffith University in Australia to develop a plan for the new network.

We support this initiative by UNHCR and have recommendations to facilitate the implementation of an ethical network of researchers and research institutions based on the experiences of the Refugee Research

Network (RRN) and the regular reviews of our work. We draw upon five key evaluation events of the RRN: 1) stakeholder interviews examining benefits and barriers to participating in the RRN by the Program Evaluation Unit of the York Institute for Health Research (YIHR) in 2009; 2) a mid-term report submitted to SSHRC (the funder) in 2011; 3) a mapping report of executive directors of institutional partners in 2014; 4) a finale workshop, "Innovations in Forced Migration," held at York's Glendon campus in 2015; and 5) the final Partnership Achievement Report submitted to SSHRC in February 2018. We have written previously about the challenges of engaging scholars at the global level particularly given deep structural inequalities among countries (Hynie et al. 2014). In the first chapter, Loren B. Landau writes about the difficulties of truly collaborative refugee research in what he considers an "era of containment," when countries of the global north are working hard to keep refugees contained in countries of the global south.

The RRN has supported and facilitated the development of new networks of researchers and practitioners across Canada and globally, including the Canadian Association of Refugee and Forced Migration Studies (CARFMS) founded in 2008, the Latin American Network for Forced Migration/*Red latino americana de migración forzada* established in 2010 (see chapter 12), the Canadian Association of Refugee Lawyers (CARL) launched in 2011, the Global Policy Network launched in 2012, and the Asia Pacific Forced Migration Connection (APFMC) established in November 2013 (see chapter 3). A highlight was the establishment of the Emerging Scholars and Practitioners on Migration Issues (ESPMI) network (formerly the New Scholars Network, established in 2009) focused on creating a cooperative and helpful professional network for those starting out in the field of forced migration (see chapter 10).

Our reflections are focused on a number of issues that have emerged: the lack of information about who is doing refugee research, particularly at the level of a local research unit; the geopolitical challenges of ethically engaging researchers globally; the lack of adequate funding in the global south for locally relevant research; the need for a funded, decentralized organizational model to support an alliance of researchers and research institutions; the challenges of disseminating research in forms and formats that are accessible globally; and the need for guiding principles for an ethical network.

# Mapping the Global Network

The number of research institutions focused on refugee issues globally is not clear although we estimate about fifty. The RRN has had partnerships with thirteen research centres (Bogotá, Cairo, Chicago, Johannesburg, Kampala, Kolkata, London (2), Oxford, Sydney, Tehran, Toronto, and Washington), but there are many more. The need for dedicated research centres and networking among academics was recognized as the field of refugee and forced migration studies was developing in the 1980s. The large movements of refugees in Southeast Asia in 1979 and the early 1980s formed the historical context for the establishment of research centres dedicated to refugee and forced migration studies. In 1981, under the direction of Howard Adelman, Canada's York University created the Refugee Documentation Project for the conservation and analysis of research documents and data collected by Operation Lifeline, an initiative to bring Indochinese refugees to Canada. The project became the Centre for Refugee Studies in 1988. In 1987, Chulalongkorn University created the Indochinese Refugee Information Center (IRIC) to observe and study the movement of refugees from Cambodia, Laos, Vietnam, and other points of Southeast Asian origin in search of asylum in Thailand. IRIC evolved into the Asian Research Center for Migration (ARCM) in 1995. The 1990s marked the launch of other centres including: the Centre for Refugee Studies at Moi University in Eldoret Kenya in 1992; the African Centre for Migration & Society (ACMS) at Wits University, South Africa in 1993; the Centre for the Study of Forced Migration (CSFM) at the University of Dar es Salaam, Tanzania in 1995 (Rutinwa 2004); and the Institute for the Study of International Migration (ISIM) at Georgetown University, USA in 1998.

Established in 1986 as the Refugee Studies Programme (RSP) under the direction of Barbara Harrell-Bond, Oxford's Refugee Studies Centre (RSC) played a central role in stimulating and facilitating research in the field of forced migration, including by holding conferences and international meetings. In January 1990, the centre facilitated the establishment and annual meetings of the International Research and Advisory Panel (IRAP) made up of national government representatives, heads of other centres specializing in the study of forced migration, and individual researchers renowned for their excellence in the field. The fifth meeting of

IRAP was held outside of Oxford in Eldorat, Kenya, hosted by the Centre for Refugee Studies at Moi University in April 1996 (Koser 1996). It was the founding meeting of the International Association for the Study of Forced Migration (IASFM) (Koser 1996). The format for the IASFM biennial international conferences was set. The goal has been to provide an interdisciplinary forum for intellectual exchange and communication across sectors including academics, researchers, practitioners, and policymakers (IASFM 2018) although the engagement of policymakers has been a challenge. The directors of the refugee research centres attending IASFM conferences usually have a side meeting; there is an informal network of predominantly English-speaking researchers.

An effort by UNHCR in 2007 to map refugee researchers and research centres globally identified twenty-one academic centres; however, the process was incomplete (Boano and Addison 2008). Several new centres have been formed since then particularly in the north, e.g., Northwestern University's Center for Forced Migration Studies (CFMS) and the University of London's Refugee Law Initiative. Centres with a broader migration mandate that incorporate forced migration have also evolved, e.g., Wilfrid Laurier's International Migration Research Centre (IMRC) and the Ryerson Centre for Immigration and Settlement (RCIS), both in Canada. The academic centres are clustered in countries that are receiving resettled refugees, e.g., UK, Canada, US, and Australia and in countries that have been coping with large refugee movements, e.g., Kenya, South Africa, Uganda, Tanzania, Thailand, Egypt, and India. The capacity of these centres to conduct research and to network with other centres varies considerably with those in the global south facing the greatest challenges. A complete mapping of research centres across the global south and north is needed so that we know the actual extent of the field.

## Global versus Regional Networks

While the RRN sought to be a "network of networks," there have been tensions in seeking to develop a global platform for research, collaboration, and dissemination while being responsive to regional needs and contexts. Participants in the RRN Mapping Report called for a more decentralized approach, "less roots and more branches." Regional networks were perceived to be more productive than wider networks (Oakes 2015). Three regional networks were formed: in Canada, Latin America, and Asia Pacific. The most successful has been in Canada building on the thirty years of experience of the Centre for Refugee Studies (CRS), the RRN network of researchers and partners, and with support from the RRN and the Social Sciences and Humanities Research Council. In 2008, the Canadian Association for Refugee and Forced Migration Studies (CARFMS) was established as a community of scholars dedicated to Canadian refugee and forced migration research. Since its founding, CARFMS has organized successful annual conferences at universities across the country and maintains a blog and a working paper series.

The social, political, and economic context of Canada has facilitated the development of refugee research and a refugee research network. Despite its modest population of about 36 million people, Canada is included in the Group of Eight highly industrialized countries in the world. It has pursued migration as a development policy (Liston and Carens 2008) and has a history of accepting refugees, e.g., Hungarian, Czechoslovakian, Roma, Ugandan, and Indochinese (Molloy et al. 2017). In 2015, a newly elected Liberal government launched the Refugees Welcome initiative, a program that ultimately brought 58,650 Syrian refugees to Canada between November 2015 and September 2018. The federal and provincial governments have sought input from researchers in the field of refugee studies in planning and assessing the Syrian resettlement program, and SSHRC offered twenty-five targeted research grants for research related to it (see chapter 13 for an example of an initiative that received funding through this program). With the support of UNHCR, the Open Society, and the Canadian government, Canada's private sponsorship program is being studied by other countries looking for new models of refugee resettlement. Canada has emerged as one of the nations taking leadership in the area of forced migration.

Establishing networks in Latin America and Asia Pacific has been more difficult. We have seen the challenges that the Latin American network experienced in sustaining itself without adequate resources (chapter 12). While the Asia Pacific network continues in place (see chapter 3), it has been more modest than the Canadian network in its level of activity. The lack of broad public or political support for refugees in both regions as well as the limited economic capacity of Colombia, where LANFM was established, made it more difficult to maintain an active network of refugee researchers—who needed funds to pursue their work. The experience of the ESPMI network suggests that the creation of global networks is facilitated by a confluence of personal communications, collaborative activities, and strong leadership (see chapter 10).

While some participants in the Mapping Report voiced a desire to see a more decentralized network, the question of who should lead such a project was not clear. One participant did identify the need for a "connector of research clusters," an entity that links international researchers in the field of refugee and forced migration studies to specific grants and topics. Overall, participants did express a wish to see more cross-fertilization among research topics, disciplines, and regions (Oakes 2015).

## Striving for an Ethical Practice of Engagement

When the members of the RRN first gathered in Toronto in November of 2008, for many it was for the first time they had met, particularly those from across the global south. While IASFM has been a forum for forced migration researchers to meet, it is often not financially feasible for those from lower income countries—particularly students—to attend the conferences. RRN provided funding for partners and the executive members of ESPMI to meet each year either in Toronto or at the site of the IASFM conference. These annual face-to-face meetings proved to be important in establishing new relationships and understandings of the different realities that members experienced. Partners shared their research and the issues they were facing in their regions.

The ability to create networking opportunities, and how this opened spaces of encounter, was seen as one of the strengths of the RRN (Oakes 2015). Participants in the RRN Mapping Report highlighted what they described as "the RRN's 'soft touch'—i.e., its ability to create an informal and stimulating atmosphere that allowed members to network at their own pace and through their own interests. It provided participants the space in which to feel out the research landscape and exercise agency and agility in choosing the topics and peers with whom they wished to collaborate" (Oakes 2015, 16). The RRN was lauded for being "a learning community that provided researchers in early and middle career stages with opportunities for personal and professional growth. Participants from less established and geographically isolated research centres indicated that the RRN had helped to broaden their exposure and strengthened their ties with institutions, NGOs and peers in other disciplines and regions" (Oakes 2015, 15). Colleagues from Colombia and India discovered that they had a lot in common, e.g., both countries had the experience of coping with high numbers of internally displaced persons (IDP). They joined the IASFM executive committee and each subsequently hosted an IASFM conference (Kolkata, India, in January 2013 and Bogotá, Colombia, in July 2014).

Virtual meetings of the partners were held two or three times per year to discuss organizational issues, plan meetings, and address any outstanding concerns. Despite access to current communications technology provided by York University, the connections were not always good. Sometimes partners could not connect or were not be able to hear and someone always had to be up late—usually our generous Australian colleagues. We relied on email for most of our communication but its effectiveness depended on the relationships that had been established through personal contact. The formation of an inclusive global network of research centres will require opportunities for face-to-face meetings and support for ongoing virtual communications. Hopefully, the technology to support virtual communications continues to improve and access to the technology increases; nevertheless, the barriers of time and language differences will need to be negotiated.

The RRN's model of research partnership based on respectful interpersonal relationships and open and transparent communications that recognize structural inequalities among researchers in low- and high-income countries has been highly productive. The principal impacts of the RRN include: 1) the building of research capacity within Canada; 2) linking Canada to new and expanded networks of researchers and research centres that span the global south and north; 3) the generation of new knowledge by clusters of researchers focused on major issues and practices; 4) the mobilization of new and existing knowledge to make it more accessible globally; 5) the development of a model of individual and institutional partnership that strives to bridge the social and economic inequities inherent in "south/north" relationships; and 6) training the next generation of refugee scholars, policymakers, and practitioners. With the support of the 2015 SSHRC Partnership Impact Award, the RRN continues to focus on the mobilization of the knowledge generated.

# Mobilizing Knowledge

On 15 and 16 June 2015, the Refugee Research Network (RRN) hosted a conference entitled, "Innovations in Forced Migration," at the Glendon campus of York University in Toronto organized by professor Christina Clark-Kazak. The event marked the formal finale of the first phase of the RRN's collaboration and brought together sixty-one scholars (faculty and students), practitioners, and policymakers from across Canada and internationally to mobilize knowledge on innovations in forced migration. Organized in a workshop format, where all participants were able to attend all the sessions, the conference was comprised of seven panels, one public keynote address, and a book launch where three recent publications were showcased. A public book fair and poster session displayed publications from the field of forced migration from the past five years and highlighted success stories of the RRN's research clusters and networks. The event concluded with a facilitated session that sought to identify and prioritize next steps in knowledge mobilization support for RRN members as the first round of funding was coming to an end. The workshop was supported with a grant from SSHRC's Connection Program.

The conference was aimed at members of the RRN and key scholars and students in the expanding field of refugee and forced migration studies. RRN institutional partners at Georgetown University, Northwestern University, Oxford University, University of London, University of East London, Makerere University, Witwatersrand University, Calcutta Research Group, University of New South Wales, Javeriana University, and University of Tehran were invited to participate as presenters, panel chairs, and/or discussants. In the closing session, participants identified the potential role of the RRN in supporting their knowledge mobilization activities and focused on the audiences, useful media and modalities, and the tools and training needed. Their recommendations have informed our subsequent work and the focus on knowledge mobilization.

Engaging political actors has been an ongoing challenge of the RRN. In December 2016, we presented four commissioned policy briefs on issues identified in collaboration with government officials to the staff of the departments of Immigration, Refugees and Citizenship Canada, and Global Affairs Canada. This kind of collaboration was not welcomed by the previous federal government, which further demonstrates the importance of the geopolitical context in knowledge production. The topics and authors were: *Age and Generation in Canada's Migration Law, Policy, and Programming* by Christina Clark-Kazak; *The Humanitarian-Development Nexus: Opportunities for Canadian Leadership* by Kevin Dunbar and James Milner; *The State of Private Refugee Sponsorship in Canada: Trends, Issues, and Impacts* by Jennifer Hyndman, William Payne, and Shauna Jimenez; and *Environmental Displacement and Environmental Migration: Blurred Boundaries Require Integrated Policies* by Michaela Hynie, Prateep Nayak, Teresa Gomes, and Ifrah Abdillahi. The papers were distributed to all interested government staff, made available in full and summary form to the larger networks, and posted to the RRN website.

Finally, a team of doctoral students at York continues to work on knowledge mobilization activities. A bi-weekly Refugee Research Digest was launched in May 2017 providing links to the latest articles and materials on refugee issues and is broadcast to over 60,000 people via the Centre for Refugee Studies listserv and other channels. It is produced in English and links mainly to English-language materials. The team is also developing the Refugee Research in Context resource, an online platform to contextualize and increase access to scholarship on contemporary refugee issues, experiences, and debates. These initiatives seek to incorporate a range of theoretical, geographical, and linguistic perspectives and resources to inform public awareness and understanding of current issues.

At the 2015 RRN conference, members of the IASFM executive committee discussed their vision for how their network and the RRN can continue to work together symbiotically. Then IASFM president Paula Banerjee reminded participants that the RRN emerged out of the IASFM and sought to extend and support the work of IASFM member institutions, promote collaboration, and develop innovative and effective knowledge mobilization tools and strategies. She noted that the achievements of the RRN in networking, research, and knowledge mobilization over its then seven-year history demonstrated what can be catalyzed with the strategic and timely application of resources in the form of seed funding and travel and research assistance support. She committed IASFM to take up these efforts and integrate the lessons of the RRN into its organizational structure, so that the IASFM can evolve into more than an organization that supports biannual conferences and that the lessons learned and achievements of the RRN can be sustained. IASFM has committed to increasing its membership, funding emerging collaborations through seed grants, and supporting the ESPMI network (see chapter 10). Existing and emerging research clusters and networks would also be supported through the knowledge mobilization infrastructure that has been developed through the RRN project and is maintained at York's CRS.

## Moving Forward

Whether there will be a new global network of researchers and research institutions as called for by the GRC, or what formation it will take, is unclear. The UNHCR has launched a consultation to determine who will be part of the network, how it will be structured, and what research will be pursued. Professor Pene Mathew, former Dean of Law at Griffith University in Australia, has been commissioned to guide the process. A discussion paper (UNHCR 2018b) was drafted under Mathew's direction and reviewed at a consultation held in Geneva in November 2018 with academics from Europe, North and South America, Africa, and Asia; ongoing consultations are being pursued. We draw on the experiences of the RRN and of the 2008 UNHCR report on a global network (Boano and Addison 2008) to comment on potential guiding principles and practices for the proposed GRC network.

The 2018 UNHCR discussion paper calls for a truly global network noting that the global south is the place of origin for most refugees, where 86 per cent of refugees are hosted, and that excellent scholars from the region would be in a position to share a more proximate, historically, and contextually informed perspective. It notes that these academics also have societal networks that will be important to ensuring that the network's research has an impact in their countries. The discussion paper (UNHCR 2018b) also recognizes the importance of maintaining academic freedom and the independence of the network and its members and cites the work of Christina Clark-Kazak in developing a model for the ethical practice of refugee research (see chapter 13). A truly global network must recognize the importance of the independent involvement of doctoral students and early career scholars (as argued in chapter 1 and demonstrated by the achievements of the members of ESPMI in chapter 10).

The 2008 UNHCR report (Boano and Addison 2008) argued that a global network must operate primarily for the *empowerment* of its southern membership. This was defined as ensuring structural equivalence between all of its members, particularly regarding access to resources and participation in agenda setting. The network must be focused towards the grassroots, and be participatory in nature. The report further calls for the network to facilitate the incorporation of southern institutions by fostering *collaborative* activities between its members. The discussion paper for the GCR network calls for the interests of and scholars from the global south to be well supported. The equitable engagement and participation of researchers of the south is consistent with the philosophy of the RRN and the position of Loren B. Landau at the University of the Witwatersrand's African Centre for Migration & Society. Landau provides some cautions and guidelines about the research relationships between northern and southern partners in what he calls an era of containment (see chapter 1).

Boano and Addison's (2008) report also called for the network to be built upon already existing relationships between institutions and individuals; it should seek to support, nurture, and strengthen already existing networks in a *complementary* manner. The RRN has engaged multiple research centres and has supported the creation of new regional networks. In his critique of the proposed global network, Jeff Crisp (a former head of research at UNHCR and an early member of the RRN), points out that the field of refugee studies is already highly networked and that there is a need to clarify the added value of the proposed new GCR network (2018).

In the call for the global network, the GCR states that "efforts will be made to ensure regional diversity and expertise from a broad range of relevant subject areas" (2018b paragraph 43). This position is consistent with reviews of the RRN recommending "more branches and less roots" (Oakes 2015) and the 2008 UNHCR report (Boano and Addison 2008) that calls for *regionality*. They proposed key institutions form "regional hubs" to facilitate the establishment and coordination of the network at regional levels. The structure and governance of the network have been key elements in the early discussions about its formation. The discussion paper suggests that existing academic networks may be tapped into for membership of the GCR academic network citing the International Association for the Study of Forced Migration (IASFM) and the MENA Civil Society Network for Displacement as examples. While the UNHCR has been mandated under the GCR to establish the network, it is not clear whether the UNHCR will act as the secretariat or whether an academic institution or an association such as IASFM will be asked to take it on; either way, the recognition of regional diversity is crucial.

A key issue for the proposed network is its *sustainability*. The Boano and Addison (2008) report argued that this entails that funds not only be available for network activities but also to southern partners in an equitable manner. Over eight years, the RRN had a budget of $2.1 million (CAD) to maintain a modest infrastructure, provide seed funding to research clusters, support student travel to conferences, and bring about fifteen to twenty partner institution members to an annual meeting either in Toronto or at the site of the IASFM meeting. A truly global network would need to be much more extensive and expensive. Crisp (2018) raises serious questions about UNHCR's capacity to maintain a global academic network covering the whole range of refugee, forced displacement, and statelessness issues at a time of serious funding shortfalls. He points out that previous research initiatives by UNHCR eventually fell by the wayside because of changing priorities and personnel.

While refugee researchers are typically striving to create knowledge that will benefit refugees, the impact of research on policy and practice is questionable. Crisp (2018) argues that academic research plays a very modest role in the formulation of UNHCR policy and the design of its programs. He claims that factors such as the pressures exerted by host and donor states, UNHCR's relations with other agencies, policy differences, and rivalries within the organization, as well as the changing priorities of its senior management, are greater determinants. Landau also questions the impact of research on policy noting that "even when research is commissioned or funded by governments and aid agencies, it is often ignored if the recommendations are politically or financially inconvenient" (see chapter 1).

What format the proposed GRC academic network will take is not yet clear, although indications are that it will be a top-down structure driven by UNHCR. It seems unlikely that there will be a fully functioning network given the cost; there may at the very least be a portal hosted by UNHCR to store relevant research and materials. The need for more cross-fertilization among research topics, disciplines, and regions is well recognized. The practices and experiences of emerging researchers and practitioners, existing researchers, and research centres as documented here suggest that there is capacity in the field to organize and support research networks although the financial capacity to do so is found mainly in the north. Existing researchers and regional networks can look to the IASFM to provide an independent platform for building on those networks and collaborations and working to expand and connect them. Established institutions and networks can be called upon to support true partnerships with emerging research centres and early career researchers in the global south. One of the goals of our work together as the RRN has been to contribute to a more global, equitable, and ethical practice of refugee research. We hope that this collection documenting the stories, practices, and contributions of a network of refugee researchers collaborating for more than ten years sheds light on both the possibilities and the ongoing challenges of such an endeavour. At a minimum, our collaboration underscores the potential of research networks to generate knowledge that is strong internationally and inclusive of multiple traditions of inquiry as Appadurai (2000) imagines.

## References

Appadurai, Arjun. 2000. "Grassroots Globalization and the Research Imagination." *Public Culture* 12, no. 1: 1–19.

Boano, Camillo, and Simon Addison. 2008. *Mapping Forced Migration Research Centres: A Report Commissioned by UNHCR.* Oxford: Oxford Refugee Studies Centre.

Crisp, Jeff. 2018. A Global Academic Network on Refugees: Some Unanswered Questions. *International Journal of Refugee Law* 20, no. 20: 1–3. doi:10.1093/ijrl/eey050.

Koser, Khalid. 1996. "Changing Agendas in the Study of Forced Migration: A Report on the Fifth International Research and Advisory Panel Meeting, Kenya, April 1996." *Journal of Refugee Studies* 9, no. 4: 353–66.

Landau, Loren. 2007. "Can We Talk and Is Anybody Listening? Reflections on IASFM 10, 'Talking Across Borders: New Dialogues in Forced Migration.'" *Journal of Refugee Studies* 20, no. 3: 336–48.

Liston, Mary, and Joseph Carens. 2008. "Immigration and Integration Canada." In *Migration and Globalization: Comparing Immigration Policy in Developed Countries*, edited by A. Kondo and A. Shoten, 207–27. Tokyo: Akashi Shoten.

Molloy, Mike, Peter Duschinsky, Kurt F. Jensen, and Robert Shalka. 2017. *Running on Empty Canada and the Indochinese Refugees, 1975–1980.* Montreal and Kingston: McGill-Queen's University Press.

Oakes, Wesley J. 2015. *RRN Mapping Report*. Toronto, ON: Centre for Refugee Studies, York University.

Rutinwa, Bonaventure. 2004. "Report on the Teaching of Forced Migration Studies at the University of Dar es Salaam: The Past, Present and the Future. Centre for the Study of Forced Migration." Faculty of Law, University of Dar es Salaam. https://repositories.lib.utexas.edu/bitstream/handle/2152/4735/3823.pdf.

UNHCR. 2018a. "The Global Compact on Refugees." https://www.unhcr.org/gcr/GCR_English.pdf

———. 2018b. "Academic Network on Refugees, Other Forced Displacement and Statelessness Established under the Global Compact on Refugees: Discussion Paper." Workshop 13–14 November 2018, Geneva, Switzerland.

# Contributors

**MOHAMMAD JALAL ABBASI-SHAVAZI** is professor of demography at the University of Tehran and director of National Institute of Population Research, Iran, and holds the position of honorary professor at the University of Melbourne, Australia. As an active member of the Refugee Research Network, he has published on Afghan refugees in Iran, and is the joint editor of *Demography of Refugee and Forced Migration* published by Springer in 2018. Abbasi-Shavazi is Laureate of the 2011 United Nations Population Award.

**PAULA BANERJEE**, vice chancellor of The Sanskrit College and University and the former honorary director of the Calcutta Research Group, is an expert on studies on borders, boundaries, gender, and critical migration. As part of her current work on borders and women, she has authored numerous papers on women in conflict situations. She has also published extensively on issues of gender, forced migration, and peace politics. She was the former professor, head of department, and dean of arts in the University of Calcutta. She has authored many books including, *When Ambitions Clash* (2003), *Borders, Histories, Existences: Gender and Beyond* (2009), *Women in Peace Politics* (2008), *Unstable Populations Anxious States* (2013), *Women in Indian Borderlands* (co-edited, 2011), and *The State of Being Stateless* (co-edited, 2015). Banerjee is the recipient of a number of awards and is on the editorial board of a number of journals.

PABLO BOSE is an associate professor in the department of geography and director of global and regional studies at the University of Vermont, Burlington, USA. He is a migration scholar and an urban geographer who uses primarily qualitative, interdisciplinary, and community-based approaches to conduct his research. His key interests lie in exploring the complex relationships between people and place and especially in the ways that flows of capital, labour, bodies, and ideas may transform various landscapes.

NERGIS CANEFE is associate professor of politics, public policy and law, in the department of politics at York University, Toronto, Canada. She is trained in political philosophy, forced migration studies, and international public law with special focus on rights violations, state criminality, accountability, and state-society relations in the aftermath of mass political violence. She has over twenty years of experience in carrying out in-depth qualitative research with displaced communities and teaching human rights and public law globally. Canefe regularly conducts some of her human rights, minority rights, and refugee rights related work on a pro bono basis and acts as an expert witness and public lecturer on subjects related to forced migration, diasporas in exile, minority rights, and genocide.

CHRISTINA CLARK-KAZAK is associate professor in the School of Public and International Affairs at the University of Ottawa, Canada, and president of the International Association for the Study of Forced Migration (IASFM). Her research focuses on age discrimination in migration policies and interdisciplinary methodology in forced migration.

DON DIPPO is a professor in the Faculty of Education at York University, Toronto, Canada. His interests include: the social and political organization of knowledge, environmental, and sustainability education, global migration, and settlement; university/community relations; and teacher education. Together with professor Wenona Giles, he co-directs the Borderless Higher Education for Refugees (BHER) project, a CIDA funded initiative designed to bring post-secondary education opportunities to people living in the Dadaab refugee camps in northeastern Kenya. He serves on the executive committee of the Centre for Refugee Studies at York University and is on the board of directors of Success Beyond Limits, a not-for-profit, community-based organization that supports high school age youth in Toronto's Jane/Finch community.

WENONA GILES, FRSC, professor emerita and research associate at the Centre for Refugee Studies, York University publishes in the areas of gender, forced migration, globalization, access to higher education, nationalism, and war. She coordinated the international Women in Conflict Zones Research Network and co-edited *Feminists Under Fire: Exchanges across War Zones*; (2003) and with Jennifer Hyndman, *Sites of Violence: Gender and Conflict Zones* (2004). More recently she published the co-edited book (with Hyndman) *Refugees in Extended Exile: Living on the Edge* (2017). She is a co-lead with Don Dippo of the Borderless Higher Education (BHER) project, which brings degree programs from Kenyan and Canadian universities to refugees in the Dadaab refugee camps. Giles is also co-editing a book (with Bhabha and Mahomed) on access to higher education for marginalized citizen and non-citizen populations.

SUSAN KNEEBONE is a professorial fellow and senior associate at the Asian Law Centre, Melbourne Law School, University of Melbourne, Australia. She supervises a number of PhD students on migration issues in South East Asia. She is currently working on two Australia Research Council funded projects: "Towards Development of a Legal Framework for Regulation of International Marriage Migration" and "Indonesia's Refugee Policies: Responsibility, Security and Regionalism." Kneebone's full CV and list of publications can be viewed at: https://law.unimelb.edu.au/about/staff/susan-kneebone.

ELLEN PERCY KRALY is the William R. Kenan Jr. Professor of Geography and Environmental Studies at Colgate University. During 2019, she is the Willy Brandt Guest Professor in International Migration and Ethnic Relations, Malmö University, Sweden. She is the chair of the Scientific Panel on International Migration of the International Union for the Scientific Study of Population, and has served as editor of the *International Migration Review*.

LOREN B. LANDAU is the South African Research Chair in Human Mobility and the Politics of Difference based at the University of the Witwatersrand's African Centre for Migration & Society. He has previously held visiting and faculty positions at Princeton and Georgetown Universities and the Fletcher School of Law and Diplomacy. A publically engaged scholar, his interdisciplinary work explores human mobility, community, and transformations in the spatial and temporal bases of political authority. He is on the editorial boards of *Migration Studies* and the *Journal of Refugee Studies* and has served as the chair of the Consortium for Refugees and Migrants in South Africa (CoRMSA), as a member of the South African Immigration Advisory Board, and as an advisor to the Cities Alliance. He holds an MSc in development studies (LSE) and a PhD in political science (Berkeley).

ELIZABETH (LIBBY) LUNSTRUM is an associate professor in the department of geography at York University, Toronto, Canada. Her areas of expertise include conservation-induced displacement, the environmental aspects of displacement more broadly, green militarization/the militarization of conservation practice, Indigenous conservation and wildlife management, and the political ecology of international borders. Her work focuses on Southern Africa and North America.

SUSAN F. MARTIN is the Donald G. Herzberg Professor Emerita in the School of Foreign Service at Georgetown University, Washington DC, USA. She is the founder and former director of Georgetown's Institute for the Study of International Migration. Before coming to Georgetown, Dr. Martin served as the Executive Director of the U.S. Commission on Immigration Reform, chaired by the late Barbara Jordan. Among her book publications are *International Migration: Evolving Trends from the Early Twentieth Century to the Present*; *Migration and Humanitarian Crises: Causes, Consequences and Responses*; *A Nation of Immigrants*; and *Refugee Women*.

SUSAN MCGRATH is professor emerita and senior scholar at the School of Social Work, York University, where she served as director of the Centre for Refugee Studies from 2004–12. She is a past president of the International Association for the Study of Forced Migration and a founding member of the Canadian Association for Refugee and Forced Migration Studies. McGrath was awarded the 2015 SSHRC Partnership Impact Award for forging innovative, interdisciplinary, equitable, and cross-sector partnerships in the field of forced migration. In 2014, she was invested into the Order of Canada in recognition of her outstanding achievement in research and policy on refugee rights and for fostering collaboration amongst scholars in her field.

MICHELE MILLARD is the coordinator of the Centre for Refugee Studies at York University, and the former Project Coordinator of the Refugee Research Network where she managed the online networking, knowledge mobilization, and dissemination activities of the project. A past president of the board at Sojourn House, former member of the executive committee at the Canadian Council for Refugees as well as of the Community Council at the Salvation Army's Immigrant and Refugee Services, Millard volunteered for organizations providing settlement, protection, and advocacy services to refugees and refugee claimants for a number of years. She holds a Master's degree in art history from McGill University and a Bachelor's degree in fine art from the University of Toronto.

PETRA MOLNAR is a refugee and human rights lawyer in Toronto, Canada, and a researcher at the International Human Rights Program, University of Toronto Faculty of Law. Molnar's work focuses on issues such as immigration detention, health and human rights, new technologies in immigration, and the politics of refugee, immigration, and international law. Along with Brittany Lauren Wheeler, she coordinated the ESPMI Network from 2012–16.

WILLIAM J. PAYNE is a doctoral candidate in critical human geography at York University, a graduate research associate at the Centre for Refugee Studies, a graduate affiliate at the Centre for Research on Latin America and the Caribbean (both at York University), and teaches in the geography department at York University and in the Community Worker Program at George Brown College, all in Toronto, Canada. Payne's research examines human rights violations against sexual/gender minorities in Latin American contexts marked by organized violence and impunity and produced through hemispheric political and economic processes. He has worked as a human rights advocate in Mexico, Colombia, Canada, and Palestine.

RANABIR SAMADDAR, currently the distinguished chair in migration and forced migration studies at the Calcutta Research Group, has for more than twenty years pursued a postcolonial method of inquiry into issues of refugees, partitions, borders, displacement, and the broader question of labour migration. He has authored works such as *The Marginal Nation* and *Beyond Kolkata: Rajarhat and the Dystopia of Urban Imagination*.

BEATRIZ EUGENIA SÁNCHEZ-MOJICA is a lawyer and has a PhD in human rights. She is an expert in International Human Rights Law and forced migration issues. Her academic and consultant work analyzes, from a critical perspective, the ability of International Law to weave a protector net upon humankind in a globalized world. Her research project is particularly focused on the most vulnerable ones, such as refugees, internally displaced people, migrants, and armed conflict victims. Sánchez-Mojica's last book, *Territorios en transformación, derechos en movimiento: Cambio ambiental y movilidad humana en Colombia* (*Territories in Transformation, Rights in Movement: Environmental Change and Human Mobility in Colombia*) was published in 2018. She currently teaches at IE University Law Faculty and at Universidad Pontificia de Comillas, both in Madrid, Spain.

JAMES C. SIMEON, Head of McLaughlin College, is an associate professor in the School of Public Policy and Administration, Faculty of Liberal Arts and Professional Studies, York University, Toronto, Canada. He is a member-at-large of the executive of the Canadian Association for Refugee and Forced Migration Studies (CARFMS) and a past president of CARFMS. He also serves as the coordinator of the International Association for Refugee and Migration Judges' (IARMJ) Inter-Conference Working Party Process. Simeon's primary areas of research are international refugee law, international human rights law, international humanitarian law, international criminal law, and public policy and administration. He has published widely in these areas and has organized and led many highly successful academic and professional conferences, symposia, and workshops.

LISA SINGH is a professor in the Department of Computer Science and a Research Professor in the Massive Data Institute (MDI) at Georgetown University. She has authored/co-authored over sixty peer reviewed publications and book chapters related to data-centric computing. Current projects include studying privacy on the web, developing methods and tools to better understand forced movement due to conflict, and learning from public, open source big data to advance social science research involving the understanding of human behaviour. Singh has also recently organized three workshops involving future directions of big data research. Her research has been supported by the National Science Foundation, the Office of Naval Research, the Social Science and Humanities Research Council, and the Department of Defense.

BRITTANY LAUREN WHEELER is a doctoral candidate at the Graduate School of Geography at Clark University, Worcester, Massachusetts, USA. Her research is located at the intersection of legal geography, environmental migration, and the temporalities of responsibility. Her long-time involvement with ESPMI included serving as a member of the executive committee (2011–12), president (2012–13), co-coordinator (2013–16), and member of the advisory committee (2016–17).

JULIE E. E. YOUNG is Canada Research Chair (Tier 2) in critical border studies and an assistant professor in geography at the University of Lethbridge, Canada. She holds a doctorate in geography and a graduate diploma in refugee and migration studies from York University in Toronto. Her research program aims to better understand North America's borders in the context of broader global processes as well as what local practices tell us about where, how, and for whom borders work. Young's work has been published in *ACME: An International E-Journal for Critical Geographies*, *Environment & Planning D: Society and Space*, *Journal of International Migration and Integration*, and *Refuge: Canada's Journal on Refugees*.

# Index

# C

Caballero-Anthony, Mely, 74, 75

Cambodia, 68, 69, 75, 82n1, 250, 291

Canadian Association for Refugee and Forced Migration Studies (CARFMS): and development of ethical principles for research in contexts of forced migration, 276, 281; Facebook group of, 200–201; founding of, 16, 152, 290, 293; listserv of, 207–8; Online Research and Teaching Tools & Practitioners' Forum (ORTT&PF), 16–17, 152–60, 161–64, 165n5

Canadian Association of Refugee Lawyers (CARL), 6, 290

Canadian Council for Refugees (CCR), 207, 279, 280–81; and development of ethical principles for research in contexts of forced migration, 276

Canefe, Nergis, 14, 45–65

Cann, Alan, 196, 208

Carnegie Endowment Foundation, 51

Center for Forced Migration Studies (CFMS) (Northwestern University, United States), 292

Centre for Policy Development (CPD). *See* Asian Dialogue on Forced Migration (ADFM)

Centre for Refugee Studies, Moi University (Kenya), 89, 291, 292

Centre for Refugee Studies, York University (Canada): and development of ethical principles for research in contexts of forced migration, 276, 279; and Environmental Displacement Cluster, 234, 237, 249; founding and history of, 161, 175, 233, 257, 291, 293; and IUSSP Scientific Panel on the Demography of Forced Migration, 175; listserv of, 207, 297; maintenance of RRN website and social media tools, 5; partnership with Latin American researchers, 257–58, 260–61. *See also* Canadian Association for Ref-

ugee and Forced Migration Studies (CARFMS); ESPMI Network; Refugee Research Network

Centre for Research on Latin America and the Caribbean (CERLAC), 257, 260, 261

Centre for the Study of Forced Migration (CSFM) (University of Dar es Salaam, Tanzania), 291

Chile, 254

Chimni, B. S., 4, 34, 67

China, 58, 260

Chubb, Jennifer, 198

civil society organizations (CSOs): attendance at the IASFM conference, 262; and the building of a Latin American network, 253–54; incorporation of demographic methods of data collection as a benefit to, 185; and relationship with states and international bodies, 67, 68, 70–71, 75, 76–78, 81, 82n4

Clark, Lance, 135

Clark-Kazak, Christina, 6, 154, 296; on developing an international network on research methodologies and knowledge production in forced migration, 19, 46, 88, 273–87, 280(f), 297, 298

climate change and displacement, 183, 194, 202, 238–39, 256, 257; Environmental Displacement cluster research on, 234, 239–45, 243(t), 250

Cockburn, Cynthia, 100

Cole, Richard T., 196–97, 206

collaborative research and publication: and development of early warning of displacement, 131–33; developing and sustaining partnerships in, 273–87, 280(f); encouragement of, 155; and knowledge mobilization, 16, 18, 195; power imbalances in, 14, 25–29, 31, 32, 33–36; reshaping partnerships in, 36–39. *See also* Canadian Association for Refugee and Forced Migration Studies

Edwards, Alice, 75
Emerging Scholars and Practitioners on Migration Issues (ESPMI) Network, 5, 18, 163, 184, 208, 269n3, 290, 294, 298; Bridging Research to Policy and Practice cluster, 229; Emerging Ideas in Migration Research cluster, 229; funding of, 226–27; *Guest Twitter Project*, 222, *224*, 225, 228; Methodological Challenges in Forced Migration Research cluster, 229; New Dissemination Practices and Public Engagement cluster, 229; *Refugee Review* (journal), 5, 216, 217, 219–22, *221*, 226, 227, 228; use of Facebook, 222; use of Twitter, 222, 224(f), 225, 228; website of, *218*, 218–19, 222, *223–24*
environmental displacement, definition of, 241
Environmental Displacement cluster, 19; *Area* (journal) special issue, 245; creation of the network, 234–38; innovative knowledge production and, 244–48; making the case for, 238–44; outcomes, challenges, and new directions for, 248–51; participants in, 243(t); *Refuge* (journal) special issue, 245, 249
ethics in research on forced migration. *See* methodologies and knowledge production in forced migration, international network on
Ethics of Development-Induced Displacement (EDID) Project, 234
extended asylum, 91, 102n1

## F

Fábos, Anita, 276
Facebook, 196, 197, 198, 277; ESPMI Network use of, 222; LANFM use of, 264, 266; RNN use of, 5, 7, 196–206, 199(f), 208, 277. *See also* Twitter
Fassin, D., 92
Ferstman, Carla, 75

Ford Foundation, 51
funding: challenges in accessing, 12–13, 26–27, 158, 165n5, 180, 198, 216, 222, 226–27, 230, 266, 273, 276, 278, 290; non-traditional vs. traditional, 18, 37; and the power to set the research agenda, 35, 36–37, 38. *See also* Ford Foundation; International Association for the Study of Forced Migration (IASFM): funding of research and networking activities; MacArthur Foundation; Social Sciences and Humanities Research Council (SSHRC)

## G

Galloway, Donald, 6
Gan-Chaudhuri, Jagadis, 112
Ganguly, J. B., 112, 124n4
Gender & Sexuality cluster, 6
gender, 6, 98–100, 102n4, 102n6, 247; in demographic data on forced migration, 178, 180, 182, 184. *See also* human trafficking, of women and children
Ghelani, Chizuru Nobe, 275
Giddens, Anthony, 90
Giles, Wenona, 6, 15, 87–106
Gleditsch, Kristian S., 135
Global Affairs Canada, RNN policy briefs to, 296–97
Global Compact for Safe, Orderly and Regular Migration, 80, 170, 173, 177, 185–87, 289
Global Compact on Refugees (2018), 17, 80, 130, 173, 177, 186, 187; call for the establishment of a global academic network, 186, 299–301
Global Policy Network, 290
Gomes, Teresa, 297
Goodwin-Gill, Guy, 74
Greece, 129, 264
Guatemala, 254, 255, 259, 261
Guattari, Félix, 58
Guterres, António, 17, 170

# H

Haaga, John, 174
Hackett, Ryan, 236–37, 243(t), 245
Hans Böckler Foundation (Germany), 51
Hardman, Frank C. et al., 96
Harper, Gary W., 274, 279–80, 280(f),
    281–82
Harrell-Bond, Barbara, 291
Hassan, Robert, 153
Hedditch, Kaitlyn, 185
Helsinki Citizens' Assembly, 51
Himley, Matthew, 243(t)
Hirsch, Rachel, 243(t)
Hockett, J. et al., 139
Hooley, Tristram, 196, 208
Houwer, Rebecca, 95
Hove, Thomas, 196–97, 206
Hovy, Bela, 177, 180, 184
Hugo, Graeme, 175, 176
human rights, discourse of, 61, 71, 72–76,
    78, 173. *See also* security/insecurity,
    discourse of; transitional justice
human security, discourse of. *See* security/
    insecurity, discourse of
human trafficking: Association of South-
    east Asian Nations (ASEAN) Con-
    vention on Trafficking in Persons
    (2015) and, 76, 82n3; of women and
    children, 120–22; human traffick-
    ing, 32, 69, 70–71, 76, 79, 274
Hussain, Manirul, 116, 124n5
Hussain, Wasbir, 119, 124n8
Hyndman, Jennifer, 6, 15, 90, 94, 100,
    243(t), 297
Hynie, Michaela, 3, 87–88, 195–96, 281,
    297

# I

Igoe, James, 243(t)
Immigration, Refugees and Citizenship
    Canada, RNN policy briefs to,
    296–97
India: colonial background, 109–14; histo-
    ry of anti-foreigner agitation in As-
    sam, 110, 113–14, 116–19, 122–23,
    124nn6–7; IASFM conference in,

295; political economy of resources
    and violence in, 114–20; trafficking
    of women and children in, 120–22
Indigenous peoples, 95, 246; Canada, 245;
    India, 116, 118–19, 123
Indochinese Refugee Information Center.
    *See* Asian Research Center for
    Migration (ARCM)
Indonesia, 68, 69, 70, 76, 82n1; and Ro-
    hingya refugees, 67–68, 78–79, 80;
    scholarly engagement with issues of
    forced migration by authors from,
    73, 73(t)
Institute for the Study of International
    Migration, Georgetown University,
    16, 291
Instituto Latinoamericano para una
    Sociedad y un Derecho Alternativo
    (ILSA), 253–54
Internal Displacement Monitoring Centre,
    137, 254–55
internally displaced persons (IDPs), 11,
    171–72, 176, 177, 184, 185, 238; in
    India, 295; in Iraq, 139; in Latin
    America, 254–55, 265, 295; in
    Southeast Asia, 68, 70
International Association for the Study
    of Forced Migration (IASFM):
    biennial conferences of, 4, 19, 162,
    163, 175, 178, 215, 217–18, 225,
    253, 255, 262–64, 294–95; code of
    ethics, 283; Facebook group of,
    200; founding of, 292; funding of
    research and networking activities,
    5, 276; and Global Compact on
    Refugees academic network, 299;
    and knowledge mobilization, 162;
    listserv of, 207-8
International Center for Transitional
    Justice (New York), 51
International Centre for Climate Change
    and Development (Dhaka, Bangla-
    desh), 250
International Convention on Civil and
    Political Rights, 71
International Labour Organization (ILO),
    171

International Migration Research Centre (IMRC) (Wilfrid Laurier University, Canada), 292

International Network for Education in Emergencies (INEE), minimum standards of, 96–97

International Organization for Migration, 71, 137, 139, 171; and the Andaman Sea crisis, 78–80; competition with APFMC for "protection space," 68, 76

International Research and Advisory Panel (IRAP), 291–92

International Union for the Scientific Study of Population (IUSSP), 173, 175–76, 177, 178

Internet. *See* Canadian Association for Refugee and Forced Migration Studies (CARFMS): Online Research and Teaching Tools and Practitioners Forum (ORTT&PF); Facebook; Twitter; YouTube, RRN use of

Iraq, 10, 203; climate change and displacement in, 202; using media data to predict and track displacement in, 129, 134, 136, 138, 139, 141

ISIL, 136, 140

## J

Jacobsen, Karen, 29
Jazeel, Tariq, 2
Jenkins, J. Craig, 135
Jensen, Krista E., 194–95, 197
Jimenez, Shauna, 297
Jones, Martin, 77

## K

Kaomea, Julie, 102n4
Kateb, George, 89
Keely, Charles, 174, 176, 177, 181, 187–88
Kellerman, Aharon, 153
Kenya. *See* Borderless Higher Education for Refugees (BHER) Partnership
Khan, Badrul H., 154
Kneebone, Susan, 14, 67–85, 218

Knowledge Mobilization (KMb), conceptual framework of, 4, 16, 153, 162–63, 194–96, 197, 296, 297–98

Koehn, Peter, 8
Kothari, Uma, 37
Kraly, Ellen Percy, 17, 169–91
Kunz, Egon F., 174
Küpeli, Ismael, 193
Kurdi, Alan, photo of, 193–94, 200

## L

Landau, Loren B., 14, 25–43, 46, 88, 290, 299, 300

Lao PDR, 68, 69, 82n1

Latin America: extractive industries and displacement in, 245, 260–61; peace-building in, 262–63, 269n4; trade and investment-induced displacement in, 256–58; violence-induced displacement in, 255, 258–61, 263, 268–69. *See also* Latin American Network for Forced Migration (LANFM)/*Red latino americana de migración forzada*

Latin American Network for Forced Migration (LANFM)/*Red latino americana de migración forzada*, 19; achievements of, 255–64, 267–68; challenges and demise of, 265–69; formation of, 254, 265, 290, 292–93

Lavia, Jennifer, 92, 93, 94

laws regarding refugees and migrants, 34, 108, 124, 274, 292; effectiveness and relevance to refugees and migrants, 36; and human trafficking, 120; in India, 113, 117–18, 123; international refugee law, 6, 48–49, 72, 76; in Latin America, 259, 265, 270nn7–8; refugee status determination systems, 6; safe country of origin policies, 6; in Southeast Asia, 71–76, 73(t), 74(t), 79–80. *See also* human rights; transitional justice

Lewis, Rhonda, 274, 279–80, 280(f), 281–82

Lingard, Bob, 92, 93, 94

Ryerson Centre for Immigration and Settlement (RCIS) (Toronto, Canada), 292

## S

Saad, Aaron, 243(t)
Sadeghi, Rasoul, 180
safe third country rules, 60
Salehyan, Idean, 135
Samaddar, Ranabir, 15, 46, 107–25
Sánchez-Mojica, Beatriz Eugenia, 19, 253–71
Sandberg, Anders L., 243(t)
Sanlaap India, 121
*sans papiers*, 58, 60, 70
SAPA (Solidarity for Asian People's Advocacy), 78
Saxton, Gregory D., 197, 207
Scarry, Elaine, 92, 97–98, 100
Schmeidl, Susanne, 134, 135, 177, 185
Schoenholtz-Read, Judith, 154
Scholey, Pam, 33–34
Schweigman, C., 30
security/insecurity, discourse of, 15, 60, 172, 173; and India, 107–9, 110, 113–14, 116–19, 120–23, 124nn6–7; and Southeast Asia, 72–76, 78–81. *See also* containment, strategies of; human rights, discourse of
sexuality, 6
Shandy, Dianna, 276
Shellman, Stephen M., 134, 135
Silverman, Stephanie, 6
Simeon, James C., 6, 16–17, 151–67
Singapore, 68, 69, 82n1; scholarly engagement with issues of forced migration by authors from, 73(t), 74(t), 75, 76, 82n2
Singh, Lisa, 16, 129–49, 180
Skeldon, Ronald, 74
Skoric, Marko M., 197
social media. *See* Facebook; Twitter; YouTube, RRN use of
Social Sciences and Humanities Research Council (SSHRC): funding of CARFMS, 293; Strategic Knowledge Research Cluster/Partnership

Grant, 8, 165n5, 266; funding of early warning project, 131, 132; funding of the ESPMI Network, 225, 226, 237; funding of a methodology project, 276, 281, 293; funding of the RRN, 174, 216, 225, 226, 290, 295, 296; popularization of the concept of KMb (Knowledge Mobilization), 194
Somalia, 129–30. *See also* Borderless Higher Education for Refugees (BHER) Partnership
Song, Jiyoung, 75–76
South Africa, 28, 291, 292; IUSSP conference in, 173, 178
South American Network for Environmental Migration (RESAMA), 269
South Asia. *See* Afghanistan; Bangladesh; India; Sri Lanka
South Korea, IUSSP conference in, 178
South Sudan, 129–30
Southeast Asia. *See* Andaman Sea crisis; Asia Pacific Forced Migration Connection (APFMC); Association of Southeast Asian Nations (ASEAN); Cambodia; Indonesia; Lao PDR; Myanmar; the Philippines; Thailand; Vietnam
Sri Lanka, 56, 68, 268
Statelessness Convention (1954), 72
students, training and mentoring of, 10, 11, 184–85, 187, 234, 237–38, 283, 289, 295; in Borderless Higher Education for Refugees (BHER) Partnership, 96, 102n3
Suarez-Balcazar, Yolanda, 274, 279–80, 280(f), 281–82
Sutherland, Peter, 172
Syria, displacement from, 129, 134, 202; and Syrian refugee settlement in Canada, 276, 277, 279, 293. *See also* Kurdi, Alan, photograph of

## T

Tanzania, 250, 291, 292
Terras, Melissa, 197–98
terrorism, 10, 256

Thailand, 68, 69, 82n1, 291, 292; and Rohingya refugees, 67–68, 70, 78–79; scholarly engagement with issues of forced migration by authors from, 72–75, 73(t)

Tibet, 110–11, 115

trafficking. *See* human trafficking

transitional justice: arguments for bringing together with forced migration studies, 14, 48–49, 55–56, 61; traditional approaches to, 49–50, 51–55; understanding displacement and mobility in relation to, 56–61. *See also* laws

Turkey, 58, 193, 268

Turton, David, 29

Twitter, 136–41, 194, 196, 197–98; ESPMI Network use of, 222, 224(f), 225, 228; RRN use of, 7, 196, 206–7, 208. *See also* Facebook

## U

United Kingdom: scholarly engagement with issues of forced migration by authors from, 72–75, 73(t), 292; use of online research materials in, 207, 222

United Nations General Assembly, 170, 171

United Nations High Commissioner for Refugees (UNHCR), 35, 72, 265; and the Andaman Sea crisis, 78–80; competition with APRRN for "protection space," 68, 71, 76–78; data on number of displaced persons, 17, 49, 70, 129, 160–61, 171, 184; and development of ethical principles for research in contexts of forced migration, 276; and development of a global academic network, 289–90, 292, 298–300; funding of APRRN, 82n5. *See also* Borderless Higher Education for Refugees (BHER) Partnership; Global Compact for Safe, Orderly and Regular Migration; Global Compact on Refugees

United Nations Relief and Works Agency for Palestine Refugees in the Near East (UNRWA), 49

Uruguay, 263

## V

van der Werf, Ineke, 30

Venezuela, 254, 269

Vidal, Roberto, 19, 253–54, 262, 264, 267

Vietnam, 68, 69, 82n1, 250, 291; scholarly engagement with issues of forced migration by authors from, 73(t)

violence, 135, 160, 246; using big data to predict, 130, 134, 137–40. *See also* human trafficking; India: history of anti-foreigner agitation in Assam; Latin America: violence-induced displacement in; Myanmar; security/insecurity, discourse of; transitional justice

## W

Watermeyer, Richard, 198

Wheeler, Brittany Lauren, 18, 215–31

Wilmoth, John, 177

Wilson, Mark I., 153

## Y

Yemen, 129–30

Young, Julie E. E., 1–21, 3, 87–88, 195–96

YouTube, RRN use of, 196, 207

## Z

Zalik, Anna, 234, 235, 243(t), 245

Zingerli, Claudia, 26

www.ingramcontent.com/pod-product-compliance
Lightning Source LLC
Chambersburg PA
CBHW051441270326
41932CB00025B/3399